OUR CULTURAL AGONY

OUR CULTURAL AGONY

by

VINCENT VYCINAS

MARTINUS NIJHOFF / THE HAGUE / 1973

PRINTED IN BELGIUM

To Audre-Audrey
  my daughter and
    co-operator.

GRATITUDE

Is expressed to Audre-Audrey Vycinas, Grade X student at Mount Prevost School, Duncan, B.C., for editorial work concerning the language and idiom of the study.

TABLE OF CONTENTS

PREFACE

Cultural twilight means cultural disintegration or death. It means cultural agony. Such agony gradually fades into the dawn of tomorrow's culture, just as the twilight of a summer's evening proceeds into the daylight of the forthcoming day. Consequently cultural twilight or agony simultaneously is the dawn — the milieu of birth — of future gods.

With these words a close interbelonging of the recently published SEARCH FOR GODS with the present study, OUR CULTURAL AGONY, is stressed. Both of these books belong together and constitute one and the same "story".

While SEARCH FOR GODS deals with man of tomorrow in his venture to find the way which would lead him to his dawning gods, OUR CULTURAL AGONY attempts to disclose contemporary man's ways of erring — his straying ways. Moreover, just as the way towards man's future gods is simultaneously his way to his true cultural self, so are his straying ways his ways of a lack of self. Man's way to his true self is his authentic, innermost, "bloody" or "ex-istential" way, while the way of his lack of self is his inauthentic way. The inauthentic ways, generally speaking, are "democratic" ways : they are the public and common ways of modern society, most typical or characteristic of it. Accordingly, while SEARCH FOR GODS has an individualistic character, OUR CULTURAL AGONY has a social character.

The close relation of both of these studies frequently results in an overlapping of passages here and there. This overlapping constitutes a praiseworthy, rather than a blameworthy, trait due to the importance, and especially the difficulty, of the central points in both studies.

Perhaps the most significant difference between the two studies consists in the individualistic or personal character prevailing in SEARCH FOR GODS and the social or cultural milieu in OUR CULTURAL AGONY. Here modern technology's global venture with all its immense strength and undeniable weaknesses comprises the whole of humanity in every part of the world and rapidly eradicates the ancient ways of life.

In spite of this difference, in the problematic of both studies prevails the same abysmal ground of Nature's play. In SEARCH FOR GODS man's innermost self consist in his response to this dynamic transcendental ground, while in OUR CULTURAL AGONY humanity's cultural life serves this ground in its disclosure or concealment.

In spite of the apparent supra-individualistic character of the present study, it, nevertheless, seeks to help the contemporary reader, thinking or meditating, or entangled in his daily tasks and looking for a way out, to gain firm steps, one after another, in understanding his cultural inheritances, the phase of Christianity of his times and perhaps most of all the mightily prevailing technology along with the "unquestionably true" democratic liberties. Attempting to provide the modern reader with this understanding, the present study helps him in finding his ideals, in freeing himself for the sight of future gods and thereby in acquiring his true, profound self.

Duncan, 1971
Dr. Vincent Vycinas.

THE CONTEMPORARY ANTHROPOCENTRIC WORLD

Today's man is caged in one or another cell of his gigantic technological world, where he has his function and his place. With hardly any effort of his own he occupies his place and begins to function there. Similarly he "discovers" his ideals and the mission of his life in his cell; the very meaning of his being is given to him without any real struggle, effort, or his own contribution to it.

He conveniently receives his well structured world as a gift from his ancestors. These — having emerged from a dark cultural background, from caves, gradually throughout the millennia have built a splendid world for themselves and their progeny. Their work was crowned by a technological world in the final cultural phase which excels all previous phases.

In spite of this, we, the modern men, know well that our world is not completed : we are still improving and developing it. We, however, do not question the brilliance of our technological world. We feel that we have attained a true world, even though we still can improve it constantly to a higher and higher degree.

1. *A Dynamic World*

The constant improvement of our environment means that we live in a dynamic world. Thus we do not fit ourselves nicely into our cells, functioning there in full comfort. We are restless and creative, even though we do not question the basic structure and character of our world. We are tempted here, already in the introduction, to express a doubt of the true meaning of modern man's dynamics. It could be that these dynamics, ultimately taken, do not mean mere improvement of a nearly perfect world. They may very well be deeply rooted dynamics by which man creates his cultural world over and over again, instead of just improving it. Perhaps, the real reason for modern man's dynamics — for his not resting in his technological cell — is the same as that of primaeval man who did not rest peacefully concealed in a cell outlined for him by Nature. Instead of blindly following Nature's codes (the way animals do!), mythical man rose to seek openly, by his own sight, Nature's fundamental ordering and guiding principles : he rose to encounter and to follow his gods.

Modern technological man, buried in the cells of his world, now and then gets an urge to rise and get hold of the ultimate principles governing his world. In the mythical world, such principles have been known as gods. Seeking these principles, contemporary man is out unawares on a search for gods, while mythical man sought gods with full awareness.[1]

A search for gods necessarily means a standing out (ex-sistence) from the world clearly organized by clear principles. Anyone who is out to search for the gods will find today an abundance of "founded" or "proven" theories of the "right" outlook on the world or reality. Because of a multitude of these theories, which often deviate far from each other or which even contradict each other, to get lost and become confused amid these is almost inevitable. Clearly laid out streets in a town may be just as misleading to man as are abruptly ending trails in some wilderness. Once the principles of a world become invalid, man is set back from a well organized world into a chaotic wilderness, and therewith he may be set on the ways of a search for gods.

A search of this kind must transcend all proven theories with well established principles. This means that man must leave the highways and roads of his clearly organized world, and he must get lost in the wilderness in order to become a searcher for the gods. It is comparatively easy to take up the beaten path of some doctrine, theory or philosophy, and follow it. Such a doctrine, theory or philosophy explains everything from its origin to its end; it explains the ways of men, of nations, of humanity in general; it establishes clearly articulated codes for right and wrong, valid to everyone in the very same way, and so on. In the wake of all this clarity, the ultimate, ever elusive, background of reality which alone is the true birthbed of fundamental cultural principles, is overlooked and ignored. Following the well laid out and maintained highways of his cultural world, man will discover everything in his world in a clearly explained manner. He, however, will never find and face by his own self — face existentially — the true principles of his world; he never will find and face his gods in a living way.

While highways or roads are public, wilderness trails are individual or personal, and these — the latter — are the ways of a search for gods. They

[1] The reading of the present study should be preceded by reading the author's *Search for Gods*. (The Hague : Martinus Nijhoff, 1972).

are the ways for lonely travellers. Today the gods are silent — are dead — in the milieu of contemporary culture. They, however, may be eloquent and alive in some individuals' inner lives. True or genuine culture smoulders today less in a "public" world than it does in a searching, restless self.

2. *Man's Supremacy in the Technological World*

In the perspectives of the anthropocentric world, man's greatness is his ability to make everything around himself servile to himself. Man does this mainly by using various technological devices increasingly more as time goes on. These devices digest raw materials and transform them to a dignified and standardized condition. These materials then become suitable for man's purpose. Surrounded by these, man *quasi* becomes wrapped in a glaring artificial world. In such a world — as we will see later — man lives a godless life.

Originally understood greatness is intimately connected with enthusiasm. Here greatness means principally that the being-man is realized only then, when man serves powers which are superior to him. These powers are gods, Nature, God.

Anthropocentric greatness needs a "godless climate" to thrive. This means that the anthropocentric enthusiasm (if we can use such an expression!) is rendered possible by a firm conviction that there is no power in reality which would be superior to man. This conviction — if not manifestly, without doubt concealedly — maintains that the gods are gone from the modern cultural world, that God is dead. Nietzsche's famous saying : "God is dead!" is not an expression of his personal disbelief in God, but is the fundamental stroke of our modern world. How else can today's man move a hillside, cut thousands of square miles of ageless forests, fill up lakes or create new ones, make extinct whole breeds of animals and birds or create new ones by crossbreeding, pollute the oceans and atmosphere and eventually control the weather, and — in the near future — perhaps completely enslave the earth? Man can do this only when he is sure beyond any doubt that there is no hand above his to direct and sway his world, or else if there is such a hand — the hand of the Almighty — it has given to man the whole world for his unrestricted exploitation. According to the latter outlook, God smiles submissively seeing his childrens' uncontrolled use and abuse of their living world. Theology of this kind is anthropocentric : it is godless.

To a superficial observer, technological man seems to be the master of his world. Is it so? Man occupies the very heart of the anthropocentric technological world. A multitude of arteries have their start here, and by going in thousands of directions, they penetrate nature around man. Raw, unrefined or uncultivated elements pulsate through these veins into man's diverse cultural institutions. Here man produces his values by issuing well-founded and refined cultural things or realities.

The rich diversity of arteries and of the entities which channel through them requires a great variety of human activities. No man can ever master all of them. In archaic times, when life was less complicated, man had his all-surveying stand in his world. In this sense he was lordly — a master of all functions assigned to him by his gods. Contemporary "godless" man is subordinate to his own complicated anthropocentric machine. Serving it, he is no master.

Technology stands in an unquestioned esteem in the Communistic as well as in the free Western world. It sways modern man just as Nature swayed archaic or mythical man. How are technology and Nature related? Could it be that technology is the concealment of once conquered Nature? We might be able to gain some insights into this problem as we proceed with our inquiry.

The technological approach to reality means a consideration of things around us without any hue of holiness or respect; they are viewed solely under the perspectives of their value — valuableness to man in one way or another. In such an approach, man's everything-determining worth is stressed : man is the subject wherein all the objects are founded. Man's perspectives, comparable to the beams of a flashlight, take everything into the anthropocentric eye-angle and determine it as to what it is or can be. A huge fir tree in such a perspective can be a cluster of 4" × 10" beams of timber to construct an impressive "A-frame" dwelling. Presence of iron ore in a mountain, along with layers of coal can be conditions for the founding of a steel industry. A waterfall may become a center piece for laying out a public park where touring people can escape noisy cities and find relaxing environment for a few days' stay. These attitudes have been observed and philosophically presented initially by Kant. His philosophy emphasizes subjective human principles *a priori*, that is, anterior to things or phenomena (beams, ore, waterfalls). Things become things by becoming objects on the grounds of subjective anterior principles.

Prior to Kant, there was no philosophical grasp of *a priori* reality. Anything which was not a thing or not an object, was not real. Things were not founded in *a priori* (anterior to things) reality, but in other things with a greater intensity of being (greater realness or actuality). All things ultimately were founded in the supreme thing or being. This being was God.

Such an understanding of reality was maintained by St. Thomas in medieval ages and by Aristotle in ancient times.

In modern times the emphasis was shifted from God as the all-determining subject, to man. Methodically this already was done by Descartes. With Kant, man became not just a central thing or being, but reality which is implied in everything or every being, as that without which no thing or being has any meaning or makes any sense.

Hegel was a philosopher of absolute spirit. This spirit was understood as God. It reveals itself firstly by estrangement from itself in nature and then it reacquires itself throughout the history of mankind. Man in his ultimate development merges with divinity. Such an attitude is inherited by technological man, except with the by-current that "God is dead" and only man is developing throughout history towards his self-completion in the technological phase of the cultural world. Man becomes sole lord of the world, the king of a godless reign.

Basically, the very same outlook is held by the Communistic world. Communistic philosophy is an outcome not of Hegel's brand of anthropocentrism, but that of Marx. His philosophy interprets man's history as exclusively consisting of exploitation and consummation of materials in man's world. The early man was "communistic" in that he used all things of nature around himself equally with others. In later times a few landlords held wide areas as their own and the rest of the people were their slaves or servants. In modern times, with the birth of industry, the means of production (machinery) was concentrated in the hands of "lords" and the working class, "the proletariat", was exploited and abused. The solution, or rather remedy to this malady is Communism. When all materials and all means of production are equally possessed by everyone, ideal culture is attained. This state responds to the Hegelian Absolute's becoming absolute. After the Communistic ideal is attained, culture has reached its fullness, and progress after it is unthinkable. Man here is the axle of the world. Everything in the world is determined or set in its meaning by man and his needs.

Technological man has a variety of positivistic or logistic thinkers behind himself. All of them, however, consider man as a stable basis while everything else is in motion. Moving in the beams of technological man's perspectives, everything acquires its meaning and being — it becomes stabilized. Positivistic (scientific) and logistic systems, using man as this stable basis, stabilize everything by systematizing it in accordance to man into a well articulated system of things. In this way, not just material things are systematically determined in their meanings (stabilized) but also "spiritual" ones. Things of entertainment, television shows, songs, paintings, and so on are established in their significance and value by the tastes of the majority of the people.

Thus technological man today is predominantly democratic. Determining all things or their meanings; he is their master. However, by being determined himself by his established systems, he is a servant of such a system, and thus he is no master.

3. *Anthropocentric "Stabilization" of Things*

In public places (especially during the summer months) there are stands for "soft" drinks. Here by a push-button method one can get either "cola", or "root beer", or "ginger ale", or "orange" or some other of the popular soft drinks. Ingredients for these drinks may come from far away places and they may be of totally different origin and require a totally different method of preparation. Nevertheless, all of these drinks are offered as *the same* (as soft drinks) to the public at its convenience. They all run into a white paper cup; they are cold and they have sizzling qualities.

This is a simple example of anthropocentric stabilization of things. By human perspectives, by man's needs or demands, totally different things are determined in their meaning as the same — they are "stabilized". Things acquire their meaning and their being within man's world. What is a thing in itself (outside of the perspectives of the human subject), as Kant first observed it, we do not know. At any time that we know a thing, we have it "humanized" : taken under our subjective *a priori* principles.

Analogically to the soft drinks, anything in the modern world is set or stabilized in its meaning and its being by its being related to or its getting into the perspectives of modern man. For instance, Canada's southwest sea shores since pioneer days, and until the last decade, had been considered of considerably lower value than the lands further inland. This was so mainly because of their rocky constitution and because of the prevailing winds here. Under these conditions their agricultural value has been low. During the last few years these coastal lands became highly desirable as view properties for permanent homes or for summer cottages. Their value exceeded several times the value of the lands deeper inland. Their meaning, and thus their being, as view properties are determined by present day man's perspectives.

In these approaches, the "democratic" aspect is noteworthy. People themselves decide what is meaningful, worthwhile and real, and what is meaningless, worthless or nothing. At this occasion we would like to state that the Western free world differs from the Communistic unfree world.

In this latter world not the people determine the values and meanings of things, but their guardians, namely, the ruling party leaders. For this reason, anthropocentric determination of all things in the Communistic world seems to be firmly set or stable, while in the West it fluctuates with the impulses and moods of the public. We know, however, that the former stability is not true; it merely is imposed upon people by strict laws and measurements. If these would be relaxed, we definitely would observe very much the same fluctuation there as we have it here, in the free world.

Accordingly we will not go wrong stressing that the "stable" axle which determines the meanings and being of all things, fluctuates itself or is unstable : man, the center of our world, is restless. The ultimate standard of measurement of reality is variable. American democracy — or, for that matter, the whole Western free world — expresses technological anthropocentric subjectivism as that which must be determined over and over again. Such a determination is sought by a survey of public opinions. The survey is taken not just with regard to the preference of "soft" or "hard" drinks, but also with regard to any technological products. Moreover, it is taken regarding anything whatever of any interest to the wide masses of people. Thus fashions for clothes, hair styles, entertainment programmes, real estate properties, political preference of one leader or another, or even the "true" solutions for some international or domestic political crises are determined.

In some of these surveys opinions are sought not just from adults, but quite often from teen-agers or even children. In this way a "democratic" opinion becomes that to which anybody can have a claim. Often today students try to determine the setting up of school programmes, the methods of teaching and even the selection of lecturers.

The above mentioned implications direct us to two basic observations. The first one can be summed up to a statement that the subjective anthropocentric axle of the contemporary world — unlike the one understood by Hegel and to a certain extent by Marx — is not absolute and stable, but always in flux. Marx did not speak of idealistic, and in that way divine, reality; however, he maintained human nature as always the same in its very essence. Because of this, the rearrangement of things or objects — economical values — around man was the sole issue of his philosophy.

The second observation concerns the understanding of freedom. Freedom today is understood "democratically". Understood this way, it means everyone's unrestricted own contribution to, or a co-operative with others in the setting up of all values, their handling, and simultaneously the setting up of people's mutual interrelations.

The first of these two observations tells us that our world is relative, while the second states that freedom is not freedom for truth but freedom for opinion. Freedom in this sense is liberty, and opinion takes the place of truth. Both of these observations reveal instability, lack of firmness and therewith a danger of disintegration planted in the midst of our world. Chaos lies very near to our seemingly very solid contemporary technological superculture.

No danger or chaos is felt by the average contemporary man. He, on the contrary, is inclined to consider present day democratic society as standing on most true and most firm principles. At least we know now that this can be doubted, its presuppositions investigated and — if need be — the growth of our cultural future adjusted.

In our technological age, circumstances (public demands) encourage a rapid growth of inventions — be they new technological devices or new models of former ones. For instance, each year cars in new styles are put out. The same must be said of appliances or furniture, record players, and so on. Technology by its new devices spreads into ever new areas, substituting ever more natural things by the technological. Just as we have today substituted butter (margarine), we will tomorrow have steaks made of weeds or sugar made of tree bark. This inevitably brings man into dependence on his own created technological world. Man no longer can live or get along without his technological products and — what is most essential — without his own technological world. Technology — that which is considered man's creation — becomes his ruler. Man first produces machine and then he acts, dances and thinks in the rhythmics of the machine. To some this seems to be a disturbing sign of ill-turn within our culture. "The real danger of our technological age is not so much that machines will begin to think like men, but that men will begin to think like machines".[2]

Whether this really means a danger at this time we cannot make any definite statement. However, we must indicate that prior to attaining technological thinking, man had to go through "unchecked", unsystematic thinking of archaic or mythical kind. In addition to this, it had to go through genuine philosophical thought. Contemporary "survey-taking" man substitutes mythical and genuine thought by mechanical probing of "democratically" expressed multiple opinions. Not just the current issues today are decided in such a "democratic" way, but also the traditional ones taken over from mythical times. Generation after generation of man inherits ancestral moral codes. Through centuries or even millennia some of these

---

[2] Sidney J. Harris, *Publisher's Newspaper Syndicate*, p. 31.

codes remained unchanged. Now the "democratic" all-powerful surey investigates such codes without leaving a stone unturned and determines which of the moral laws are to be maintained and which must go. Family bonds today are falling off because this issue, like any other, becomes a matter of society's choice.

Since we — ourselves or through our elected representatives — establish or found the norms of behaviour along with the sanctions for their breaking, we assume that the ancestral codes or norms governing man's behaviour were, too, established the very same way. Here we are wrong! Ancient man, unlike contemporary "democratic" or technological man was not standing under a godless sky. He acted in response to gods of earth and sky. The codes of his moral laws, along with the principles of understanding his reality and world, grew up under the influence of Nature like an oak firmly grasping into the earth and swinging mightily high up in the sky.

Present day thinkers (the "opinionists") would be inclined to consider early man as spineless for his inability to establish his own order independently. Whether this is true or not cannot be aswered now. Only if one firmly maintains that the movement of fundamental reality, from where the principles governing all things get their start, is best manifested by the cross section of public opinion, then to him the "opinionists" are right. And in such a case, then, any other kind of truth is either subjective in the sense of its being dream-like, totally personal, odd opinion, or else it is a superstition brought into our cultural world since bygone "unsober" or "undemocratic" times.

According to mythical thought, man is not a completed being. The serving of gods by him manifests his way towards completion. Contemporary technological man contrastedly differs from mythical man by being self-sufficient, and therefore godless. We have seen that even modern man is not complete; he — the stable axle, which stabilizes all things — is in motion. However, this man himself — and no gods — guides himself towards completion by creating his brilliant technological world. Man's completeness foremostly consists in the arrangement of everything around himself into a harmonious and meaningful order. Such an order is attained by weaving the humanistic trend into the fabric of everything, that is, by "humanizing" all things. When all things are completely "humanized" as if being digested and restlessly incorporated into the human household, then they, and likewise man himself, become complete.

In sea food stores we can see glass tanks with live lobsters. These are sold alive to please man's culinarian discriminating tastes. Lobster meat is at top quality, when it is thrown alive into boiling water. In ancient times sacrifice of live animals or even men was usual. It was a part of the rites of cults by which man was serving his gods. Today only animals can be sacrificed and only for man; — not, however, as a part of cult, but simply because of consideration of man as the supreme reality. Man is the central being, according to which everything is directed, valuated, determined and established. Edible or poisonous mushrooms, beneficial or harmful plants or animals, valuable or worthless metals or minerals — all this is firmly stabilized to what they are only by their being exposed to man and his needs.

Man himself today is not utilized, applied or sacrificed to any gods or to Almighty God. If we still talk of man's self-sacrifice or of his heroic works resulting in his death, we mean his sacrifice for other men : for his beloved individuals, for his fellow men, compatriots, or for his nation. Religious cults today are "humanized" to the extent that human sacrifices for gods or God not only are not encouraged, but they are even forbidden. Contemporary religious cults are anthropocentric.

All this shows that man is the supreme reality, the all-determining subject. However, as we have seen, he is relative : is himself in motion towards completion. Man grows. Whereto does he grow? Are there any standards for his growth? If there are, they — according to anthropocentric principles — cannot be transhuman or godly standards. There are no such standards in the anthropocentric world. If man, then, cannot be boiled for any of the gods or any reality transcendental to man, wherein does that man's ultimate worth, his realness, consist? Does it consist in his static being-a-subject or in his dynamic growth? In the latter case man's ultimate realness is manifested by technological standards or criteria. Are these criterias truly and exhaustively human?

Man's pre-eminence to everything whatever is real, on the one hand, and his incompleteness, on the other, can perhaps be best expressed symbolically by a ball, which, even though complete, rolls to completion. Such an understanding of man is presented by Nietzsche who, by seeing the whole reality as a stormy sea of the Will to Power, sees man as constantly riding the white foaming crest of these waves — free and dominant! This great image of the superman is worth exploring in order to investigate the extent of man's freedom in his self-completion. Is man's freedom simply a principal independence on anything but his own self? Or is it a dependence on the sea, on Will to Power, on the background of man's world? Does Nietzsche's superman underline the world as anthropocentric? Or does he present man as thrown around helplessly in the play of mightier powers — Nature's powers?

4. *Things of the Technological World*

Rapid and mighty growth of the modern world to a great extent was due to the becoming impotent or falling apart of the early mythical cultures — of godly cultures. When cults die, the soil is ready for the upswing or growth of technology. Cultlessness is godlessness. Technology thrives in a godless climate. Such a climate is a vacuum of non-belief, non-serving; — the vacuum of man's self-affirmation in his own naked human brilliance.

The symbolic image of technological man is the outstanding ball which stabilizes all things around itself in their meanings and being and which itself is always rolling. This means that modern technological man is never in a state of perfection or completion. What then, is man's true greatness? Wherein consists the greatness of technological culture? What is its future? Is man totally free in his anthropocentric world? — totally self-supporting and thus absolutely godless?

Technological movements, which substitute and refine Nature's movements, often fall upon man as a heavy burden. Man then makes adjustments or improvements which often are obviously analogical to adjustments or improvements done by creative Nature, governing things, plants and animals. Technology, and nothing but technology, is burdening us with pollution and overpopulation in our megalopolises, the city chains. Closely related to it are various upheavals, revolts or street battles in the central cities of technological culture.

A careful observation of the process of our technological culture would discern in it forces which unplanned and uncontrolled by us, get us into their grip and direct or even drive us to the opaque and obscure ways of technology itself. Such observations would show modern man's implication in technology's own rhythmics, just as mythical man was implicated in the rhythmics of Nature. On the other hand, just as mythical man depended on Nature's sway, so does modern man on that of technology. In no way is technological man totally self-sufficient. Who of the members of technological culture can live today outside of thechnology and still be a cultural man? Hardly anyone! Mythical times are gone, and it is not in our power to bring them back. Instead of a return to the standards of the past, a genuinely cultural man, seeing the shortcomings of technology, must stand in the technological world firmly and from there gradually guide mankind into new horizons, other than those of anthropocentrism. He must enter a way of a search for gods. Such a way, first of all, must overcome the shallow ("unholy") meanings of things in our technological world.

My grandfather had a deep respect for the things of his living environment. An old oak tree for him was permeated by the power of reality of Perkunas, god of thunder and lightening. Whenever he had to cut off a small tree or even its branch for a horse whip or for a cane, he could not do it totally without pain. In such cases he tried to cut a sidebranch, rather than the tree top, carefully avoiding an interference with the proper growth of the tree. Everywhere when handling things he tried to preserve them as much as possible in the way they are set by mother Nature. When picking nuts, wild apples, berries or mushrooms, he made sure that the plants or their roots would remain unharmed not just not to interfere with next year's crop, but — most of all — not to interfere with Nature's order which prevails over all things.

He understood Nature to have a remedy (in the way of healing herbs) for each disease or ailment. In Nature there also were many harmful elements or plants. A wise man is the one who knows all beneficial or harmful things in Nature, along with the ways of drawing them from her. He knew that from the same plant a bee gets her honey, a snake her poison; from the same black soil delicious as well as poisonous mushrooms get their nourishment. All things — whether beneficial or harmful — are holy because they originate in holy Mother Earth along with other mighty spirits in Nature's milieu. All these powers ultimately stand under the influence of Almighty God.

God, in my grandfather's understanding, was not exclusively loving, protective, and a softhearted father, but often demanding, condemning, punishing and even coldly and mercilessly playing with men.

Man's exposure to often merciless and painful blows of destiny can even be felt in our modern times, where Nature seems to be more and more subdued to the will of man. The events of our world often befall us in a beneficial or harming way. Rarely does everything around us flow just the way we want it to. Not purely by our willful efforts do we get into our possession some valuable property. Not all of us find a pleasant and rewarding job. Not everyone of us meets a dear person, enriching our life and filling it with happiness. These or many other beneficial things may or may not befall us, just as in ancient times similar or different events or things befell the ancient man by the destinies of Nature's powers. Contemporary man, the measure of reality or the master of his world, himself is exposed to a great extent to things or events of his environment which more and more exclusively are dominated by the sway of technology. This means that man today is swayed by technology in much the same way as the mythical man was swayed by Nature.

Mythical man's respect for things was rooted in his respect for Nature. Things were holy because Nature was holy. We, Christians, know that the the Bread and Wine at the altar are holy. To a mythical man — including my grandfather — holy was water, fire, dew, dawn, a tree; — even a hut, a well, a table, a loaf of bread or anything whatsoever. These things were all gifts of gods, even those which were man-made. "Man does not really make a thing", my grandfather used to say, "anything he makes he actually receives from God as His gift through his work and sweat".

An old Lithuanian proverb says : "Bread does not arrive to us on wind"! Even though it is a gift, it must be received by man's efforts and work. Bread does not come to man freshly baked with a pleasant odor. Man must work for it : he must receive gods' gifts by his own active participation in their becoming what they are. Things — the gifts — only when received are fully manifestations of the presence of godly powers in Nature; only in that way are they holy.

Things in the technological world have lost their aspect of holiness. This is so because of contemporary man's godlessness. Nobody would add an epithet of "holy" talking of a pair of size 10 rubber boots, of a sheet of plywood, or a new model of Pontiac. These things are "soberly" known as the products of man — a fruitful result of man's efforts to tame raw Nature by making her an obedient and willful slave. Anyone considering things and Nature with a hue of holiness, today would make an impression of being naive, romantic or even odd.

When living in Pittsburgh, a large industrial city, I would at times tell those around me about my childhood in Lithuania. During the summer months, every morning I used to run to Mituva, a nice clear creek, to wash my face or to take a bath. "I find it quite different from washing my face now at the faucet of hot and cold water". "There cannot be any difference"! I used to hear an indifferent voice say : "Except, perhaps, that washing at a sink or lavatory is so much more convenient than in a cold creek"! "There is a difference"! I used to insist : "By washing my face in Mituva, I used to be overcome by the touching realness of mighty Nature's backgrounds, whence all the waters originate. I was acutely aware of the clouds above my homestead, of the rains and heavy dews. Along with all this I was aware of green fields sloping towards the creek with cattle on them and the home- stead further above; I was aware of the hard work by my parents on their fields and the happy days when the crop from these fields was taken home in the golden days of autumn. The whole life and destinies of my parents and ancestors stood before my eyes, along with the holy forces of the heavens which direct everything on their ways in the valley of Mituva. There was something holy about my washing up in the waters of Mituva"! Of course, such talk of mine sounded poetical rather than real. In the present study I may gradually show that such "poetry", when seriously taken, is more true and realistic than "sober" technological approach to things.

Water running from a faucet speaks of a widely branched-out system of water lines of various crosscut dimensions. Such a system points necessarily to men who have planned and laid it out and men who use the water for their daily household needs. There is nothing romantic, poetical or divine about the water running from a faucet. This water is not holy!

Are things of the technological world, clear down to their core, objectively or scientifically true? This can be doubted! Is water for us always a compound of oxygen and hydrogen in a proportion of 2 to 1? Are stars, when we look up to them in a clear night, huge celestial bodies many times larger than our Earth in immensely varied distances from us? Is a monument on someone's grave a mere chunk of granite? When we hear a song, do we just hear various vibrating sound waves? Is our grandmother just a huge cluster of molecules? If we would sincerely try to think into the meaning of these or many other clearly scientifically explained things, we would in each case run into romantic, poetic or religious overtones. This means that we would find mythical traces right in the midst of our anthropocentric society and its technology.

When contemporary people buy antiques, build log cabins in hide-away places, go on tiring and unprofitable hunting or fishing trips, admire music and art, read philosophy or get interested in religious problems — they manifest the insufficiency of the purely technological anthropocentric criteria or ways of life. The clear scientific world with exhaustively and objectively explained things in it can no longer satisfy many contemporary people, and as time goes on dissatisfaction tends to increase.

Perhaps all this indicates that there is a hidden stream in our cultural life which had preceded it, which prevails in it in a concealed way, and which finally will outlive it, upsurging into a dominance in the post-anthropocentric cultural phase of the future. If this is so, technology does not present the ultimate phase in our Western culture; nor does it indicate the total control of Nature by man.

In order to gain a more detailed insight into the meaning of culture and thereby to be better equipped for an evaluation of the contemporary technological phase of our culture and in gaining insight into the future phase of it, we must once more in a more detailed way, make a deepened and more extensive inquiry into present-day man's cultural standing. In this inquiry, in spite of modern man's godlessness, we must try to see hidden, distorted, nevertheless present godliness in his living days. Moreover, in spite of his kingly domination of Nature by his technology, we must try to see Nature's hidden sway in the midst of his technological world.

Prior to the birth of man there had been some nutritious roots available as a source of food. Along with this there had been animals who were in need of such food. Nature provided these animals with teeth just right to efficiently dig into the pulp of these roots.

There is a great variety of teeth well fitted for various purposes that Nature has created through millennia. We can also find in our technological world many kinds of "teeth" of machines or appliances for various purposes. Is there any relation between Nature's work and that of technology?

In many situations Nature has built channels to get the subsurface water high up into the leaves of tall trees or to carry milk into a young mammalian body's organs, or for blood to flow into brains. Technological man constantly builds channels; for instance, he drills wells to gain access to stored-up resources in Nature needed to promote man's well-being. Are these human ventures just the new ways of following age-old Nature's lessons? Or are they purely man's inventions? When we try to view without any prejudices Nature's work and that of technology, we can see a remarkable resemblance. Similarity between Nature's work and man's technological enterprises may help us to evolve some noteworthy conclusions in that area.

A consideration of the technological world under a renewed (non-anthropocentric) grasp of Nature is bound to help us attain a more appropiate insight into the meaning of culture. Properly understood culture — as we we will see — stands under the sway of Nature.

An investigation of culture cannot be completed without an inquiry into Christianity. Throughout the history of the Western world, Christianity permeated all the European cultures to such an extent that the elucidation and treatment of cultural and Christian principles separately became almost impossible. Due to this, Christianity, culture, and Nature hardly ever were properly explored as far as their differences and interrelations are concerned. We hope to gain some insights into these delicate intricacies in the course of the study.

Insights into the meaning of technology, into culture and into Christianity are bound to result in a renewed understanding of Nature. Instead of nature (which we know well), we must try to open our eye toward Nature (whom we ignore). Since Nature is dynamic — always playful — we will attempt to understand Nature's play as far as this is possible.

Once we understand Nature in her play, we simultaneously will understand the true meaning of culture. With the knowledge of culture we may gain a better insight into man's innermost self and his mission in his world. This will provide us with a firmer stand in our confused present and — what is most important — will open up new vistas, new directives, towards the future of modern mankind.

CHAPTER I

GODLESSNESS

To an ancient man all things were holy : fields, creeks, sky, fire, and all realities around him. This was so because the ancient or mythical culture was in its very core a cult — a cult of Earth, of Nature, of gods.

The "sober" technological man of today cannot but smile when he hears about his ancestors being filled with fear of gods. To consider all things holy to him seems to be a sort of theistic materialism. This is so because in the eyes of contemporary man gods are nothing but the products of the vivid imagination of early man, who was not as yet capable to grasp things soberly, that is objectively. With gods deleted from the ancient world (in the eyes of modern man) the epithet "holy" preceding things is also dropped off, and therefore the ancient world seems to consist of things alone — seems to be materialistic.

An unprejudiced reconsideration and evaluation of the meanings of gods, applying, along with it, some aspects of Kantian *a priori*stic and contemporary existentialistic philosophical approaches would show that gods are realities anterior to things and that things become meaningful only in the light of transcendental — godly — background.

1. *Some Traits of Mythical and Modern Man*

Mythical man in no wise was a materialist. He sheltered himself and gathered valuable things, especially nourishment not to make things servile to him, but primarily as the media for serving his gods. Each thing was a realistically true channel for encountering a god or gods, and therefore it was holy. The mission of his life was to serve his gods, to bring their light to shine into his living days. Holy things were holy because the light of the gods was arrested in them and it broke forward with clarity reflected from them.

Mythical man was a man of culture in the sense of his tender and devoted

care for the cults of his gods. A cult meant man's responsive acceptance of
the gifts of Nature and her gods along with his gratitude and indebtedness
to them. By such a responsive acceptance and gratitude he regarded his
gods as really — almost tangibly — present in his living days. Mythical
man's world — we can say it without a danger of erring — was Nature-
or gods-centered, while contemporary man lives in an anthropocentric or
man-centered world.

In modern man's world, not Nature's system, a harmonious interaction
of a rich variety of gods, founds things and their meanings, but his own
consciousness. Today's man sets the meanings of all phenomena, just as he,
in a wider or narrower sense, produces all things. He does this by his own
organizing principles. There is no genuine cult left in contemporary man's
world. The *logos* of his conscious takes the place of the *logos* of gods.

We have already seen and will see again, that the flourishing or thriving
human mind, which orders and arranges everything, is rendered possible by
the withdrawal, by the absence or by the silence of gods. The downfall of
gods — their retreat into the twilight — makes man the sole "spiritual"
power in the world. To care for man and for the *logos* imbedded in him is
the real culture. Such a culture is cultless, because it is godless.

An animal eats his food without knowing that it is divine. The modern
man eats his bread knowing that it is his own product. He "produces"
bread using Nature's (*qua* nature's) resources just as he produces a wooden
box by using hammer, lumber and nails. Beyond the modern, *humanistic*
things prevails a firm knowledge or conviction that *there are no gods*, and
that only man, his mind, is the principal originator of things. Such an attitude is the attitude of godlessness. Human "spiritual", technological
efforts — with no cult whatsoever — dominate the contemporary world.

When gods withdraw from man's world, they leave a transcendental
vacuum behind. This vacuum is fertile soil for the nourishment of human
logos which — instead of that of the gods — sways all things and determines
their ways. Human *logos* determines not only the meanings of things but
also of man himself : it assigns and directs all man's ethical, moral or cultural ways in his world.

There is no clear-cut anthropocentric *logos*. Rather there is a multitude
of systems in the light of which things and reality are variously interpreted.
With the constant development of modern democracy in the direction of
individual freedoms (which we would rather call liberties as they are freedoms of peripheral selves), in contemporary society, everyone has his own
credo, his own world-outlook, his own interpretation of the ultimate
principles of reality. Instead of truth — which is often painfully hard to

conceive and, after conceiving, to hold — now a confused multitude of opinions prevails everyhwere. Everyone feels entitled to his own opinion and no one can impose his *credo* upon the others.

Consequently, everyone has his own code of life, his own interpretation of everything in his world, his own religion or his own irreligion. In today's "cultural" conditions prophets of various brands of religious or semireligious outlooks arise and effectively revolt against the "old ways" of the elders. Such new societies with world-outlooks of religious admixture are mushrooming. Beatniks, hippies, "Vietniks", "Peaceniks", and so on create disorder in the cities of North America. Moreover, they do so in the major cities around the globe. Only Communistic countries seem to lack these ailments under which the whole free world is suffering. This is so because Communistic regimes rootlessly suppress and oppose any free opinions or outlooks. They ascribe to everyone a clear-cut Communistic doctrine which stands beyond anyone's doubt or criticism.

Man in the early days stood in a whirlpool of Nature's powers, equipped with many-sided capabilities which were due to his acute responsiveness to his living environment. He built his shelters, worked his fields, made his wagons, tools, traps for the forest wildlife and weirs or nets for fishes; he sewed his garments and made his footwear; he fashioned his musical instruments and jewels; created songs and stories.

Contemporary or modern man is necessarily fragmentary : he is specialized in a narrow field in the great multitude of works in his modern world. A man in the field of construction of residential homes, most of the times is incapable of building a home from beginning to end. He is an expert in building foundations, framing-in the outer shell of the house; he may be a plasterer, a cabinetmaker, a plumber, a painter, a roofer and so on.

Today's unionized society even demands man to restrict himself to a narrow scale in a great variety of occupations and to function efficiently in it. Outside of his own field such a man most frequently displays his ignorance or even stupidity. The lack of respect toward their parents and to their elders in general in our youngsters, to a great extent, is due to the incapabilities or impotencies of the former in the wide areas of life. A youngster who asks his father to help him build a tree-house immediately notices that his father is just as "green" as is he himself in this enterprise. Moreover, the universally prevailing right of everyone to his own opinion makes even a youngster feel as standing on equal ground with his parents or elders.

A youngster of a mythical society could never match his parents or elders in any of the areas of their life. The strength of mythical man's standing in his world meant the presence of superhuman powers of Nature in it. In the world of modern man the absence of a world order (the sway of gods) which dominates things, animals, men and cultures, is substituted by a multitude of ordering systems (human *logoi*), which deviate far from each other, conflict with each other or even contradict each other. Nevertheless, almost all of them claim to be scientifically proven and therefore absolutely valid. When in the vacuum of the absent gods, diverse human absolute theories thrive, we have a state of confusion rather than a true anthropocentric or humanistic order, *logos*. This disunity of various anthropocentric systems, under the principle of democratic tolerance, instead of a confusion is seen as a "mosaic" harmony. This misleading cover-up of confusion can be unmasked by a genuine inquiry into the very meaning of order or *logos* along with the inquiry into the very essence or mission of man. In this way the harmonious interbelonging of the "tiles" of the contemporary cultural mosaic would appear to be without any interbelonging and only as accidentally lying along each other in confusion rather than order.

Confusion of this kind possibly is an intermediary phase between a godly order which is drifting away and one which may be advancing from the impenetrable veils of the future. Just as an entity in chemistry must be dissolved into its original elements in order to produce a new entity by a different combination of these elements, so the order of withdrawing gods of the past must be substituted by a godless confusion before the approach of future gods announces a new godly order. Perhaps, the flourishing of today's democratic liberties lies between the freedom towards the withdrawn, and thus silent, gods of yesterday and the freedom towards the unborn gods of tomorrow — that is, between the twilight of the ancient gods and the dawn of the gods of the future.

Our theme, here is not an opposition to American democracy nor is it an attempt to restore the harmonious sway of the ancient gods in man's cultural world, but rather is an endeavor to reveal the necessity of preparing ourselves or becoming open to the silently advancing gods of tomorrow. If we, now in the graveyard of the gods of various cultures of earth would become alert to the silence of these gods, we would already hear gods *in their silence*. Such an awareness would be our way of responding the gods or our having our stead in their absence.

2. *The Anthropocentric Character of the Modern World*

An observer from the bygone mythical world, seeing the way of life of contemporary modern man, would definitely be shocked. We know that today "a guy" working in a mill often is unable to participate in religious celebrations on *holy* days. The mythical man would ask a question : where-from does this man draw his strength to disobey his gods and to break their laws? Man can only be man — a mortal — by serving gods — the immortals. If someone breaks a god's law, he can only do so by the power of some other god. Only a god can be the source of power to oppose another god. In no wise can man alone do so, as man is "a shadow of a dream" (Pindar).

We know, that technological man draws his strength to oppose the *logos* of the gods from his own human *logos*. The unrestricted sway of human *logos* is rendered possible by the withdrawn ancient gods, by the silence of their graves. The death of these gods is the soil which nourishes the anthropocentric world.

The absence of gods makes man an unprincipled being. Contemporary man's work consists of the establishment of principles, which he lacks and which are needed to accomplish the mission of his life.

Unlike in the ancient world, it is not certain men (prophets or kings) who transmit the ultimate truths, which regulate human ways to the broad masses of their people, but every man is the peak or the highland in the cultural technological territory. Nietzsche compares the superior man to a wheel, where — at each phase of life or at each movement of the cultural world — he is the ultimately dominant power with no gods above his head; he is the Will to Power, Nature's sway itself.

Nietzsche, however, did not say that every man is great or is a superman. Only the ones who are aware of godlessness and who thus have the strength, a backbone, in themselves to sway the meanings of things and to determine man's ways, are supermen. Nietzsche was aristocratically, rather than democratically, minded. Democratic man is godless without being aware of his godlessness; Nietzsche's superman has the greatness — not possessed by democratic man — which consists of his awareness and willful under-going of his godlessness. Mythical man's greatness consisted of his participation in the play or in the dance of his gods.

The godless masses of the contemporary world ignore their godlessness and thus are no superman. However, they certainly live in the vacuum of unprincipledness. Instead of principles, technological democratic humanity possesses the rights of its own outlook and interpretation of everything. It has the right to speak out its "holy" opinions and a right to confess the church of its choice.

Because of democratic liberties, no religion or social system common to everybody is maintained. Man has a right to be irreligious or godless. With the American expulsion of religious teaching in schools man's position as standing above any religious principles is emphasized. Man selects his church, just as he selects a pair of shoes for himself. He does not serve a god or gods. but these implied in the flow of his life and utlilized by him as a means of satisfying his religious needs, are brought by man to significance or importance. Contemporary man maintains the laws of a church hoping for a better afterlife. The meaning of his religiousness is manifestly anchored in his own well-being, and in no wise does he live for the sake of his gods — for transmitting their divine light and majesty into his living days and his living situations.

We can find much the same aspect of serving man's well-being in the systems established by man which govern his life. For instance, the Communistic system is considered by its enthusiasts, as the ideal example of man's domination, utilization and exploitation of reality. According to these enthusiasts, through the Communistic doctrine the "earthly paradise" can be realized, where everyone will enjoy equally the highest possible well-being. Communistic heroes do not die for the Communistic system or Communistic gods, but ultimately — for the realization of man's well-being.

The realization of the well-being of man in the "earthly paradise" of the future is strictly godless. The ideal Communist serves no gods; he serves only humanity — serves men. Communism — just as American, European or world democracy — ignores the age-old truth that man's very being-man, his inner self, consists of his surrendering to superhuman, that is godly, principles. "Man is a rope stretched between the animal and the Superman — a rope over an abyss".[3]

Whenever Communistic armies invade, occupy and "liberate" a hitherto free country, they instantly delete, supress or make obsolete the country's own cultural principles — they kill its gods. "Liberation" in Communistic terminology means the destruction of hitherto existing ways of life and the forceful introduction of strictly Communistic ways. After these ways are established, a watchful eye is kept for any unrest, in order to efficiently oppose the smallest attempts to change the "iron clad" social machinery which determines every man's place and function in the Communistic world. Communism triumphs over the ruins of cultural worlds, over the graveyards of gods.

The "Cultural Revolution" of China is a clear manifestation of the denial, denouncement, removal, and destruction of everything traditionally cultural — be it originated at home or brought in from abroad; it is a denouncement of everything non-Communistic in Mao Tse-tung's brand of Communism.

[3] Friedrich Nietzsche, *The Philosophy of Nietzsche* (New York : The Modern Library, 1927), p. 8.

This denouncement and destructiveness is considered heroic. In a Shangai newspaper three girls, Lu Yang-ping, Lu Yang-bing and Lu Yang-min wrote their story in which they expressed their being in very low spirits at the time their father was dragged out by proletarian revolutionaries, was tried and condemned for his anti-Communistic outlooks or attitudes. Only after attending classes of Red Guards, these girls realized that their father was a "dangerous enemy of the people" mainly because of his refusal to study Mao Tse-tung's works and live by them. Since then these girls have fully supported the expulsion of their father and of those with views similar to his from Communistic society.

A similar radical anti-cultural or godless movement is maintained in Russia. It was especially harsh and inflexible in the initial days of the Communist revolution in Russia. Churches were completely closed and believers were sternly persecuted; families were dissolved and the government took up the education of infants with the purpose to make of them ideal Communists; private possessions were strictly prohibited and no individual food storage or wardrobe was allowed. The sudden dissolution of traditions led to a critical economic, social, and cultural bankruptcy. Because of this the process of Communisation was eased up, and the ideal state of Communist society put off until it was prepared for by a gradual education or training.

The free Western world is to a great extent no better than tyrannical Communism as it triumphs, like Communism, over conquered cultures and their gods. The British Empire, for instance, is proud of its widespread "culturalization" or civilization of "backward" countries. The French, Spanish and other once mighty empires have a similar attitude. All of them succeeded in planting provinces of their own "superior" culture all around the globe. They did this mainly by killing the gods of occupied countries. The "barbarian" customs, rites and ways of life of conquered nations had to be made extinct by the conquerors before the introduction of "true" cultural principles was possible.

The roads of the "culturalization" of "backward" countries by "highly advanced" European nations or cultures, are marked with the tombstones of "barbarian" gods. These roads were broken open and built with Christianity's co-operation, since the European "advanced" cultures were Christian. Christianity, just as Communism and Western democracy, attained its widespread domination by its unequaled ability to kill the gods of various cultures. This was done by means of well equipped military crusades as well as peacefully, with love and charity and missionary works. Is it possible that in recent times Christianity has begun to show signs of unsureness as to its hitherto unquestioned duty to destroy pagan cultures and their gods? In any case, since the days of Pope John XXIII Christianity has acquired tendencies toward cultural tolerance.

Theocide, philosophically formulated by Nietzsche's famous maxim : "God is dead", is nothing other than a declaration of the anthropocentric character of the modern "highly civilized" world.

3. *Technocracy*

While mythical man was holy, the "sober" contemporary technological man is fragmentary in his functions as well as in his tools, which have only a certain, narrow application. The former mythical man was standing on his own feet. He was a stout supporter, defender, teacher, and highpriest of his family. Today, for all these functions we have a series of experts, and a series of insurances for our protection : fire insurance, car insurance, unemployment, medical, and life insurance. We moderns are no longer the masters of our lives. Mastery consists of man's response to his gods.

Ancient gods, ancient wisdom, beauty, workmanship, valor, and many grand individual qualities or talents lose their importance in a technocratic society. Instead of holy, individual, unique abilities or traits, today's man must first become a naked zero before becoming a useful and efficient member of his society. Becoming a zero is a precondition to enter a certain area of the ultramodern technocratic world. By entering such an area the individual acquires his place, function and his meaning within his world.

An "old time" tailor, before he is accepted in a modern tailor shop, must first of all abandon his own individual ways of tailoring — cutting and fitting — and then he can learn a certain single function of the complex functions of his workshop, and he must learn it with precision and accuracy. This means, that he must first become a zero before taking up a function with robot-like precision.

Man, whose holiness (integral wholeness) is dissolved into atoms, and who becomes an expert, resembles a cell, a brick in the structure of technocratic society. With a complicated system of living cells operating highly efficiently in very narrow segments of the technocratic world, our anthropocentric society becomes an immensely complex human-machine power which can "chain the earth and draw its juice dry" for the better growth and well-being of humanity. Nothing can stop this gigantic technological sway of the world, since its gods are dead.

Many millions of years ago Nature arranged unicellular organisms composed of atoms into groups and each group performed a certain function of several. All these groups, working harmoniously, resulted in multicellular organisms, and thus Nature started a new phase in life's development. A cell lost its primordial meaning; it became an insignificant particle in a large organism.

Today's technological man is gradually developing a man-made organism of humanity, where an individual serves the whole of humanity by simultaneously losing his former individual significance.

Technology is man's creation. However, we become more and more aware that modern society, a technological organism in a broad sense, consisting of groups of unionized experts, sways our lives : it draws us into itself, wears us out, and then discards us as pensioners. It replaces us with new living human cells, by young faceless individuals of rising generations.

It is quite obvious today that in the near future the technocratic super-organism will govern every phase of human life with robot-like authomatons. Various such devices, then, will determine the capacities, inclinations and talents lying in a person. It will determine his education, training, and his way of life according to its discoveries in order to extract from him his top efficiency and usefulness to society. He will be placed in the areas of gigantic technocratic machinery, where he will function like a living cell as long as he is useful. After he loses his efficiency — like a worn out cell in a living organism — he will be ejected to a convenient retirement home. The family is bound to disappear as a disorderly and unbridled social unity, when looked at from the viewpoint of the technocratic whole. There will be semen stations (similar to blood banks of today), supplied by men with the great abilities, and only "qualified" mothers will be privileged to partake in the well rationed quantitative and qualitative preservation of the human race.

The social systems dominating the world scene are American democracy (including all the free world) and Communism — both working towards the technocratic society roughly described above. America's "silk glove" society and China's despotic Red Guard herding obedient masses of Chinese people are bound to merge both in theory and in practice in the futur's technocratic world.

In this "ideal" society of tomorrow, the world will have changed imperceptibly. It will no longer be an anthropocentric world, since every individual will function like a tiny wheel in a complex mechanical device or like a cell in a complex living organism. In this phase of technocracy, the height of his anthropocentric world, man will realize that it is not he who sways his world and that everything does not work for him. He will begin to see that on the contrary he functions by serving the man-made superstructure —

his technocratic world. This man-made or manufactured technocratic world will sway and dominate him and his function will be to serve it faithfully. Anthropocentricity brought to its extreme will prove to be the opposite of what it is : now it will be revealed as a net-work of cross-roads (*logos*) in which not human, but technological forces set and determine the meaning of everything, including man. Man will be exposed to technological *playing* powers just as the mythical man was exposed to Nature's playing powers.

What are these mighty technological powers? What are these unknown gods? Nietzsche first and Heidegger later stressed that Nature's powers (Will to Power; *logos*) prevail in man's technological world. All technological devices or creations — ultimately speaking — are not of human making : they are the outcome of the swaying and playing technological powers (a mode of Nature's sway or play) which, responded to by man, determine the place and meaning of all things and the ways and aims of men in their peripheral selves.

Nature (*physis*) sways or playfully comes forward into the open (*logos*) of any culture, including cultureless or godless technology. The discovery that the technocratic world is swayed by unknown forces will set man on the ways of a search for gods. In the midst of technocracy man will awaken to the search for gods. Godlessness, which succeeds the twilight of gods apparently will precede the dawn of new gods. Man is inevitably a being bound by gods.

4. *Godlessness and Philosophy*

A mythical world enters a crisis when its gods display tendencies to withdraw from the ways of men. Man in such cases no longer stands under his gods : he fails to stand under their sway and fails to be surrendered to Nature's dominating powers. When a mythical world is in a crisis — that is, when the swaying or dominating powers of the world are lost from sight and no longer govern man's life convincingly, philosophical thought begins; it is thus rendered possible.

With the event of philosophy, Nature ceases to be the all-dominant holy play of ever-concealed fundamental reality, brought to man by his gods. It comes to be considered as "wholy". Wholy, rather than holy, Nature is *physis* or Being, a transcendental reality which breaks into the open of man's cultural world, where it founds or renders possible all things and their meanings.

In the advanced phase of philosophy (in the philosophy of Plato) *physis*, remaining unentitative, is no longer transcendental reality; it is considered unreal in itself and becomes real only by being enacted by the "spiritual" powers of ideas. To consider Nature as being matter demonstrates sheer ignorance of her. Just as Nature is ignored in Plato's philosophy, so are the gods. These, even though the prototypes of ideas, are no longer thought of mythically. In other words, ideas, being disconnected from Nature (*qua* matter), cannot be properly interpreted as a philosophical conception of gods. Gods, then, are ignored in Plato's philosophy.

Plato's ideas, nevertheless, are transcendental realities : they are not things, but rather realities anterior to anything entitative. Entitative reality is founded or rendered possible by the ideas. What is the world of ideas? What is this "spiritual", immaterial, transcendental reality? Plato does not seem to have given a satisfactory answer to the above question. We, however, know that the world of ideas is not Nature and not gods. Plato's philosophy, consequently, must be considered godless.

Plato's emphasis of goodness as the highest idea was taken over by Aristotle and later by St. Thomas as God, the first mover or supreme being. In this way the transcendental reality of *logos* was localized in one of the entities — in the highest entity or being. *Logos* was considered the mind of the divine subject, which is the founding ground of everything-there-is.

Such an understanding of reality as consisting merely of things or entities actually means abandoning reality's transcendental character. Reality thus comes to be seen and treated as immanent. One of the entities (supreme being) founds or "creates" all others.

While Plato, having abdicated *physis*, still maintained *logos* in his own way, his successors dismissed *logos* as well, by locating it in an entity. God, as the *locus* of *logos*, was the divine, all-founding subject. After the abdication of *physis* as well as *logos*, whole reality was seen as consisting of things, the entities, alone. Whatever was not a thing, an entity, or a being, was not real. A system interpreting reality entitatively, is necessarily a *godless* system. This status is not changed in principle, even though most philosophies throughout history stressed and emphasised God. Once God is understood as an entity, he is not really God, but a philosophical or speculative god; he is the god of a godless world. Philosophy is born with the withdrawal of gods, and it is developed with the deletion, overlooking, ignorance, or "non-under-standing" of gods. Because of this, philosophy necessarily is godless. It remains godless until it begins to look into its own origins and thereby unnoticingly embarks on the road of the search for gods.

A drifting in this direction has already occurred with the re-discovery of pre-entitative or transcendental principles of reality, located, however, in a subject, the human consciousness. Such a re-discovery took place with European "continental" rationalism and "insular" empiricism during the XVIIth century. Kant synthesizing both these major systems ingeniously created the doctrine of transcendental principles, the subjective *logos*, located in the human, rather than in the divine, mind. He created the philosophy of anthropocentric subjectivism.[4]

Since man is a finite reality, *logos* in man — subjective *logos* — acquires the aspects of relativity. Hegel sees the eventual completion of the historical development of the human subject, of the Spirit, in its coincidence with divine *logos*, the *logos* of the Absolute. In his philosophy, therefore, subjectivism is absolutistic. In the succeeding philosophies (Nietzsche, Heidegger) *logos* is thought of again under the aspects of finitude. Here, we regard the subjective *logos* of modern philosophies, unlike that of medieval philosophies, as transcendental. This is so because the divine subject is definitely an entity, while the human subject of modern philosophies has the status of pre-entitativeness or of *a priori*. This latter view, however, became obvious only with Heidegger's understanding of the human subject as *Dasein*.

The rediscovery of *logos* gradually was followed by the rediscovery of *physis*, known in Hegel's philosophy as Nature, the Spirit's self-estrangement. This event of the movement of the Spirit from its self-estrangement to its self-repossession is a pre-condition for anything entitative to be or to have a meaning. Hence, both — *logos* and *physis* — here are preentitative or transcendental. However, *physis* (Nature) in Hegel's philosophy is obviously inferior or subordinate to *logos* (Spirit). A shift occurs with Nietzsche, who elevates *physis* or Nature's play (Will to Power) over *logos* which means the coming of truth in various ways in cultural enlightenment. *Logos* to him is a solidification of the ever-living event of Nature.

Heidegger's existentialism has, as its most prominent problem, the Event of Being (Nature's play) which always occurs in the human cultural world, in *Dasein*. The Event of Being is brought to light by the foursome (*Geviert*), the interplay of transcendental powers of earth, sky, gods and mortals. Mortals here are not taken as entities, but as the participants in the transcendental interplay of the foursome and thereby as transcendental co-founders themselves of the meanings and thus of the being of things in their cultural world.

Heidegger's thought concludes the course of philosophy by bringing it back to its original native ground of the mythical world. In Heidegger's

---

[4] Cf. Vincent Vycinas, *Greatness and Philosophy* (The Hague : Martinus Nijhoff, 1966).

major problems lodge highly mythical characteristics. They are no longer philosophical problems, since they can be thought of or interpreted by pre-philosophical or trans-philosophical means rather than with purely philo-sophical ones. His thought stands closer to godly mythical thought than it does to the godless thought of the "classical" philosophies.

The spirit of this return of philosophy to its original godly ground is nicely expressed by Bernard Boelen who says : "The 'actual' beginning of philo-sophy is a dialogue with the 'pre-philosophical' beginning of philosophy, and philosophy points 'from the very beginning' *beyond* philosophy. This paradox, this tension between immanency and transcendency is the actual beginning of philosophy and the mainspring of all our philosophical explorations".[5]

Philosophy begins in the twilight of gods, where man becomes an outcast from the dance of the gods, and because of this he, already with his very first steps is directed into the process of his struggle, pressing his way back into the works of the gods — he is on the way of a search for new gods. The process of philosophy is, historically, the process of its deviation from mythi-cal thought. During this process philosophy seems to acquire its own stand on its own grounds. Only gradually during its historical development, does philosophy begin to realize that these grounds owe themselves to the abysmal or chaotic ground of pre-philosophical or mythical thought. By seeing itself as merely a province of mythical thought, philosophy overcomes itself; it does so by heading towards the dawn of new gods.

5. *Godless Man*

More often than any previous time men today are sitting at the conference tables trying to reach full mutual understanding. More than any previous time these mutual understandings fail, in spite of frequent phrases of "full accord has been reached" issued after such conferences.

Today — at a time when a multicolored diversity of opinion flourishes, "democratically" backed up by majority votes or by long series of signatures — we live in confusion. We consider ourselves as the most advanced human-ity of all time, and many men, randomly picked from the streets of our bril-liant megalopolises, when asked about the cultural principles of their world or about humanity's ultimate ideals, according to which social and family lives must be guided, or about the meanings of things in man's environ-

---

[5] Bernard J. Boelen, *Existential Thinking* (Pittsburgh : Duquesne University Press, 1968), p. 56.

ment — by their answers they would demonstrate primitive, immature and childish "wisdom". Hardly any of these people, thus asked, would show any grasp of humanity's cultural principles or its ideals. Everyone, most probably, would speak of the well-being, economical securities, commodities, pleasures and such like. Answers of this kind, principly viewed, could be sooner called biological than cultural, as they would be concerned with the well-being of the human race, rather than with man's mission of the inner self serving gods.

Contemporary man does not cultivate his inner self and because of this, he lacks integrity or greatness. The cultivation of the inner self is not principally concerned with the well-being of man, but with his destiny or the mission assigned to him by the ultimate governing powers of reality. The cultivation of man's inner self — of his soul — transcends the man-centered (anthropocentric) grasp of reality; it is open to superhuman powers.

A man of the pre-modern era cherished the beauty of works of art, for instance, not merely as objects of entertainment, but as the "assemblers" of Nature's godly powers. He respected ethical or moral norms not as attained by the mutual agreement of society, nation or humanity, but as inherited from the great men of the past who received them from the nation's gods. He felt a love for his fellow men which he demonstrated not by shallow get-togethers with his next-door neighbors, but by regarding them as people all of whom undergo the blessings and hindrances brought upon them by their gods, who thus determine their destinies and bring them closer to mutual togetherness, occurring mainly during the holidays of their cult, the days of festivity. And finally this mythical man maintained a respectful attitude toward things. Instead of treating them as mere objects exposed to himself, he saw in them the light of the gods; his respect for the gods was displayed by his respect of their gifts, the things.

Henrik Ibsen creates a successful image of a typical member of modern anthropocentric society in his drama *Peer Gynt*. Peer Gynt grew up in a fatherless home in a small mountain community in Norway. His home, like everyone else's there, stood on a patch of soil, the land of the family, passed down from generation to generation, from father to son, and which, this land, in the eyes of the people of the village, was considered holy. Peer Gynt felt no respect either for his land or his community.

Already in his years of adolescence he embarked on his life with no reverence of the ancient Norwegian moral traditions or for his own mother. He disobeyed her disgracefully, and left home, leaving her behind. During a wedding which took place in the village and to which Peer Gynt was uninvited, he intruded in the midst of the wedding dances and, "like a mountain troll", he captured the bride Ingrid, and carried her away to the forested mountains. Thus he manifested his total disregard of the holy rites and customs rooted deeply in the ancient traditions of the community.

A short while later, he left Ingrid, and Solveig, a girl he had met at the wedding, became his wife. He cleared a site and built a hut in the mountains and soon left her with no intention to care for her. He travelled all over the world. He took up and dropped a variety of occupations in various parts of the world. He was a sailor, a prophet, a treasure hunter, a millionaire, and so on. Not just because of his extraordinary clerverness, but perhaps more because of his enormous versatility, due to his rootlessness, he seemed to be able to attain whatever he wished.

Peer Gynt's life seems to be the manifestation of the idea that the man of the peripheral self — a man who serves no high reality and has no genuine ideals but his own bare self—is the acme of man's world. The one who serves nothing but himself seems to dominate everything around himself, and thereby he seems to be the realization of man's mission — the mission of self-centricity. In his own eyes Peer Gynt was a superior man — brilliant and unequalled, and the others — especially those who remained faithful to their small community and its ways, seemed to him but human dwarfs.

Travelling all over the world he was at home nowhere. Nevertheless, he felt the opposite as true : he was at home everywhere. This was so because of the significance to himself of his own individual self, his conscious subject as the holy of holies. Besides himself there was nothing holy, and thus there was no holy place, or home. The presence of a "holy" self (uprooted, conscious self) makes a place holy, a home.

Solveig, on the contrary, remained faithful to her holy patch of land, her mountain homestead, where Peer had built a cabin for her. All her life she waited for his return with unbroken fidelity and love. All her days she maintained the ancient traditional ways, and never lost hope that Peer would return.

However, before Peer could return home and join Solveig, he got into the hands of the ruling powers of Nature and had to stand trial in front of the tribunal of mountain trolls, the spirits (gods) of Nature. Here he was carefully checked by these spirits who weighed every bit of his human valor and significance. These powerful and just spirits of Nature screened the merits of every human individual minutely and accurately as regards his realization of his innermost self. Those who have no worth at all dissolved into the materials of which buttons were made. According to the Norwegian mentality "good for buttons" means having a lack of any dignity, any worth, or any human greatness; it indicates the respective individual as being a nuisance.

In this tribunal Peer Gynt had a shocking experience. He was fully convinced that his inner worth would prove to be of lordly or kingly grandeur; — he would be judged a superman. He was stunned and bewildered when the tribunal judged him good for buttons, that is, good for nothing. This first judgment was quickly reviewed and modified. Instead of being immediately dissolved into materials for buttons, he was given a chance to go back to Solveig. The motive for the altered sentence was Solveig's love for Peer.

She was old when Peer Gynt — an old man as well — came back. He was estranged to everything in his humble native village. Only under the roof of Solveig's hut could he feel warmly accepted; he felt to be firmly standing on his once forsaken ground again.

None of the many "great" roles he played during his life — prophet, sailor, gambler, millionaire — provided Peer with a continuous existential "essentiation" of himself. All of these roles were mutually disconnected fragments, leaving Peer spineless as regarded his inner self. Solveig's love, however, held him continuously in Nature's play and granted him coherence, continuity, and valor as far as his very being-man was concerned. On the ground of Solveig's love, the tribunal of Nature's spirits gave Peer Gynt another chance to accomplish his mission of being-man by sending him back home to Solveig, for here alone had he a possibility of building up the true worth of his self — his inner self.

In spite of his brilliance, kingliness, wordly wisdom, endowment with manifold capabilities, and cleverness on the level of the peripheral self, Peer Gynt was only "good for buttons" — a shallow, substanceless, and selfish human entity — in the silent and ever-concealed play of Nature. Solveig, on the contrary, modest, simple, earthbound, dutiful, and loving, was strongly implied in Nature's play, in the works of the gods.

As we know, Peer Gynt had founded the homestead — the holy abode — for himself and Solveig. Even though he deserted it, Solveig's fidelity preserved and guarded the milieu, in which the inner selves of both were rooted. This preserving and guarding of the holy sod of home's land simultaneously preserved, guarded, and developed through devoted care and love not just of her own inner self, but also of that of Peer Gynt.

A person's peripheral or individual self means a series of disconnected, incoherent decisions or acts. Without an existential unity of the inner self, these acts of the person — in spite of their seeming brilliance — indicate that his being lacks the true self which is needed to accomplish his lordly or godly mission of being-man.

The inner self belongs less to man, as a conscious entity, than it does to his world, his *Dasein* — to the dance of the gods which sways his culture. Thanks to Solveig's love Peer Gynt was involved in Nature's play itself. His greatness did not occur in the manifest, strikingly noticeable events of his conscious day, but in the silent, concealed, obscure night of his inner self, in which he was rooted by his joining Solveig and founding a holy stead with her.

In spite of the manifestly "godless" ways of his being, Peer Gynt was "godly" in a deep corner of his inner self, a shrouded corner of his soul. This shrouded corner meant a chance and possibility of his embarking on the road of the search for gods.

Man may be passive, backward, indifferent, and even stupid as regards the anthropocentric conventional enterprises of his peripheral self. However, he may be active, enthusiastic, and devotedly involved in the ever-concealed play of Nature, wherein his inner self is rooted. He is then existentially alive.

There are times in cultural development, when man loses interest in his *Dasein*. This is the time when gods die or withdraw themselves from man's ways. Festivities, then, cease to be *holy* days, the days of gods. They are merely days of comfort, of longer sleeping hours, — days of fishing or picnicking. They are days of activities purely of anthropocentric entertainment value. Holy days in the anthropocentric world become mere "holidays", the days of leisure, breaking the monotony of the days of work.

Both of these, work and leisure, do not have inner unity or coherence in the modern man's world. Such a man — taken by himself (his peripheral self) is a "jerking entity" moving in various directions without any truly sequential interbelonging. Kierkegaard effectively compares such a man (called by him "aesthetic man") to a frog which, when having attached to itself an electrically charged wire, moves senselessly in a jerking manner in random directions. This experiment illustrates the "activities" of man's peripheral self in its isolation from his inner self. Such activities are marked by confusion.

As regards his inner self, a man of confusion, a Peer Gynt, is a bloodless corpse even though he has a strong pulse and rosy cheeks. A godless man, a Peer Gynt, is dead in his inner self, — good for buttons.

The difference between contemporary and mythical men consists in the godlessness of the former and the godliness of the latter. "Our age stands farthest from the pristinity of the early ages, where everything was still full of gods. Our age is the time of the most extensive gods emptiness, — the time of the most extensive withering of religiousness, which ordinarily is termed 'nihilism' ".[6]

A godless man, a Peer Gynt of our times, is a strange child of our world which has become empty of gods — a vacuum suitable for the godless plays of such men. Having only his own peripheral self in his control (as the inner self always is godly — belongs to or is controlled by gods), he sees all the possibilities around himself from his "firm" human perspectives. We must keep in our minds here, that precisely this "firmness" is weakness by being the manifestation of man's inner confusedness. Peer Gynt, who in the eyes of some of his fellow men, and most of all in his own eyes, seemed a brilliant, strong, superior man, was weak, confused, shallow, lacking integrity, and good for nothing in his very inner self.

In a magazine article a reporter speaks of "Joe the Cat", an apartment burglar.[7] In the major cities of North America there are clusters of high rise apartments which may be 30 to 40 stories high. Apartment dwellers are to a great extent strangers to each other. One more stranger in their midst (Joe the Cat), a burglar, is not noticed.

When a tenant leaves for work in the morning, there is a pause before the garage door closes automatically. Joe the Cat uses this advantage for sneaking in, often with a small truck. When he is in, he can use an elevator and get into a certain apartment he has noticed as being "promising". With hardly any danger, he can load his truck with color television sets, tape recorders, expensive cameras, jewelry and some loose cash.

Joe the Cat, being thoroughly "godless", has no scruples about the moral norms regulating his actions. Why should he? In "democratic" times with freedom — or rather, liberty — to have his own opinion and chosen ways, he outlines his own mission in life.[8] Responding to all the circumstances around himself, he sees everything from his own viewpoints or perspectives; he weighs it purely by how this or that factor is beneficial or dangerous to him. A bobcat in the northern wilderness of Canada acts in the very same way : there are things on which this cat keeps a watchful eye and some day she captures one with a quick and nimble leap. There are also things which it is better to leave alone. In this way, a godless man stands much closer to an animal than does a godly man. However, the actions of an animal are

---

[6] Eugen Fink, *Spiel als Weltsymbol* (Stuttgart : W. Kohlhammer Verlag, 1960), p. 205.

[7] Don Bell, "High-Rise Crime" in *Victoria Daily Times*' Weekend Magazine, July 19, 1969 (Vol. 19, Nr. 29).

[8] Joe the Cat differs from a fully pledged "democrat" by his ignorance of the basic validity of the "categorical imperative" in modern democracy.

governed by Nature without the animal's responsive or irresponsive participation in this governing. Man — be he godly or godless — partakes in
Nature's play constructively or destructively.

The world of Joe the Cat is not Nature's wilderness, but that of technology
— the man-made jungle of the technocratic world. He lives in these jungles
like the bobcat in hers. He does not know, however, that the same powers
which dominate the bobcat's world, ultimately dominate his world of concrete, steel, and glass. His irresponsibility to any gods is his responsibility
to their absence, and it could very well be that this absence, when fully
"under-stood" may point to the misty dawn from where the future gods
will rise. In other words, the technological world understood in an "under-
standing" way may become a godless stepping stone toward a godly future.

An unbiased glance into the backgrounds of the lives of Peer Gynt or
of Joe the Cat would discover there a distance from the godly way of living.
In the atmosphere of contemporary technocratic man one can experience
directly on his own skin the breat-taking realness of godlessness. No theo-
rization or meditation could ever provide such a real, living contact with
the world's godlessness. The attempt of some few truth-searching individuals to escape modern ways, and their failure to fully do so, nevertheless gives
them the experience of realizing how contemporary man is tossed about by the
winds of godlessness. Such an experience is a prelude to the experience
of the gods of tomorrow, who announce their coming — as yet soundlessly
and lightlessly.

6. *Poetical Aspects of Culture*

In the contemporary specialized world those who work in the "cultural"
field constitute a small segment of society which is pre-occupied by scientific
research, aesthetic activities, educational work, servicing the community's
religious needs, and similar activities. The majority of people perform their
daily routine work without being considered "culturalists".

Against this view, we must state here that culture is no specialization.
Man as such is cultural. Not everyone is a shoemaker, but everyone — openly or in a concealed way — is cultural. Culture means wholeness rather than
specialization, and a culturalist is not an expert on a certain segment of the
human *Dasein*, but a man who preserves the prisitine "waylessness" of
being-man.

Today only a peasant seems to maintain the traits of wholeness (and thus
of holiness).[9] He seeds his fields with the variety of plants required by his

---

[9] A farmer, unlike a peasant, is specialized just as is any tradesman in the modern world.

own family and animals. He provides his family with vegetables, fruit, eggs, milks, meat, and so on. He provides his animals with hay, grain, shelter, bedding, and similar needs. Peasants, besides having a thorough understanding of plant and animal life, are butchers, taxidermists, implement makers, seamstresses, tailors, sanitarians, constructors of buildings, and masters of many other trades. All their knowledge is inherited from their ancestors, and only a small part of it is discovered by their own experiences.

A peasant's knowledge of his world covers the whole range, the whole world of peasantry, from horizon to horizon. This knowledge is not pieced together from various things which he handles. On the contrary, any thing in a peasant's world is grasped or approached from his understanding of Nature in her wholeness.

This understanding, inherited from his ancestors, throughout the ages, is to a great extent shrouded in obscurities. Even though obscure itself, however, this knowledge renders the things of a peasant's world clear, comprehensible and manageable. Moreover, this knowledge or understanding is the "under-standing" in the sense of standing under Nature's all-swaying, unentitative powers which elucidate, explain, or make clear the things of a peasant's world. This knowledge, thus, is of the existential kind; such a knowledge is pre-scientific or pre-philosophical.

The peasant's activity is not just the cultivation of soil and the making or creating of almost all the things in his world. It is principally his understanding of Nature's powers by his standing responsively under them and thereby by bringing them to disclosure within his living days. A peasant is not a soil expert or specialist; he is in the first place a culturalist.

Culture in its own "essentiation" has the character of wholeness: it brings to light reality's (Nature's) principles which form and found the meanings of all things. Reality's or Nature's principles are gods, and man's responsive standing under these gods is his participation in or co-action with their works. This participation or co-action is his cult, and this is why man is a culturalist.

We know that animals maintain the features or traits of their distant ancestors long after they have left them and have become a species irrecognizably different from them. In this way, for instance, birds and mammals have some reptilian features. Insects, the most numerous type of animal, survive by becoming specialized or becoming "experts" in a certain function of their lives, very rigidly determined by their instincts.

So called intelligent animals are less specialized in this way or less "expert". They become so purely by the works of Nature. Intelligent animals may learn new ways in their limited habitat. They can transmit their learning to other individuals, usually to their offspring. The flexibility of intelligent animals, however, and their discovery of new ways, is rather their ability to modify their primarily instinct-bound situation. In other words, by their flexibility intelligent animals never do step out into the "wayless" whirlpool of Nature's creative powers in order to originate a totally new way from there. An animal — be it instict-bound or intelligent — never starts his own way. While an instinct-bound animal proceeds rigidly on his way, the intelligent animal has a broader scale of variation on the very same way.

Only man can step back into Nature's creative source and — responding to her playing principles, the gods, — he can be a co-paver of his way with them. Such responsiveness in the breaking-open of one's ways (*Be-wëgung*) is cultic or cultural.

Culture — as we have already seen — is not a "spiritual" activity such as meditation on transcendental principles of reality *in abstracto* by closing oneself off from the "impure", "material" entities. On the contrary, man is a culturalist handling the things of his living situations in such a way that in these situations he guards the dynamic transcendental truth of powers which are presupposed by things and which render them meaningful.

A culturalist in Heidegger's thought is a man who lives poetically. Poetical living or dwelling for him is not unrealistic playing with the images of phantasy with an aim to provide the readers or hearers of poetry with an aesthetically satisfying experience. One who allows a thing to be what it is in Nature's play lives poetically. To allow thus is man's response to Nature's play. It guards the interplay of transcendental or pre-entitative powers by guarding the meanings of the things founded by these powers.

Midus was an intoxicating beverage well known in the mythical Lithuanian world. This thing, logically defined is an intoxicating beverage made of wild bee honey. Approched "poetically", *midus* is variously interrelated with many other things and, most fundamentally, it discloses the transcendental background in which its meaning, and those of things, related to it, is founded.

Bee honey is brewed in the cool water of forest springs with the admixture of various spicy herbs. Water and herbs are things granted to men by the rainy skies and the sun which bring flowers to bloom and shed warmth on the bees which gather the honey. *Midus* was one of the basic sacrificial offerings to the Lithuanian gods, especially to Patrimpas, the god of Nature's gifts and to Medeine, goddess of the wealth found in forests and their rivers and lakes. *Midus* was the major item in the ancient Lithuanian menu.

It was served, as everything else, on heavy oak board tables in rustic archaic log dwellings during national or family festivities.

To know *midus* as solely man's beverage, is to know it in an anthropocentric, and that is, in a godless, way. To know it poetically — according to Heidegger's way of interpreting poetry — is to know it as the spot wherein this thing is firmly established and wherein the transcendental powers of the foursome flash into the light. These powers are earth, sky, gods, and men, as far as these are responsive to or implied in the other three. "A poetically dwelling man brings the pristine light of earth, sky and the holy ones /the gods/ into that which then acquires its own stance by preserving the wholeness /the interplay of the foursome/. He brings the pristine light by granting a meaningful stability to this thing".[10]

Man's participation in Nature's break-through (her guilt) in a thing — which is always a thing in man's living world — man's existential guilt by which he is the guardian, in the first place, not of things in their meanings but of powers in which things are founded or firmly established — brought to stability. Culture is thus concerned with the unentiative or *a priori* reality no more than it is concerned with the entitative or *a posteriori* reality. Things as things cannot be thought of without unentitative powers of Being which are presupposed by the things. Moreover, not some of the things are cultural, but things as things — things in their "essentiation" or their being established on or their owing of themselves to the unentitative grounds.

Man's expertise or specialization means his ability to handle a certain "line" of things. A culturalist does not have a "line" of things. He understands things as things, that is as the spots where the unentitative or transcendental powers of Being flash up. By such an understanding of things, man stands under these unentitative powers of Being by responsively participating in their action (the play) of founding or establishing things in their meanings. Here we can see why the culturalist's way of being is "poetical". To guard a thing in the pristine light of Being is to create (or rather co-create) it.

In the traditional conception culture means a forming of matter by spirit. In the theocentric world of the medieval ages God, understood to be the supreme thing, was the spirit forming all other beings, entities, or things. In our anthropocentric times man's spirit forms and molds things. It does this most manifestly in the field of sciences, especially in that of technology.

[10] Martin Heidegger, *Hölderlins Erde und Himmel* (Pfullingen : Verlag Günther Neske, Long play record, NV 7,8,9,10 — 33-0195A,B and 33-0196A,B.)

Even if things are not approached just purely scientifically or technologically, they still — in our times — do not refer to any transcendental powers, but to man as the main entity. A poet today does not serve any gods by letting their light flash up into the human world. He serves men. Aesthetic values are those which arouse and enhance enjoyment in man by appeasing his feeling or craving for beauty, exclusively as that which makes his living environment more pleasant and attractive.

Poets, or men of art in general, today are entertainers. To a great extent they are comedians. This is so because enjoyment tends more and more to brighten or to elevate society's happy mood which manifests itself by laughter. The early Greek plays, which brought great, divine powers down into the real, living situations of the Greek *Dasein*, placed men into the experience of the somber and often startling superhuman powers which often mercilessly ruled human destinies. Today's heroes of the stage are jokers. They dominate almost all poetical segments of culture in literature, on stage, and especially on television screens. A culturalist today is a comedian.

A comedian does not create things poetically; he reveals them in a distorting light (comparable to bent-glass mirrors which distort the true reflections of things) and thus makes them appear ludicrous or amusing. A poet is serious. A genuine poet does not twist real things, beautifying them by symbolic, allegoric, or some other aesthetic means. Poetical living or dwelling views and presents a thing on its pristine innocent ground on which it paradoxically is still "guilty" by being a spot where Nature's guilt fllashes into the light. Poetical living is innocent because of its sincere response to Nature's pristine guilt, her break-through into the light of man's world. To live poetically is to plunge into Nature's primordial innocence (peace), or her guilt (play). Pristinity here consists of transcendency; it means anteriority to any thing. Poetical plunging into Nature's primordial guilt is a plunging into Nature's still innocent working powers — powers which found, give a start to, or establish things whose "essentiation" consists of bringing to light Nature's background, that is, disclosing that which is ever-concealed and thereby committing the cosmic guilt.

An animal is placed in a situation in which he has a definite pattern by which to manoeuvre. Man falls into a misty pathless milieu where he must establish things of his living world and break open his own paths. The diclosure of the meanings of things and the breaking open of his trails brings the light of *logos* of reality (*physis*) and thus carries on the guilt of Nature's self-disclosure.

Poetical, or *ipso facto* culturalistic, living is pristine; it is anterior to any occupation or specialization, anterior to any "objective" or scientific interpretation of things or formulation of their meanings. To regard poetry as a way of playfully distorting the "realistic" traits or meanings of things is a failure to see poetry in its original sense which prevails or plays in the pristine chaos wherein it founds things or gives a start to them. By his plunge into Nature's creative abyss, a poet comes up with a totally new word. Such a word is holy — not only because it evokes the name of a god governing a wide range of reality, but because it brings along (discloses) the whole of Nature's play.

As time goes on, poetical things or poetical words lose their pristine shine : they gradually wear out. In times of cultural decline, holy words, like worn-out coins, lose their poetical gleam and become profane. Their meanings are then definable with logical precision. These, however, cease to relay the godly light into human life; they speak only of purely human affairs and become godless. Language, originally poetical (language of *logos*), becomes logical — a handy instrument serving man, an instrument for the humanization of his world.

The cultural way of man's being his innermost self is creative. It is so because it lets or allows transcendental or godly powers to prevail in man's world, in his living days. In this milieu things are poetical : they are pristine, godly, holy or wholy.

At the time of the pharaoh Tutankhamen's coronation, Egypt had experienced a phase of "prosaic" life. In this phase things, along with man's loss of poetical living, seemed to have lost the halo of holiness, a trait of the whole. This attitude outwardly manifested itself by the crumbling of the sanctuaries and temples and by the holy walks becoming overgrown with weeds. Pharaoh's cultural mission consisted of the descent of his own self (his *Ka*) into the holy creative source of Nature's play. Nature's play was expressed by the rising of Atum, the ever-concealed, as the life-bestowing, brilliant sun, the god Ra, over the Egyptian nation. Such a disclosure, guilt, or distortion of the Ever-concealed, necessarily had to be made good or repaid by the sun's dipping back into the shrouds of concealment. At the end of the day, Ra returned to the dark region beyond the horizons and became Atum again. The cycle of Osiris' birth to Isis, followed by his matrimony to her, and completed by his return to her (to Mother Earth's holy Throne, her womb) was a modulation of the same basic truth. This latter cycle of Nature's play was especially manifested by the birth of the holy stream, the Nile, followed by its harmonious marriage (to marry is to harmonize, to fill, to merge or to become one) with earth. This marriage resulted in a multitude of *holy* things, which were holy because they reflected or manifested the "wholy" play of Nature. The Nile's drying-up or death turned all things to dust, and the Nile itself, the god Osiris, disappeared into the dark depths of earth (Isis' womb).

Each pharaoh was a god by his response to Nature's play. Pharaoh's response was a trigger for the eruption of the light of the gods and of Nature's play, which then settled in the midst of the living days of Egyptian society. During the reign of each pharaoh a new cultural phase was realized by the erection of new grandiose monuments along with the restoration, rejuvenation and renewal of the light of the old ones.

During Tutankhamen's coronation, Horemheb, the supreme general of the Egyptian armed forces, said in his speech that the new king "would supress evil in all the land and cause the ruins to 'flower again' and become once more 'monuments of eternity' ".[11] These promises, unlike those of contemporary "democratic" statesmen, show the king as serving the gods and thus, as simultaneously indirectly serving men (the nation) as far as men are concerned with their responsibilities to the gods. Contemporary "democratically" minded statesmen have primarily no "poetical" (cultural) aspirations or interests; their interests lie in serving men not with regard to their innermost mission, but as what concerns their peripheral demands, needs, or desires. If they had any "poetical' 'or godly aspirations, they would inevitably lose their election to a "sober"-minded competitor who is concerned only with man's self-centered well-being.

The "poetical" (cultural or godly) vocation of a king is well expressed by Tutankhamen's name itself. Literally it means "the king 'who spends his life making images of the gods' ".[12] "Making images" here must be understood as "bringing the gods to light; their disclosure or manifestation". This trait of kingliness must be applied to any great man in the mythical world. It stresses such a world's "poetical" and thus properly cultural nature. The anthropocentric world, being prosaic, is principly cultureless or godless.

7. The Twilight of Gods

Pharaoh's mission was to restore the nation's *Dasein* by healing its prosaic ailments, which distort the pristine light of the gods which is in it (in *Dasein*), and thus restoring its "poetical" innocence. This mission expresses or reflects the same tendency which lies in Nature herself. As we have already seen, in the mythical events of Atum-Ra or Isis and Osiris Nature comes for-

---

[11] Christiane Desroches-Noblecourt, *Tutankhamen* (New York : Graphic Society, 1964), p. 182.

[12] *Ibid.* p. 173.

ward in the innocence of her pristine light. She discloses herself in this light and becomes guilty by making a breach in her essential concealment — breaking through into disclosure. Nature then heals her breach by drifting back into shrouds of concealment again.

Such a pulsation of Nature is responded to by the pharaoh from coronation to burial. Both of these magnificent events in the cultural life of ancient Egypt were cult events — they were "poetical" — because they responded to the play of the gods.

Cultural pulsation occurs not only within cultures themselves, but each culture as such is often one immense pulsation. History tells us again and again that cultures, like plants or other living organisms, are born and die. Neither cultural birth nor death is primarily man's constructive or destructive work or accomplishment. Culture is born with an entering of gods into man's world and it dies with their recession from it.

Man, a cultural being, has nothing to say about the gods outside of his cultural milieu, his world. Gods, when breaking into the cultural *Dasein*, rise from their misty dawn and thus they *quasi* are born. When mythical cultural standards or norms lose their hold upon man's way of life during the late phases of his cultural life, his gods seem to lose their power or realness : they withdraw from the openness of human *Dasein*; — they *quasi* die by pluging into cultural twilight.

This shows that the reign of gods is not eternal. Greek myths present several cases where the ruling of the gods shifts from one deity to another. Mother Earth was the supreme deity in the earliest (Chthonian) phase of Greek mythical culture. Later Kronos, her son, became the ruler of the world and of all other gods. Zeus took over this ruling power from Kronos by some tricks with the help of Mother Earth. With Zeus, the most brilliant personage in the drama of the Greek gods, the Olympian age of mythical culture was realized.

In spite of Zeus' supreme might, in many Greek myths a foreboding of his fall can be felt. This was expressed most clearly in the prophecies of Prometheus, while he was suffering, chained to a rock by Zeus' order.

The Teutonic myths were more concerned with the struggle among the gods and the end of their reign than were the Greek. "The Teutons did not believe that the world would endure for ever nor even that the gods were immortal. Like men the gods had ceaselessly to struggle against enemies who were full of envy and deceit. To maintain their pre-eminence over these demons they had incessantly to remain on the alert".[13] The struggle of the

---

[13] *Larousse Encyclopedia of Mythology* (New York : Prometheus press, 1959), p. 282.

gods and the shift of ruling supremacies among them must be understood to have a close relation with the fluctuation of man's cultural life.

At the time when the early Europeans hunted mamooths and later, wild horses, they did not have much contact with their more distant neighbors and no towns with concentrated populations; likewise they did not have strong warring kings or kingly, dominant or conquering gods, such as Odin or Zeus. Their deities stood close to undisturbed Nature and to the living situations of peaceful communities of hunters or peasants. Such, for instance, where the early Athena or Artemis in Greek society. These deities originated as being assembled by skillfully made things such as implements for hunting or for agrarian work. The making of these things required wisdom, dexterity or ingenuity. Along with them the aspects or motives of the awesome beauty and purity of Nature entered the *Dasein* of these people. Not only manufactured things, but human ventures in the chase and in travels displaying insight, understanding, or wisdom on forest trails, rivers, streams, or on the waters surrounding the sea islands brought these godesses as living presences into the human world.

We know nothing of the beyond-*Dasein* — the beyond of Nature's play — nor do we know anything of gods ouside of the limits of our world. The appearance of gods in our *Dasein*, their dominance there, their withdrawal and their being absent from there — all this is known to us through the wisdom of our inner selves. Moreover, our response to these gods in their appearance, prevalence, withdrawal and absence from our world depends much on our own responsive co-operation, or lack of it, to this birth-life-death, to the play and dance, of the gods in our world.

In spite of the necessity of man's response to the invasion, prevalence and withdrawal of gods in his cultural world he remains the subordinate power in this world. The world is dominated principally by the gods even when they are withdrawn and still rule our world in their absence. Cultural origin, its height, and its decline are foremostly in the hands of transcendental powers, the gods. Man has only a subordinate or secondary role in the cultural movement (*Be-wëgung*).

Culture necessarily is a disrupture : gods invade man's world, ordain it and withdraw from it. Their invasion and ordinance is their self-disclosure, which — as we already have seen — disrupts their essential concealedness. By their withdrawal from man's world, by their dying away in their twilight, they redeem their cosmic guilt and thus they restore their pristine peace of concealment.

The "play" of gods in a peculiar mythical way is presented by the Teutonic motive of the Twilight of the Gods. "In the dawn of time the gods in their palaces in Asgard had led a peaceful and industrious life. They had taken pleasure in building temples, erecting altars, working in gold and forging tools with hammer and anvil, or in playing draughts together. Had they only been able to dominate their passions this golden age of peace would never have come to an end. But the gods brought down the blows of destiny on their own heads".[14]

The above passage, of course, must be understood as parallel to the Egyptian mythical structures of Isis-Osiris or Atum-Ra, pointing out Nature's disclosure as her disturbance of her own peace. The need to restore this peace makes it requisite that gods plunge back into the twilight of the approaching cultural night — they plunge into godlessness. Gods and their disclosed cultural *Dasein* are pregnant with disorder and downfall. With the downfall of his gods man's cultural world inevitably crumbles into ruins.

During the phase of the Twilight of Gods, gods of light, disclosure, and order fight a losing battle against obscure godly powers of concealment and chaos. In the *Edda*, a collection of Teutonic myths, the powers of chaos are presented as monsters, serpents, fire giants and so on.[15] In the Greek myths they are generally known as Titans. While this battle is fought, divine order (*logos*) becomes impotent in the human *Dasein*, and this precisely is a pre-condition for a mighty sway of purely anthropocentric *logos* — the *logos* of godlessness, of irresponsiveness to gods and their sway.

The *Edda* already sees far ahead when speaking of new gods who are bound to rise after the era of godlessness (after our era!). In fact, the dawn of the new gods announes itself with the twilight of the old gods. However, they — not being invited or introduced by man's *godly* responsiveness into his *Dasein* — remain inactive and thus still absent. "On the field of peace ... the new gods gathered in their turn. Who were these new gods? Had they no connection with the gods of olden days? None at all. They had already been in existence, but having never shared the passions, or quarrels of the former gods, having committed neither perjury nor crime, they had not perished. To them it was reserved to renew the world".[16]

These new gods were faceless (undisclosed). Gods can acquire their faces only in the cultural milieu — in man's world. These gods, remaining absent from our contemporary world, make it shallow. In such a world, conditions are favorable for the thriving of a small weed, the subjective or anthropocentric human entity, which stupidly seeks very-human (*allzumenschlich* — Nietzsche) happiness and who thus is a true "democrat".

---

[14] *Ibid.*, p. 283.

[15] *Ibid.*, p. 284.

[16] *Ibid.*, p. 285.

Man must penetrate the vast realm of godlessness, if for nothing else, but to realize the truth or destiny, according to which, man without the gods is but "a shadow of a dream" (Pindar). This idea is known in a Teutonic myth where man is seen as having sprung up from the vegetative world.[17] Before man was originated, three "gods, Odin, Hoenir and Lodur, one day were travelling together on the still deserted earth. On the way they came across two trees with inert and lifeless trunks. The gods resolved to make mortals of them".[18]

The cult of trees was widespread in the Teutonic and also in the Lithuanian mythical world. The tree symbolizes pristinity. Plants are more primitive than animals, and thus they stand closer to the original source of Nature's creative play. Primitivity is a trait of an entity, while pristinity is a transcendental quality. Taken symbolically, primitivity, and thus a tree, may mean pristinity — the being-implied or belonging in the pathless whirlpool of Nature's movement (*Be-wëgung*), wherein all ways have their start and all things are born. Man's relation to trees must be thought of as his being-implied in Nature's pristine play, anterior to things and their ways. A tree trunk can be symbolically seen as Nature who founds and supports all things. "The Germans believed that the universe was supported by a gigantic tree".[19] In man's most delicate, refined, and genuine cultural achievements there is — and there must be — the tone of Nature's pristinity. We indicate this tone symbolically by the wailing of a dead tree swayed by Nature's winds. This sound is the pristine song of Nature, to which gods dance.

Gods, invading the human *Dasein*, man's cultural world, introduce into it the transcendental light which holds things variously interrelated or located on the roads and crossroads of the world's openness. This light is *logos*. It is the light of the Ever-concealed (of Nothingness) — the light of *physis*. This light (*logos*) distorts concealedness (*physis*) wherefore it is always relative. It is always going out or dying into the transcendental twilight of the gods.

Even though "relative" — that is, non-absolute — the *logos* of a cultural world is always its ultimate foundation or ultimate truth — of things and of man's behaviour. Consequently, each cultural world has its own gods, and only with these present in it can a man of respective culture live an ultimately founded life. No cultural norms, or rather no gods, of any one culture can be imposed upon the other cultures. This is so because there is no absolute culture, nor are there any absolute gods.

[17] Cf. *Ibid.*, p. 254.
[18] *Ibid.*
[19] *Ibid.*, p. 256.

In history frequent attempts have been made to introduce the "true" culture to "backward" countries. The first step in such an introduction was always a denial and rejection of the native gods. This was done by proclaiming them either negative (devilish) forces or the products of an erring imagination.

Christianity especially is prone to oppose and destroy the gods of various cultures (pagan gods). Christianity's road through history is marked by a series of silent graveyards of the gods of various cultures. The number of theocides in the history of Christianity is remarkable. Rome directly, and perhaps more so through various European *Christian* cultures, committed most of Earth's theocides. With the death of its gods a cultural world collapses and therewith becomes ready for digestion by "true" Christian culture.

Christianity is proud of its missionary works — of its spreading of the "true" faith around the globe. The same pride is shared by all *cultural* European countries, especially England, France, Spain and others, who have "civilized" wide areas of "backward" barbarian countries around the world. British culture apparently is to be considered the most efficient here. Britons consider themselves the founders of cultural and social freedom wherever they have flown their flag. In contemporary times Russian despotic Communism considers itself the "true" apostle of freedom and culture who "liberates" the people of any country it invades and brutally occupies.

Let us see what an old Indian chief, Dan George in Canada, has to say about the freedom Canada gave to his people : "But in the long hundred years since the white man came, I have seen my freedom disappear like the salmon going mysteriously to sea. The white man's, strange customs which I could not understand, pressed down upon me until I could no longer breathe.

"When I fought to protect my land and my home, I was called a savage. When I neither understood nor welcomed this way of life, I was called lazy. When I tried to rule my people, I was stripped of my authority".[20] These few complaints by a great Indian man give only some fragments of what happens to a nation whose cultural principles are taken away. Indians, to a much greater extent than the people of most other cultures, were incapable of adjusting themselves to the gods of conquering alien cultures, who "liberate" them from their own gods.

The death of the gods of a culture is the death of the culture. The most efficient conquest is not attained by slaughtering the defenders of a defeated nation, but by killing its gods. A nation without its own gods falls into

---

[20] In *Victoria Daily Times*, Weekend Magazine, May 23, 1970.

confusion, into a meaningless way of being, into chaos. Only in this state is a nation ready to accept the gods of the conqueror and live under the new cultural standards.

The Western culture which successfully buried most of the gods of various other cultures around the globe today has almost completed the theocide of its own gods, or rather, its own God. "God is dead!" says Nietzsche. "God remains dead! and we did kill him ... The holiest and mightiest that the world hitherto possessed bled away under our knives".[21]

Just as we killed the gods of almost all of Earth's cultures we finally killed or dethroned our own Christian God. We did this in the technocratic phase of our culture in which all things and all ways of man are determined by man's own decisions, domination, regulation and order. We are holding fast onto our wholly-human stead, as the nerve centre of the swaying and governing of everything in the world. We are the true dwellers in the world of godlessness.

We Christians, who for centuries have eagerly combated the enthusiasm of people of all other cultures by trying to inspire them with our "true" faith, stand today in a world vacated by our own God — we stand here ourselves without a faith. Does Christianity and do Christian norms still dominate the ways of our lives? Let us think momentarily of the centers of our contemporary cultural world — New York, Paris, Tokyo, Moscow, and so on — aren't they all alike in being the manifestations of our glorious technocratic civilization? In the various forms we fill out in various offices, there is a line which asks us to indicate our faith, the church we belong to. This in no wise means that faith is the main driving force in a man's life. It is only a small characteristic among many other characteristics, such as nationality, age, marital status, physical handicaps, weight, and so on. It is the mighty technocratic machine which today drives or governs the movement of men in the anthills of modern cities. Technocracy determines man's position, job, occupation, family and social life, even his reading, vacationing, art enjoyment, and way of thinking. Technocracy has taken the reins from theistic hands. Undoubtedly, the average man would state that he is a Christian. that he believes in God, and partakes in Sunday worship. However, the main question here is whether his life, his existential traversing of his living situations, his accomplishment of the mission of his life — does this stand principly under the sway of God's Gospel? Is Christ?, is the Church the true driving power operating modern humanity's world in

[21] Quoted by Martin Heidegger, *Holzwege* (Frankfurt a.M. : Vittorio Klostermann, 1950), p. 198.

its glorious cities, in its administrative structures, in its daily life on streets, on roads, in offices, in markets, in stadiums, in art galleries, in libraries, in homes, in kitchens, in easy-chairs, and so on? No! The technocratic clock dictates man's pace on his routes of his public and private life; it determines his goals and aims. Our world is godless.

The downfall of gods, their extirpation, by invading alien cultures or their cessation to exist, principally or ultimately is not accomplished by man. It is not his plans and willful decisions or his overpowering of people of other cultures, but the transcendental powers behind him that are the true destroyers of the gods of invaded countries. When cultures fall apart and their gods die, they fall victim to the brighter light of other gods who produce a mightier response from men "under-standing" them (standing under them). Modern man's godlessness, too, is not an accomplishment of man, but is due rather to the withdrawal of his gods — by their cessation to be principal driving powers in the late phase of modern culture; — their cessation to be present in the cultural life of man.

We have already seen that the cessation of gods to prevail as active cultural powers in the human *Dasein* means strictly speaking, a cessation of cultural life as such. A godless man, fundamentally speaking, is culture-less. Consequently technocratic culture should not really be called a culture or cultural phase, but rather a, or the, civilization. The Latin word for "citizen", *civis* in the root of the word "civilization" underlines man (the citizen), and not a god, as the culture-bearing power. American democracy is a civilization as being the domain of man. Communistic proletarian dictatorship, no doubt, should be seen in much the same way.

In godless times gods remain inactive, impotent or absent. Gods who die, who withdraw from man's cultural *Dasein*, never return or are never reborn as what they were. Neither Zeus, nor Ra, nor Odin, nor Perkunas will ever come back in the dawns of future cultures, which are bound to follow this phase of civilization. Only Nature remains a transcendental power in godless times. However, her play is concealed during these times. Nature is ever young. Mother Earth is always youthful, a bride. Yet she sways in her concealment. She needs gods to raise herself to the light of disclosure. Accordingly, Nature's sway during the phase of technocracy, the phase of civilization, is concealed despite her being ultimately active there. This sway can be and will be disclosed with the dawning gods, responded to by men on the way of the search for gods.

Gods arise in their dawn, they reign over man's world; then they withdraw into the cultural twilight and remain absent during the night of godlessness. New gods arise, reign and withdraw. Man seems to outlast the gods. Man, by his very essence (or "essentiation"), is primitive, or rather, pristine. His pristinity is due to his ever remaining in Nature's play, her womb.

Man is thus the son of chaos. Perhaps we should say that he is the son of Prometheus who represents Nature's pristinity or chaos. Man is essentially man by maintaining or upholding his pristinity; — by always having its abysmal, chaotic ground beneath his feet. Man can be a faithful servant of some gods or an arch enemy of some other gods. He can commit theocides (being, of course, responsive to the works of those gods who oppose the gods being killed). He can lose his fidelity to his gods and become godless. And then again, he can go out on a search for the new gods of the future. Man may be godless, yet he never leaves Nature's play, even though this is to a great extent concealed from him.

Man may be constructive, following the lead of Zeus and the other Olympian gods, and just equally he may be destructive, following Prometheus : revolting against transcendental, yet chaotic, ways. Nature is creative and destructive. She constantly rises into light with the dawns of gods and dips back into darkness with their twilights. So does man : he is creative and destructive. He partakes in Nature's play by his constant dips into her pristinity.

Investigating the poetry of Georg Trakl, Heidegger points out man as being essentially implied in Nature's play, by seeing him as a child of light and dark, a child of "blueness". Nature is neither light (disclosure) nor dark (concealment); she is "blue". "Light concealed in darkness is blueness".[22] Man, due to his pristine participation in Nature's play, is the child of "blueness". "Blueness" is the milieu, wherefrom gods are born and wherein they die.

8. *Godlessness and Things*

Even as man is always involved in the transcendental movement (*Bewegung*) of Nature — be it in godly or godless times — so things in their being and meanings are founded in Nature even in godless or anthropocentric times.

Things of the anthropocentric world ultimately refer to the silence of the withdrawn gods. This silence founds the anthropocentric world. In the night of godlessness, with the dawn of new gods still afar, only the silence

[22] Martin Heidegger, *Unterwegs zur Sprache* (Pfullingen : Verlag Günther Neske, 1959), p. 44.

— the absence of these gods — can be experienced. Today "the sign of gods", says Antoine de Saint-Exupéry, "is silence itself." (from *La Citadelle*).

Here, of course, silence is not simply the absence of sounds. In the latter sense silence, just as sounds, can be grasped on an entitative or objective level. Silence here is a mighty transcendental power which ultimately founds the current things of our world. In the following words of Christiane Ritter, which speak of winter's dead lull on a remote northern island of Spitsbergen, we can feel the realness and the might of silence : "I have an inkling, or rather I know with certainty, that it was this, this terror of nothingness, which over the past centuries has been responsible for the death of some hundreds of men here in Spitsbergen.

"It wasn't only scruvy. Often enough they died though the larders were full and there was plenty of fresh meat. They had guns and cartridges; there were reindeer grazing in all the valleys. But they did not dare to venture out. The terror lay in wait for them just outside the door of the hut; it sprawled over the entire bleak land like a monster. It riveted the most courageous hunters and seafarers to their huts. It was the image of the immense deadness of the country, the fearful immobility of all being, that had been graven in theirs souls, crippling all their energies and emptying them of strength. Physical disintegration was bound to follow".[23]

The preceding words, it is true, can be understood from a psychological standpoint as describing a phobia; however, it also illustrates well the point of the intense realness of basically non-entitative reality. Silence in this sense illustrates well Heidegger's problem of Being, which is experienced in the mood of dread, when all things — all entitative reality — drift away and the realness of Being itself, as "not-a-thing", as Nothingness, falls upon us. Such is the experience of transcendental reality, — of that which is ever-concealed, the experience of Nothingness, the silence of gods.

Being in its disclosure, or gods in their presence, are always experienced through things holy — things which are the assemblers of the interplay of the transcendental principles of Nature. Nothingness also (concealed Nature), can be experienced with the absence of drifting away of things. A sensitive or poetical soul in these godless, modern technocratic times now and then is suddenly overcome by the ultimate meaninglessness of things. We, surrounded by an abundance of products of technology, stand in the midst of the desert of a meaningless world. Much the same experience can suddenly occur to those who, being extraordinarily wealthy, surround themselves with

---

[23] Christiane Ritter, *A Woman in the Polar Night* (New York : E. P. Dutton & Company, Inc., 1954), pp. 171-172.

all manner of material goods and still look about for more. All that they can desire is more and more of these things. What else? There can be nothing else, since beyond all things lurks the merciless, horrifying vacuum of godlessness, the silence of gods.

When earth becomes merely a huge cluster of crude materials to be "dignified" by technology, it becomes useless in itself. Only in the technocratic world can earth acquire its worth. Only those few who still have a poetic life in themselves or who live closer to earth, can still feel earth's holiness. Christiane Ritter was able to experience earth's transcendental supremacy over things only after going far from the technocratic world. "Only now", says she, "do I grasp the real meaning and the world-transforming element in the saying : 'Become as the peasants, understand the sacredness of the earth' ".[24]

In spite of the Christianization of the Lithuanian nation during the XIII-XIVth centuries, people in the villages maintained the archaic mythical customs as late as World War I and even a decade after it. For instance, the longest day of the year was still celebrated with rich mythical ceremonies in which both old and young participated with fervor. The true meaning of most of the ceremonies, however, was no longer properly grasped or understood. Even the holiday itself was no longer considered the feast of the sun-god, but that of St. John.

The meanings of things were drawn mainly from the archaic cult ceremonies or rites. All the main work of the peasants was not guided by the calendar, but by the archaically known or transmitted *natural* signs. For instance, peas were seeded one month (one moon) after the vernal equinox, while the seeding of oats occurred during the bloom of the bird-cherry. Immediately after the holy day of the Sun or after the "sun's return" (after the feast of St. John), was the true time designated by gods, for seeding linseed. Rye was mowed at the time of the Holiday of Herbs (August 15th); its time of sowing coincided approximately with the autumnal equinox. These are only a very few of the natural dates taken at random in the Lithuanian peasant's life.

Nothing in this peasant's world can have a meaning without a recourse to Nature. Nature is generous with her gifts, although she often burdens man with ill fortunes. Man must have respect for Nature. He must have a respectful, yet at the same time cautious, attitude toward her. He must be an agile co-player in Nature's play in order to live a life amid holy things

[24] *Ibid.*, p. 181.

and simultaneously avoid being harmed by the misfortunes dominated by ill gods.

A knowledge of Nature provided the ancient Lithuanian with the qualities of good craftsmanship. He knew that a certain tree (and no other) was suitable for making the fellies of the wheels, which for the hubs, for a scythe or rake handle, which for a trough, for a barrel, for a spinning wheel, and so on. He knew the materials and the ways of making ropes for various purposes : for reins, for fetters, for lashes, and other such things. He knew where to obtain the materials for his garments, his footwear, his harness, and so on; and knew also how to make these things. All this entitative knowledge was supported by or rooted in the knowledge of the holy earth from which all the above things of man's world originate. Such knowledge was the earthly wisdom of the ancient Lithuanians.

According to this wisdom, Earth was the mother of all things. She is seen as purifying and rejuvenating everything. Whatever dies and rots helps to support other life, whether it is the living juice in plant fibres or milk and blood in animal veins, when acted upon by the powers of Earth. Earth heals wounds and takes away the pain. According to the ancient wisdom and customs, a sick person or someone dying with great suffering used to be laid on the earth, as she calms and soothes pain.[25] Only a few decades ago, elderly Lithuanian peasants used to kiss the "holy Earth" with devotion before sowing the first handful of grain in the spring. They used to pray with the words : "Earth, my mother, I arise from you. You feed me, care for me; you carry me and you accept me after death".[26]

Earth used to be called the "blossom-raiser".[27] By this poetical expression the black earth was indicated to be the source of all colors. Earth here can be seen as the concealment which breaks open to disclosure.

After World War I the cult of Earth, generally speaking, disappeared. Earth was treated just as everything on it — rocks, plants, animals — from a utilitarian, objective point of view. Only poets or men of literature preserved in themselves some reverence for Earth. It is in a very mythical manner that Jonas Avyzius speaks of earth in one of his novels : "Earth must be venerated like one's true mother. If this is done, she too will love man. She is alive and wise like man. If you listen well, with your ear on the earth, you will hear her breathing".

[25] Cf. Jonas Balys, *Lietuviu Liaudies Pasaulejauta* (Chicago : Lietuviu Tautinis Akademinis Samburis, 1966), p. 11.

[26] *Ibid.*, p. 12.

[27] Cf. *Ibid.*, p. 14.

Needless to say, this poetical description of earth is "unsober" and unrealistic in the eyes of a logical objective thinker. The sciences cannot look into their own bases *scientifically*. If they could, they would become aware of the great shift which took place with the modern philosophies of rationalism, empiricism, and Kantianism — the shift which makes everything objective dependent on the subjective. Once the grounds of objectivity are understood, the meaning of the subject or subjectivity as rooted in *Dasein*, can be properly approached. With *Dasein* and thus with the interplay of the foursome, a more adequate understanding of earth and other transcendental powers of reality can be acquired. Only then can the evaluation of the previously quoted words, demonstrating a mythical understanding of earth, be adequately performed.

Once scientific objectivism begins to search into its own grounds, it will inevitably embark on a search for gods. This, of course, will require its overcoming of itself. Sciences, the offspring of godlessness, are bound to overcome their shallowness and thus outgrow themselves with the dawing of gods. With this, poetical and mythical thought will once again become "sober".

With the dawn of future gods, man is bound to return to his "essentiation" *qua* man. Such an "essentiation" is attained by the upsurge of man's inner self which is implied in the sway of gods. To stress man's implication in the works of gods, we would like to recall to our attention the wild horse hunters of central Europe some 25,000 years ago. These early Europeans hunted large herds of horses by stampeding them and making them run over a high cliff, and thus killing them *en masse*.[28] Immediately after the massacre, religious rites were held right on the site. The high priest of the hunters' society used a magic staff with the insignia of the offended gods to chase away — it was believed — the ghosts of the dead horses. The best cuts of horse meat, or even the best of the dead horses, were sacrificed on the altars of the offended gods. With these rites the hunters were cleansed of their offensive deeds and their succeeding guilt, and became entitled to use the meat and hides for their own purposes.

The above description provides a glimpse into man's involvement in the works of gods. Any cult or culture, to a great extent, consists of the appeasement of its gods. Because of this appeasement man becomes entitled to use that which he attained by breaking the laws of the gods or of Nature and thus by becoming guilty of the disturbance of the godly order. The appease-

---

[28] Cf. Otto Zierer, *Bild der Jahrhunderte*, Band I (Gütersloh : Murnau Gesamtherstellung & Co. G.m.b.H., n.d.), p. 10.

ment is a reconciliation with Nature or a redemption of man's guilt; it is the restoration of Nature's peace.

In much the same way the Lithuanian peasantry maintained its agrarian cult. A Lithuanian plowman would plow a crust of bread into the first furrow of the year. This bread (*duona*) was a sacrificial gift (*duonia*) to Zemyna, Mother Earth. The peasant, to a certain extent, would "rob" Mother Earth by gathering her gifts (by mowing grain) and taking them to his home for use during winter. To appease her ,or the gods of earth and sky, in whose care stands the growth of plants in general, man must give the gifts of these gods back to them. Such gifts entitle man to eat bread and other fruits of Earth with the consent of the gods. By returning to the gods what is theirs, man becomes *quasi* a partner of the gods and as such he can be the co-user of that which is theirs.

Modern man — especially the industrial or technological man of today — is recklessly using Nature's gifts with no thought whatsoever of giving anything back to Nature. Technological man is a plunderer, a robber of the earth. In his eyes earth or Nature deserves no respect, esteem, or reverence.

In the last decade, the problem of pollution and of ecology has become increasingly more and more acute. This problem reminds man of his need to respect Nature and give some gifts (*duonia*) back to her, instead of merely stripping her naked. Today man has begun to plan to keep Nature clean, that is, he plans to repair the damage he has inflicted upon her. As yet, he plans to do this with his own well-being in mind. He has become aware that by reckless disruption of Nature's own processes of self-purification or self-rejuvenation, he will inevitably end up by making his continued existence on the earth impossible. It is quite conceivable that in time man will begin to esteem Nature not only because of his anthropocentric point of view, but for her own sake. To have respect for Nature *ipso facto* is to have respect for gods. With this respect for Nature and gods man will again become a cultural rather than a civilized being. Only a cultural man "essentiates" (realizes) his very own mission of being — the "essentiation" of his inner self. Moreover in his inner self he can become aware of the true "essentiation" of things : instead of seeing them as objects, he will become aware of them as the assemblers of the transcendental powers of reality — of earth and gods.

It is about time for modern man to understand that the highest assignment (mission) of man is the remedying of the disruption inflicted on Nature by technological devices by the use of the same means (with technological devices). To do this, the man of the future will have to discover gods in the midst of his technocratic world. The search for gods does not mean that it is necessary for modern man to escape his living situation; it means rather an attempt to look into the presuppositions which are cornerstones or the pillars of his technocratic world.

The meaning of man's life does not consist of the mastering of his world, but of his *responsive* "under-standing" of the ultimate powers which dominate his living world, his *Dasein*. *Dasein*, the stead of man's life, is principally the playground of gods. Serving gods by his surrendering, responsive cult, man lives culturally. A cultural life is not executed by measuring and evaluating all things around man by his anthropocentric, objective, or logical standards or by the scale of values adopted by him, the all-powerful subject; it is attained by man's making himself available to the measuring devices of Nature's godly *logos*.

In the mythical world man's responsive cultural attitude was expressed by his giving gifts (*duonia*), consisting of the first and best fruits of his work, to his gods, while technological man only takes, grabs, robs, and holds everything that his hands or his technological instruments make available or attainable. Such a mastering of the earth is the way of civilization, but not of culture. The mastering of earth, rather than a way of serving any gods, is the motto of technological man. Does such a man attain the fulness of being-man? Not at all! Rather he betrays the mission of his life, his own inner self. Even this treason of godlessness is rendered possible by gods : there must be gods, there must be a cult, and there must be culture for man to be godless, cultless, and cultureless.

After the coronation of a new Egyptian pharaoh, treasures and works of art were brought to the king from all parts of the country as gifts from the people. This, according to the Egyptian cultural tradition, was not the respect shown to a dignified person trying to please his individual or peripheral self. It was the respect to the king's *Ka* or soul, by which he — more than any other person of the Egyptian nation — was implied in the play of the gods, in the drama of Osiris' birth-death. By the king's participation in the play of the gods, he himself became god-like. Gods — just as Nature herself — are concealed in themselves. They are disclosed in the human cultural *Dasein*, wherein the king is the most god-filled, the most divine reality. This is why the god Osiris' statues in the tomb of a king have a resemblance to the king. Moreover, all the statues of the king's servants or staff, which are also found in the king's tomb, have features identical to those of their king. This can be extended to all of Egyptian society or rather, to every individual in the nation under the king's rule. By this, the Egyptian mythical culture attemtped to state that the king merges with the gods. On the one hand, he brought the gods into his *Dasein*, and on the other, he related his nation to the gods. The Egyptian pharaoh, the god-man, was a mediator between the gods and men. The king's inner self, his *Ka*, was the god Osiris' entrance into the Egyptian *Dasein*. The king's *Ka*, *ipso facto* was the *Ka* of every member of his nation. The *Ka*, the inner self, of an Egyptian was a form of his king's *Ka*. This means that his participation in the play of the gods occurred with his recognition of the lordly sway of his king.

Treasures and works of art, brought from all corners of the land of Egypt to the king after his coronation, principally were things not for the use of the king's peripheral self, but for his use in his aspect of the place-holder of the gods, that is, for his inner self, his *Ka*.

In King Tutankhamen's grave were preserved a great variety of things, given to him after his coronation. For instance, the Nubian nobility "presented the pharaoh with superbly wrought furniture, eminently fit for his palace, folding stools of precious wood with fur cushions, arm-chairs, beds, shields covered with animal skin, and bows and arrows. At his feet their attendants laid gold rings and bags of gold dust, cornelian heaped up in bowls, jasper, elephant tusks, ebony boomerangs and even a gold-plated chariot. There were also a golden shrine and a masterpiece of Nubian craftsmanship — a sort of stool upon which a long tray held a complete re-presentation in gold of a characteristic landscape of Wawat".[29]

Gifts to the pharaoh are gifts to his inner self, to his *Ka*, which ultimately means that they are gifts to the gods. The Egyptian world was not man-centered, not humanistic, but god-centered. In such a world, the meanings of things are rooted and founded in its gods. A man, a craftsman or an artist, by making things serves his gods, rather than men. The pride of a craftsman or an artist is in making or creating a thing in such a way that it becomes a spot where the light of the gods enters man's *Dasein* and thereby this thing introduces the gods, or assembles them into man's world. The mission of a man is not to grab goodies and to hold them in his possession, but to attempt to attain the highest excellence possible in making *holy* things — things which reflect the godly ever-concealed light shining brightly in the midst of his living *Dasein* and reflected by the things of his making.

The holy aspect of godliness, typical of mythical things, was carried over into the early phase of philosophical thought which sprang up from the mythical world. Even Plato still maintains the holiness of things. Properly understood, the prototypes of ideas are gods. "An idea is a true god. Out of this speculative conception of a god, according to which a god is thought

---

[29] Desroches-Noblecourt, *op. cit.*, pp. 199-200.

of as viewed from an idea, Plato conceives also the essence of *Mania*, the essence of man's being captivated by the might of a god.[30]

Ignoring Nature in her concealedness (*physis*), Plato nevertheless maintains man's and things' subordination to Nature as understood to be the world of ideas. We know that Nature as the world of ideas is Nature in her disclosure — is *logos*. For Plato this disclosure has an absolutely lasting or static character. Ignoring *physis*, he ignores Nature's movement of self-disclosure, — Nature as dynamic. Excluding Nature in her concealedness, he in addition degrades her to a realness inferior to that of things. Concealed Nature to Plato is mere matter. Because of all this, we can state that Plato makes an incision into mythically understood Nature who constantly breaks through into openness and discloses herself, after which she falls back into the shrouds or veils of concealment. This pristine event of reality is thought of by Heraclitus as *physis*-is-*logos*. Plato differentiates between *physis* and *logos*. For him only *logos* is transcendental reality, while *physis* has not even the status of the immanent or entitative reality of things.

Even though Plato initiated the downhill way of transcendental reality, by still maintaining the transcendental world of ideas, he maintains — we can say — things as being holy, that is, as standing in the light or the shine of gods. As far as man is concerned, Plato properly understands him as having memories or knowledge of pre-entitative or transcendental reality — ideas or gods. Because of man's relation to ideas, his mission is to guard things in their light, that is, to preserve them as holy.

For Plato human thought is principally a thought of ideas (thought of gods). Such a thought is enthusiastic in the sense of the thinker's captivation by the gods. Human thought, thus, is not simply *human*. This is why Fink indicates that philosophy to Plato is *Mania*, which can well be understood as enthusiasm in the primordial meaning of this word.

The thought of philosophy as *Mania* does not master things by "iron-clad" logical principles rooted in the human mind (subjective *logos*); it instead avails itself to the *logos* of reality — the light of ideas. By such a thought things are disclosed not in the light of the human mind, but in the light of Nature (the world of ideas), brought down or reflected (assembled) by things themselves. By guarding things in the primordial light of Nature (of ideas), we guard by our thought this transcendental light itself. We reponsively co-operate with Nature's light, with her self-disclosure by means of ideas.

Philosophy after Plato abandoned the transcendental reality of *logos*, or ideas, and therefore it ceased to be *Mania* — ceased to be enthusiastic.

[30] Fink, *Spiel.*, p. 91.

It became a "sober" exploration of things, of their immanently contained essences by the means of logical principles based on the metaphysical or ontological ones. The basic principle of metaphysics states that there are beings (things) only; and whatever is not a being (a thing), is not real.All other principles are restricted to the make-up of beings or entities; they are purely immanent or entitative.

Starting with the modern philosophies, especially with Kant, a concern with transcendental reality was revived. Once again, that which is not a thing, not a being, or an object, was, nevertheless, real. Moreover its realness — the realness of a subject — was understood as anterior, that is, more fundamentally real, than the realness of objects or phenomena.

Modern subjectivistic philosophies, instead of being Nature-centered became man-centered. Only with Nietzsche and Heidegger did philosophy once again become *Mania*. Now it is again pointing to the dawning gods, while Plato's philosophy was adrift from the gods during their twilight.

Philosophy as *Mania* is gods-bound : it stands under the sway of gods ("under-stands" the gods). The "under-standing" of gods (standing under their sway) is not restricted to philosophy or philosophical thought alone : it comprises man's whole life — his standing or holding a stead in his living world, in his *Dasein*. Man's life as *Mania* means his cultural way of being — his culturalness, not just his thought.

Greek dramas present man with a mask, playing the role of a god or a hero (godly man). They evolved from the earlier mythical cult plays. Their meaning consisted of showing that man's mission is his belonging in the play of the gods. The mask can be understood as being the concealedness of a god on the stage of man's cultural *Dasein*. The Egyptians, on the contrary, thought of their gods as participants in the human *Dasein* not with a mask, but with the face of their king. Osiris always has the features of the pharaoh, the living god of the nation's cultural phase.

In spite of the "open-facedness" of the god in the Egyptian *Dasein*, he, nevertheless, like a god in the Greek *Dasein*, is always a concealed god. While a mask conceals the god of the Greeks in the openness of their *Dasein*, the king's facial traits conceal the god in the Egyptian *Dasein*.

Man's relatedness to gods, his *Mania*, helps him to see things with the meanings set by the shine of his gods, that is, it helps him to see things as holy. Just as Plato sees things in the light of ideas, so does a mythical man in the light of gods. Plants, animals, and the ways of men acquire their meanings and directions in the play of gods. Osiris, the life-granting stream of the Nile, sways everything in the span of its being. The Nile determines when plants germinate, flourish, ripen, spread their seed and dry out and become fragile twigs. Likewise it determines everything else; it guides men in their laying out of their fields, of their irrigation systems, in their erecting of their villages, towns, roads, temples, and tombs. All things and all men have their beginning, duration, and end in the openness of the world. There is nothing everlasting, except Nature and her gods.

The king's *Ka*, however, in the fullness of the "essentiation" of his inner self, becomes eternal by merging with the god Osiris. Pyramids and sphinxes — lasting realities amid everything perishable — are not built for men, but for their gods; or more precisely — for their king-gods. The lasting things — the temples of the gods and tombs of the kings — stand amid the chaos of everything which rises into the clarity of the cultural morning only to drift back into the veils of its night. This means that only man with his cultural works can set out or display the light of the immortals within his mortal world. Only in such a light are things holy.

Man can display the lasting shine of Nature and her gods in his dying days because he — even though a mortal — is, or can be, responsively "under-standing" the immortals. Responsive "under-standing" of transcendental reality by man is possible only because this reality itself comes into disclosure and withdraws from it back into concealment. The Nile rises and then sinks into the motherly dust of Earth. Ra rises, shines and sinks into the Ever-hidden, into Atum.

This pristine play of Nature — her disclosure-concealment — is — as we know — her cosmic guilt, and man's responsiveness to this cosmic guilt makes him *existentially* guilty. Existential guilt does not means man's deviation from his way of being -man, but, on the contrary, it is his way of being-man.

Hebrew myth states that in the midst of the first man's *Dasein* stood the tree of knowledge. The first man's responsiveness — or rather irresponsiveness — to the cosmic law brought a disturbance into the pristine peace of Nature and made him guilty. By his disruption of Nature's harmony, man became aware of his nakedness — his being a nothing without the gods. Thus, by breaking the law of Nature's peace, he not only became aware of Nature as transcendental reality, but he discovered his own inner self, his *Ka*, which consists of his involvement in Nature's order.

The tree of knowledge must be seen as discord planted in Nature's peace. Man did not plant this tree; he was merely a stumbling block, by colliding with which Nature revealed her own — cosmic — guilt; the disclosure of her concealment. Nature's guilt, her play, responded to by man, breaks into culture, which, therefore, is principally under the domain of Nature (and not of man!). The Hebrew myth of Adam and Eve — remotely resembling the "event" of Isis and Osiris — interestingly relates knowledge, and thus disclosure, to guilt. Without discord in or disruption of Nature's peace, her Ever-concealedness, there could be no truth or knowledge; there could be no being-man or any culture. Culture is the playground of Nature, where gods dance with men as their co-dancers. This playground is an outcome of the transcendental discord or cosmic guilt.

Immanent philosophies stress reality as consisting of things only, and rationalistic philosophies stress the absolute static axle of all finite things. This axle is centered either in God (theocentric subjectivism) or in man (anthropocentric subjectivism). Immanent as well as rationalistic philosophies overlook Nature; they overlook the reality in which things, men and gods have their beginning, Nietzsche was the first to have courage enough to look at Nature directly and to have seen her as chaotic, ever-playing ocean waves which give a start to everything and then swallow it up again. The waves of Nature's ocean (her play) alone last, while everything started in them perishes. The Will to Power is the ever appearing and ever withdrawing movement or play of Nature.

9. *Godless Confusion and Godly Ambiguity*

Nature plays incessantly. She does not have a definite goal as her own self-completion. By having no direction, she is always young and the same. Nevertheless, at every instant she is new, different, and ever beginning like "a self-rolling wheel".[31]

Essentialistic or rationalistic philosophies try to discover some aim in Nature's eternal play — some end at which Nature finds her fulfillment. The most exemplary of such philosophies is that of Hegel. By trying not to become overwhelmed by any of these philosophies and by biasedly observing Nature's eternal play amid things and within various cultures, we cannot fail to see that there is a striking progressive build-up, development, and diversification of various species of things and that there is build-up, development, and diversification of various cultures. We, however, then cannot fail to simultaneously notice that there never is an ideal breed or species of living things, nor is there an ideal chulture which, in its completed form, would crown Nature's works, be her ideal goal.

There is perfection in almost all ways of things, animal life, and cultures, but there is never an end which, when attained, would eliminate further creative works of Nature. There are no absolutely perfect things, organisms,

---

[31] Nietzsche, *op. cit.*, p. 65.

men, or cultures. Consequently, no living being — be it animal or human — and no culture — be it insignificant and ordinary, or chosen and elevated over all the others — can impose itself on all others.

There are *holy* norms in every culture; yet there are no absolute, unquestionable and universally ideal standards for all cultures. An ideal is always an ideal of a certain culture within the network of *Dasein*'s ordering plan laid out by its gods. A man of such a culture may die the death of a hero — if need be — in various situations of his cultural world, supported by his gods. No man, however, or rather no culture may impose its own standards, norms, or credos on all humanity. This applies to Communism, American democracy, Christianity, and even to the scientifically proven, "right" ways of our advanced technological society.

Like plants, cultures are born, grow, and pass away as lifeless twigs. Empires and cities which in their time seem "eternal" and indestructible fall into ruins and their grandeur sinks into oblivion. The names of great kings are in time worn out of the memories of people. When Assurbanipal, who ruled the mighty Assyrian Empire, and whose authority was extended over the whole universe known at that time, triumphantly entered Nineveh, the world's capital, after his victory over his united enemies, there it did not seem remotely possible that he or his empire would ever be shaken. The triumphal chariot, in which he and the Queen rode, was drawn by "three princes of Elam and one sheik of the Arabs. Thousands of war prisoners, cattle herds, looted temple treasures and precious implements followed them".[32] All this was an impressive manifestation of the might of King Assurbanipal and of his empire.

When, in the evening of this day of triumph, during the splendor of the victory celebration, the King was overcome by a feeling that all this would perish, the Queen spoke to him : "Assurbanipal will not die like the other men; he is king and god at once. The kingdom which he has built will last until the end of time, and will make him immortal".[33] The King's answer to this was : "Even Assurbanipal will die ... Also the Assyrian Empire will sink down; because wise is the saying which is in the ancient writings : "Behold the body which you take hold of; it will wither away and become dust' ".[34] These sober words of a king manifest his true grasp of the ultimate powers which sway everything, all men, empires, and cultures.

[32] Zierer, *op. cit.*, Band I, p. 110.
[33] *Ibid.*, p. 112.
[34] *Ibid.*

There are frequent cases in history where a nation is conquered by another. However, as long as the gods of this nation prevail firmly and sway mightily in its *Dasein*, in the daily lives of its people, its culture remains alive and strong; meaningful and hopeful. No other culture can destroy a conquered nation unless it manages to destroy its gods. Even if a nation having a certain cultural life is not conquered and enslaved by another nation with a different cultural life but, for some circumstance, it ceases to *under-stand* its own gods and if its people no longer cultivate or uphold enthusiastically the cults of thier gods, such a nation loses its strength and firmness, and its culture disintegrates. It falls into confusion and loses its way in its *Dasein*. "In the history of mankind there is perhaps no more terrifying event than the collapse of the beloved images of the gods ... When cults fall apart and lose their securing and upholding power, man is driven into sinister confusion, where he knows neither a way nor a trail, where he no longer knows what an upright life is, what good and evil are, honour and fame are, or shame and disgrace. The divine is the great star according to which mankind has plotted its perilous course for millennia and which has guided nations as they embark on the courses of their destinies".[35]

The technological man of today has long lost the sight of gods' twilight and still has not caught the shine of god's dawn. In his godless night he is surrounded by the brilliance of the world of his own making. Godless, he no longer knows enthusiasm. His thought is "sober". The thought of *Mania* is outlawed. It is restricted to emotions and phantasies. At the very best, it can find room in poetry, but poetry is clearly degraded to a level much inferior to that of rational thought. The cult today is no longer alive. Wherever it still prevails, it is a mere formal ceremony. Such a contemporary dreamless, unheroic, and unenthusiastic godless man is called by Nietzsche "the last man".[36] The last man makes everything for himself. He no longer cultivates with devotion his cultural soil. This soil becomes barren under his feet. "That soil one day will be poor and exhausted, and no lofty tree will any longer be able to grow thereon", says Nietzsche.[37]

Man's cultural soil becomes barren when he fails to respond to Nature's creativeness; when man becomes godless. To be godless is to no longer be enthusiastic and live for any high ideal, to seek a star. "Alas! There cometh the time when man will no longer launch the arrow of his longing beyond man — and the string of his bow will have unlearned to whizz".[38] Not to

---

[35] Fink, *Spiel*, p. 204.
[36] Nietzsche, *op. cit.*, p. 11.
[37] *Ibid.*
[38] *Ibid.*

launh the arrow of his longing beyond man means to lack transcendental or enthusiastic aims, to be self-centered in one's peripheral self, or to be anthropocentric.

" 'We have discovered happiness' — says the last man, and blinks thereby".[39] Here happiness is, of course, purely anthropocentric happiness; it fails to bring fullness to man's inner self. Our democratic society considers as its highest aim the realization of every man's happiness, his highest possible well-being.

The era of the last man, the godless man, may be long. Nevertheless, it is bound to end and times may gradually begin to turn toward godliness. There are some signs of such a turn. As one of these signs we can consider the awakening in man of an interest in and inclination toward the "old ways" of pioneer times.

This conservatism repeats itself in the simultaneous increase of interest in curbing the rapidly spreading technocratic civilization and to thus preserving sanctuaries where Nature's sway can go on uninterrupted by efficient technological devices and industrial projects. A newspaper man says : "As an editorial in the New York Times puts it : 'The wild places are now seen not as an enemy but as a vanishing resource. As the neon lights glare ever brighter and the miles of paved road wind ever onward, the chance to escape to the solitude of a roadless area, an unspoiled forest or an untamed river becomes ever more precious' ".[40]

In the last decade or two, many park areas and camping sites were opened along the major highways of North America, and — especially during the months of tourism — these areas or sites are filled with visitors from far away. Instead of the comforts of civilized life, people are beginning to choose the hardships of living close to Nature. Sleeping under the open sky and cooking on open fires under the trees, walking on winding rocky paths, wading in the cold waters of mountain streams, and so on, have become worthwhile ventures. Instead of being surrounded with the commodities of civilized life, man longs today to experience the feel or touch of the raw but fascinating environment of Nature unchanged by civilization.

While living in Prince George, I met Harold Dugan, a college graduate from the United States, who travelled to McLeod's Lake, about 80 miles north of Prince George, to homestead there in the unspoiled northern forests. According to him, a man in the technocratic society tends to become a brick the same as any other brick in this society. In such a society a man's

---

[39] *Ibid.*
[40] *Victoria Daily Times*, 1969, Nr. 94.

individualistic traits or features lose their significance; modern life deletes them. A man is placed in a workshop, a store, in a school, or any other humanistic institution or organization, where he functions according to detailed regulations. He resembles a bolt in a metal framework. Such a man, like this bolt, is easily replaceable by some other member of society just like him. In contemporary society a man becomes faceless, and it is precisely by being so that he functions more efficiently than if he were individualistic.

According to Dugan, the conditions in American cities "make the development of individuality impossible". The same conditions make a man "a brick" in a certain anthropocentric institution, and simultaneously they uproot him or dislocate him from his genuine family or social life. Even as a member of a family, the provider of bread and butter, the contemporary man is faceless : he leaves his family with all its living environmental details and functions all day in an environment which basically has little if any relation to his home and its problems, and he returns home much as a stranger. His main activity and attention is devoted to his occupational world rather than to his home world.

The family belongs together and all its members must be mutually involved in the projects and enterprises of their home. A homestead is such a place. Here everyone stands shoulder to shoulder facing the family's common problems. Family life on a homestead is colorful, diversified, unique, and everyone here has his own characteristic face — has developed and augmented his own individuality in particular situations of homestead life.

The emphasis of man's individualistic face here must be understood as the cultivation of man's inner self rather than his peripheral self. The latter "democratically" seeks the well-being of all by exploiting and dominating Nature, the resource of materials for such well-being.

With awakening of longing for Nature in her own unspoiled state, he is bound to cease considering her as merely a resource of materials. Gradually it may be followed by her merging with a halo of godliness. With this renewed experience of Nature man will become cultural again. "The feeling for Nature and experience of her beauty is the mark of higher culture. A man who considers Nature solely with practical motives, for whom the forest is merely a raw material for sawmills, and birds and wild animals only the means of satisfying the hunter's passion, is neither cultural nor humanistic".[41]

The overcoming of anthropocentric godlessness can be realized not only by the revived longing in man for unspoiled Nature, but principally by man's

[41] Balys, *op. cit.*, p. 91.

opening himself to the hidden principles of reality which ultimately sway all things — be they "natural" or man-made. Such an opening is easier to accomplish by looking into those technological things which stand closer to Nature than those which seem to be totally disconnected from her.

An architect who creatively designs and constructs a rustic lodge of cedar logs in some remote wild park does so not for his own convenience nor principally for his love of his fellow men. With this lodge the architect tries to respond well to the mood of unspoiled Nature by fitting the building well into its particular location. He takes into consideration the sky which gives a certain amount of rain, snow and sunshine annually. He blends the structure into the surrounding rocky slopes, into the tall cedars or pines, or perhaps into dead tree trunks with ghastly twisted branches, bleached and washed by rains or blackened by forest fires. Of course, the architect is intensely concerned with the vivid inclination of some tourists to become exposed to the unbridled and untamed sway of wild Nature and to seek an escape from the comforts of civilized life in urban environments and strive for the solitude of an Artemisian world which for millennia was the world of their ancestors. A lodge of this kind helps a man to free himself — at least for a few days or weeks — from the paved and polished ways of the technocratic world. The raw environment, "undigested" by technology, throws the visitor from totally human ways and exposes him to the silent sway of the obscure, unknown, but palpably real swaying powers imbedded in Nature. These powers — the gods unknown — are reflected in the purity of the morning dew on grass blades and on pine needles, on colorful pebbles, washed and polished throughout the ages by clear mountain streams; in the buzzing of wild bees, in the song of birds, in the leaping motions of deer and fawns. The creation of this architect definitely has religious undertones. His concern for man is not seen from the angle of his comforts, but from his "under-standing" of Nature's gods. Moreover, he is more concerned with the beautiful earth wedded with the changeable skies in their depressing and soul-lifting rhythms just as he is with men who dwell near to vague and silent gods, than he is with a detailed elaboration and realization of purely man-made blue-prints.

Man's conquest of and penetration into every region of the world — even extended recently to outer space — seems to stress that he is the master of everything around him; — the master of his own growth, development and the accomplishment of his self-outlined mission; and finally, — the master of Nature. But is he really a master, the axle of his world?

We — just as the people of bygone times — are born and die in times and places not of our own choice. We are not what we would like to be : our appearance, our physical constitution, our talents, our fortunes — all are not in our hands. We — and even our governments — are not the swaying powers of our historical events. We seem to rule our civilization or dominate our technological world; however, when we stop to think and begin to weigh our roles in our technocratic empire carefully, we soon realize that instead, hidden powers within our technology dominate technology, and us, technological men, as well.

Our civilization, which has lasted for centuries and which becomes more and more brilliant, seems to place us, men, on definite, dependable, and firm ways with which to live our lives and accomplish our human mission. When carefully viewed these ways are neither firm nor securely dependable. There are many threatening evil eyes lurking everywhere, which call for the improvement and adjustment of our technological world. The most perilous of all these ailments is the lack of a fully founded and universally accepted theory or doctrine for our civilization. A man of this world is more confused and more lost than was a mythical man of any culture. The modern man lives without principles, without moral norms, without enthusiasm-evoking ideals. We modern people no longer know of any holy bonds which bind the members of a family, neighborhood, society, or nation together. Meaning of love is lost; patriotism by some psychologists is considered a kind of insanity. Holidays are days for fishing or for riding around the country with no aim or purpose. Human life has become shallow. An individual lacks firm knowledge or firm principles by which to live. He turns to a marriage counselor for advice when the seams of his marital life threaten to break. A modern mother looks in a booklet for information on how to raise children. A man of our society has experts to plan his homes, his jobs, his vacations, his household budget, and so on. Does this indicate contemporary man's high-standing strength and superiority or does it mean the opposite?

This confusion and sense of being lost becomes more and more manifest each year by all kinds of disturbances, disorder, revolt, upheavals, demonstrations, and so on. These are carried on mostly by our youth. All this disquietude, to a great extent, is taken advantage of by Communist organizers, who seek to undermine the governments of free Western countries and thus to create chaos so as to be able to realize their aim to completely conquer the world. All of these destructive movements make it necessary for us to search for and re-discover firm principles; they call for a search for gods. Either we find our future gods or we will end up facing chaos or anarchy.

As soon as we make an inquiry into the seemingly well-proven, solid grounds of our scientific-technological world, we immediately obtain as a result objectivism or subjectivism. Truthfully, we end up with both, because and object is always an object from the perspectives or viewpoints of a subject. Briefly, we end up with Kantianism which, especially in the scientific circles, is cooled down with the objectivistic standpoints of positivism which recoil to Aristotelian essentialism, holding an emphasis on things, on objects, rather than on the subject. Kantianism cannot be properly comprehended without a recourse into the empricism and rationalism which preceded Kantianism. Moreover neither empiricism nor rationalism can be adequately grasped without an acquaintance with the basic principles of medieval, and furthermore, of ancient, thought.[42]

This means that the clarity of the technological world is not at all self-explanatory or self-founded. Contemporary man's pride of his well-founded technological world outlooks, which in his view stand far above those of the medieval or ancient world, only demonstrates his ignorance of the principles or the cornerstones of his technological world.

The technological world and man's way in it is successfully explored by the thought of Martin Heidegger. This thought reveals the technological world as lacking principles and therefore, as godless; and man as capsuled into his principles of a godless way of life. Because of this, the firm believers in the absolute truth of the technological world consider Heidegger's penetrating thought to be regressive — to be merely rejecting the "progressive" technological cultural heights.

Heidegger's philosophy is noteworthy for its efficient unmasking of the contemporary technological world by exposing its major aspects of godlessness, lack of principles, confusion, and being lost or uprooted. This philosophy is a prelude into a search for future gods with man's opening of himself to the view of the dawn of tomorrow's gods.

Heidegger's thought is often seen as retrospectively interested in the problems of early philosophy, especially those of the pre-Socratic or pre-classical era. That this is a onesided conclusion is manifested by Heidegger's definite carrying on of the vital flow of modern thought : Kant-Nietzsche-Husserl and his own existentialism of Nature, the thought of the overcoming of metaphysics and of philosophy in general.

Consequently, Heidegger's thought is pre-philosophical and post-philosophical at one and the same time. It ties the birth-bed of philosophy to its final fruits of self-overcoming. The carrying of modern and contemporary thoughts to their ultimate conclusions confronts us with typi-

[42] Cf. Vycinas, *op. cit.*

cally mythical problems, such as earth, sky, men as mortals, and gods as immortals. Heidegger evolves these problems from the *sober* and living thought of the Western world through its sequential historical development. In no wise does he abruptly break off the flow of traditional thought. He merely carries it on to its natural consequences.

Any cultural growth reveres the roots, the origins of prevailing cultural styles or modes and at the same time keeps open its vision into the future cultural eventualities which will come down with the dawn of the gods of tomorrow.

The revolutionary, disorderly and disquieting movements in our world in recent times may be diversely motivated. However, it may well be that the most pristine roots of these movements are initiated by man's awakening awareness, still obscure to himself, of the shallowness, principlelessness, "*logos*-lessness" of his confused *Dasein*. Briefly, it is the awareness of the godlessness of his world. Such an awareness leads to a search for a firmer world, for future gods.

The search for gods is a very realistic venture. In this search we are not seeking ideal realities in their sublime purity. We search for gods by viewing things in our *Dasein* without subduing them with the yoke of one or another logically built-up philosophical system or under precise scientific, impersonal, or objective proofs.

On our way of a search for gods we approach things the way a peasant approaches the plants he cultivates : he lets them be and develop in their own way — in Nature's sun-rays, rains and gentle summer breezes. He removes only those obstacles which distort or prevent the natural development of these things. To see things realistically — in the sense that Heidegger understands realism — is to let things appear in their own light — that which they bring with them. To let things be by witholding oneself from violating them is a responsive co-play with Nature.

The question, what is bread? is a question of total clarity at first. In our world bread is one of the basic food products produced by modern agricultural technology; more accurately — by men, specialized in the field of baking. To know bread *realistically* is to know it outside of the purely technological world. *Realistically* understood, bread refers to earth, its nutritious soil in which the life-supporting plant, rye, is rooted, exposed to the blessing warmth and the rains of the sky. In the early days bread was the vital thing in a man's household. In those days bread meant life, the very existence, of man. Lack of bread equalled hunger and death. Moreover, for the early agrarian cultures of peasants, it was the major sacrificial gift (*duonia*) to their gods.

Bread, thus seen, refers to the *fundamentally* (transcendentally) realistic grounds of all things — earth, sky, mortals, and gods. The interplay of these powers of the foursome constitutes the very "thingness" of the thing bread (or of any other thing). Such a way of understanding things *ipso facto* is the "under-standing" or standing under the transcendental principles of reality. By this "under-standing" we stand under gods even though they may be absent due to their being still nameless in our aging and decaying cultural phase.

Realistically understood, these things are not determined or guided by man's efforts only, independent of any transcendental powers by subjectivistic man — but they are founded, upheld and directed by Nature's laws, the "*nomoi* in the sense of grand ordering powers which direct and guide the ways in which everything must be used in accordance to its true " 'essentiation' ".[43]

A thing, as the assembler of the transcendental powers of reality, is never absolutely known or definable. Things in the light of the foursome cannot be defined once and for all. Bread has a different *realistic* meaning in the world of fishermen, hunters, or of desert sheperds. This means that a thing, even though founded in the foursome, is different in different cultures because of a different way of the powers of the foursome stepping into the openness of this or that cultural world.

A thing varies from one cultural world to another. There is never a generally defined meaning which is valid in each cultural world in the very same way. Even in a different phase of the same culture, the meaning of a thing can have been changed. Bread in the Lithuanian world, after the introduction of many domestic plants, vegetables, and fruits from abroad, "assembled" the foursome (transcendental realities of earth, sky, men, and gods) into a changed or modified interplay. *Realistically* understood, the meanings of things in a cultural world undergo vivid, colorful metamorphoses or modifications. They thus display always the same and yet always new revelations of Nature's play. Things in the mythical world, even though firm, are vague.

The dynamic life of things in their meanings is made absolute by the technological-logical freeze-up or petrification of their meanings to make them "handy" or proven for everyone and for all times. Heidegger's thought comes out against this vivisection and freeze-up of living things by his emphasis of a word as that in which the being of the thing is born. Heidegger's philosophy of language tries to free things to a dynamic life within

---

[43] Heidegger, *Erde und Himmel.*

language, understood as the language of *logos*. Man speaks authentically by responding to or "under-standing" the transcendental principles of reality.

The interrelation or interplay of transcendental, pristine realities is made inaudible and ungraspable in the medium of technological language — in the technological world. Modern technology encumbers things and their meanings in the contemporary world by the demanding, rather than responsive, attitude of technological man. These demanding attitudes are not the ultimate ones. Beyond the technologist's sway of the things of his world — beyond his demanding encumbrance of them — there are ultimate demanding powers within technology itself which are not in man's control. The true nature of these powers is uncomprehended and unexperienced so far.[44] The ultimate driving powers behind man's technological efficiency are ignored.

As soon as man becomes aware of these powers and that he himself is swayed by them in their concealment within technology itself, he will be simultaneously and inevitably set on the way of a search for these powers, for the pristine principles of technology which are harboured in Nature rather than in man. A guideline to such discovery is provided by language. With a careful inquiry into the meanings of things, the pristine swaying powers can be evolved from the background of technological or scientific proofs, which hitherto remain unquestionable.

Generally speaking all words can be traced back to the source of all things —to Nature's wholeness. A common English word "to teach", for instance, in its original sense meant "to show". This aspect is still preserved in the meaning of the word "to teach". To teach is to show. The Old English word *tacn* meant "to show". This word is closely related to the Sanskrit *dic*, from where the Latin *dicere*, "to say" originated. The English word "to indicate" has evolved from Latin *dicere*.[45] It is quite obvious that all these words — "to show", "to say", "to indicate" — are implied in the meaning of the word "to teach".

A teacher is the person who explains, presents, or points out something. To do this he must be acquainted with the background or the wholeness wherein this thing is rooted and wherefrom it draws its meaning. Only by knowing the whole, can we locate the place and thus the meaning of any thing within this wholeness; and furthermore, we can then properly show this thing by indicating its interbelonging with other things in the framework of the whole.

[44] Cf. *Ibid.*

[45] Cf. Joseph T. Shipley (ed.), *Dictionary of Word Origins* (New York : The Philosophical Library, 1945), p. 352.

To teach, then, is to "under-stand" the interplay of the transcendental principles of the whole, of Nature. Only with this "under-standing" can we point out, locate, show and properly teach anything in our living *Dasein*. The teacher is the one who stands near the gods and who thus is rooted in his lordly inner self, his *Ka*.

Tracing words which have been abused and made shallow to their original sources in Nature's play is the restoration of their pristine, poetical shine, comparable to cleansing worn coins which then reacquire their former gleam. Such tracing is in no wise a scrupulous evisceration of our words; it is rather a means of freeing ourselves from being swayed by technocratically, precisely well defined meaning of the words. Instead of "understanding" these words and being dominated by them, we should seek their respectful, living, pristine meanings. By "under-standing" the words in the pristine, mythical meanings into which they are thrown by Nature's play, we can learn to dwell under gods again.

Against common conviction, the birth of great truths occurs in a particular — perhaps very insignificant — spot on the map of the world, by the responsiveness of one or a few enthusiastic persons who have a poetical grasp of the roots of words. To utter or relay deeprooted words evokes the bysounds of the most pristine correlated words, the names of gods, the holy or "wholy" words.

When Heidegger investigates Hölderlin's profound saying "poetically dwells man on this Earth",[46] he evidently means man's dwelling in his *own* living situations, his own *Dasein*, in the sense of his dwelling in the words, unfalsified by universally definable meanings — in poetical words. The responsive poetical dwelling of man means his experience of transcendental realities. "To a poet's mood — tranquil and joyful — earth, sky and gods, concealed in the Holiness, are present in the whole of Nature, who breaks forward in her pristinity".[47]

To dwell poetically means to dwell in the roots of the words — in the words as arising in Nature's creative womb. A poetically dwelling man lives in his existential situations, unfalsified by logical, absolute explanations or interpretations. Such existential living is the holding open of a stead for Nature's own play. It is a re-play (playing in accordance) in the sense of reply (an answer) to Nature's demands, rather than replying to technology under man's domination. A reply to technology in this latter sense is godless.

---

[46] Martin Heidegger, *Vorträge und Aufsätze* (Pfullingen : Günther Neske, 1954), pp. 187-204.

[47] Heidegger, *Erde und Himmel*.

However, when this reply refers to the ultimate principles concealed in technology itself, it may mean an "under-standing" of Nature, present in the grounds of technology. She is present there by her fluctuation of disclosure-concealment, the event of *physis*-is-*logos*, implied in the grounds of technology.

The task of poetically minded great men (prophets, poets, thinkers, and the others, who are capable of freeing themselves from the current logically defined and scientifically "proven" essences of things) is to help the gods of the future to be born in *Dasein* — their own and their fellow men. Poetical dwelling means letting new gods play in one's living situations and thereby naming them. This disclosure of them (by letting them be present and by naming them) is the reply to (re-play of) the play of the gods of the dawn.

A step back into the archaic meanings of things helps us to see these meanings as founded in the sway of the pre-anthropocentric powers of reality. By taking a stand or a stead in the roots of the words, we open our eyes to a far-sighted view of the dawning future cultural principles.

A way toward the dawn of gods is by "under-standing" (*qua* surrendering to) the language of Nature, the *logos*, not mastered by man, but *vice versa* mastering man. By settling in the language of Nature (in *logos*), man never "under-stands" it exhaustively. He always remains on the way toward it, toward the language, because it, being Nature's play, is ever-living, always dynamically sparkling, and constantly changing, even though always remaining the same. According to Dieter Sinn, the title of Heidegger's work "*Unterwegs zur Sprache (On the Way Towards Language)* does not mean that man would arrive by a certain way (method) at a definite language as his final aim and that he thend could somehow dominate it. To be on the way, instead, means never arriving at an end, because the language withdraws itself from the (metaphysical) unequivocalness of an aim — withdraws from the final saying-everything".[48]

A responsive "under-standing" of language, rather than its mastering, does not result in exhaustive clarity. It instead merges into the obscurity or vagueness of Nature's or gods' play. A widely used expression "one can never predict the weather" indicates already that Nature's play is always vague, never clear or definite.

The soul of a poetically dwelling man "glides /slips/ away into the bluish evening twilight of the spiritual year. Such a soul becomes an "autumn-

---

[48] Dieter Sinn (Mannheim), "Heideggers Spätphilosophie" in *Eine Vierteljahreschrift für Philosophische Kritik* (Tübingen : Hans-Georg Gadamer und Helmut Kuhn, Mai 1967) Heft 2/3, p. 780.

soul" and thereby it becomes a "blue soul' ".[49] The poet Trakl's words "autumnsoul" (*Herbstseele*) and "blue soul" (*blaue Seele*), quoted here by Heidegger obviously mean a poetical man's pristine standing in Nature's play, — his being implied in her language. "Autumnsoul" apparently describes a man as having retreated into the twilight of gods which precedes the phase of godlessness, while the "blue soul" indicates man's openness or responsiveness to the dawn of gods, which is bound to follow the phase of godlessness.

The "blue soul" is a name for man's inner self. While to a conscious man, the subject (as the sole and exclusive place of *logos*), who grasps reality by peripheral "mindful", anthropocentric principles, everything is clear-cut and definite in its meaning, the *poetical* grasp of reality by man's innermost self (his "blue soul") is never clear and always elusive; it resists any domination by anthropocentric principles.

To occupy a precisely defined dot on the complex map of the technocratic world and to function efficiently there in some institution as a manager, a salesman, a teacher, a janitor, a reporter, a farmer, a policeman, a clergyman, and so on, is easy. It is so because each speciality has a set of clear-cut rules or regulations, by following which the "expert" functions like a small wheel in a complex mechanical device.

A life on the landscape of *logos*, the richly articulated language of reality, is toilsome, obscure, and misleading. To dwell poetically is to walk under the gods of one's own *Dasein*. Such walking has no already opened ways or trails for the walker to follow. The walker himself makes these ways or breaks open these trails not by following his own impulses or whims, but by humbly responding to the often obscure marks set by often vague gods in their accordance to the dictates of playing Nature.

The most difficult burden falls on the shoulders of the one who is capable of the ways of the "blue soul", who is a poet, that is, it falls on the shoulders of a great man. To be a poet in this sense is to "under-stand" the *logos* of reality, of Nature. Such an "under-standing" means the ability to dwell without the regulating anthropocentric or man-made principles, but according to the ever-changing rainbow principles of gods, playfully fluctuating in the holy milieu of Nature. A poet, a great man of culture, must always have a sharp eye and acute ear for the transcendental flash-ups and sounds in the midst of the immanent things and events of his living *Dasein*.

To dwell poetically or to be a man of greatness means never to become petrified on a certain walk of life. It is true that this walk has been opened

---

[49] Heidegger, *Unterwegs zur Sprache*, p. 49.

by the responsive participation in Nature's play of a man's own inner self; nevertheless, once it freezes into a definite pattern, it ceases to belong in Nature's dynamic fluctuation. To participate in the opening of a way in Nature's *logos* (in her dynamic trail-breaking movement, *Be-wĕgung*) is not a venture for once and for all; it is rather a man's continuous "essentiation" (realization) of his inner self. Once he settles down on an open way, a definite path, he is no longer "pathless" and because of this, he resembles an animal who has a way given to it. In this sense a technological man is much more animal-like than is a "poetical" man.

To maintain *poetical* freedom (the freedom of a man's innermost self) is to remain in the neighborhood of gods. Such is the creative way of being of a great man. Let us once again recall the literary meaning of the pharaoh Tutankhamen's name, "the one who makes the images of the gods". This name can be applied to any man who dwells existentially. To be the maker of the images of gods means to incessantly let the gods come to light or disclosure in one's own *Dasein* by one's own responsiveness to them. This is done by making or creating things (and guarding the things encountered which were already there) as having been born in or having evolved from Nature's holy or wholy play; — making or guarding things as the assemblers of gods and other transcendental powers.

My grandfather, the last *krivis* (highpriest) of the bygone mythical *Dasein* of the Lithuanians, was never caught by peripheral, profane things. The things of his living *Dasein* were holy, because in them he saw the eternal images of living gods. Even in the phase of Christianity, which in his lifetime maintained a strictly doctrinal, statically articulated system of things, and clear-cut and well-defined ways for man to follow in his "material" world, he maintained an openness to the obscure ways of Zemyna (Mother Earth), Perkunas (god of thunder and lightning), and many other deities which dominated wildlife, blessed cultivated fields or guided man on his way in his family and national life.

Being a Christian, my grandfather did not call the above mentioned swaying powers of Nature gods, but "spirits" in a sense close to that of angels. These spirits, in his understanding of them, had to be constantly creatively responded to, depending on the particular situations in one's individual, his family's, and his community's lives. Such a response calls for mythical wisdom instead of anthropocentric expertise with instinctive sureness or cleverness.

Poetical living takes place in the chaotic dimensions of the pathless playgrounds of Nature, while the instinct-guided (biological) or godless (technological) way of life proceeds along given roads. Even though the "given" roads in the technological world were once opened up by man's co-action with Nature, they thereafter became the clear-cut channels which determine man's movements, just as biological instincts determine the movements of animals.

The preceding remarks show once again that there can never be a clear and "ideal" cultural system worked out once and forever. Because of this, no culture — be it "true", "most advanced", or "superior" — can ever be imposed on any other or all other cultures. Moreover, no cultural phase can be crowned with complete accomplishment which then could overshadow the other phases of this culture, just as no animal can be considered "ideal" and thus be the final pattern for all animals to strive toward. In each area or phase of her play Nature is eternally beautiful, ever-mighty, magnificent and divine. Poetical dwelling, just as Nature's play, never attains its ultimate end of self-realization (contrary to what Hegel maintains); it is a constant search for gods.

Contemporary man's godless confusion is ripe for replacement by godly firmness, even though this firmness is in no wise clear, but, like Nature in her play, is always vague. In our democratic society people's minds are dominated by one or another "school of thought". It is about time for us to realize that there cannot be any absolutely true school of thought which would provide man with objectively formulated blueprints explaining everything to everyone at all times. Great men are those who can hold their heads above all "-isms" (all schools of thought) and, instead of living by these, guide themselves by obscure gods flashing up into, or withholding these flash-ups from within man's *Dasein*.

A poetical — great or heroic — life is possible today not by a direct experience of gods (as these have withdrawn themselves, leaving our *Dasein* empty of gods), but by the experience of their absence. To experience godlessness means to lack gods or to be aware of their absence. A totally godless man does not experience gods either in their presence or in their absence; he simply ignores them. A man who experiences godlessness does not ignore gods; he really and sometimes breath-takingly feels the lack of them — feels them in their absence.

A properly understood culture, just as Nature herself in her play, must maintain its peak at each stage of its development; it must have a constantly changing peak. There can be no exclusive peak which would act as an objective measure for any other phase of this culture. If there was such a peak, it would violate, rather than contribute to, the cultural life. A culture does not proceed in a more or less straight line from a primitive beginning to the state of perfection. It must rather be like a constantly rolling ball seeking the top, which — in the case of a rolling ball — is never new. To be a culturalist in the proper sense — to dwell poetically — means to be a kind of acrobat who maintains his equilibrium on an ever rolling ball of Nature's play. It means to ride the crest of the ever heaving ocean of the Will to Power. Such a rider is the Nietzschean superman — the man who can firmly maintain his standing in the chaotic. pathless territory of never-resting and ever-playing Nature.

10. *The Youth of the Technocratic World*

In recent years youth all around the globe but mostly in North America has made itself noticed by its various destructive and rebellious activities directed against the order and the prevailing cultural principles of its elders. These rebellious activities are to a great extent located or initiated jn the colleges or universities. They are, however, supported or carried out by youth in general. A typical example of this kind of youth are the "hippies".

Dr. Gutas, who observed the life of the hippies on one of the beaches of lake Erie finds them miserable because of their negligence, lack of cleanliness and their lack of integrity or self-respect.[50] They swim with their clothes on, have long hair and unkempt beards. They lack any ideals, have no aspirations, show no sign of any interest. Dr. Gutas considers them neurotics, lacking inner sanity, having a vacuum in themselves, and being totally apathetic regarding the highly esteemed values of their elders. According to him, they know no altruism, have no social or humanistic interests. They maintain a rejective, negative attitude toward the way of life of their elders in general. Dr. Gutas finds that this apathy is a result of their failure to see any meaning in human life. He quotes Freud as saying : "From the time on, when man begins to doubt the meaning and value of life, he becomes a sick man"![51]

In the framework of the following study, we intend to briefly approach the rebellious, protesting movement of our young generation from the viewpoint of the godlessness which dominates the world of their elders. We assume that the ultimate motives of our rebellious youth are unknown not only to us, but also to our youth itself. We intend here to provide some glimpse into these hidden motives.

It is obvious that our youth is protesting not only some aspects of our world, but it in its entirety with all its fundamental principles. Their neglected

---

[50] Dr. J. Gutas has treated the problem of contemporary youth in *The Lights of Homeland*, (Lithuanian weekly newspaper, 941 Dundas St. West, Toronto, Ontario), 1969.
[51] *Ibid.*

appearance, unattended hair, and "wild" beards are merely an outward sign of their inner attitude which further manifests itself in their disregard to our ways and their refusal to prepare themselves for some speciality and thus to enter constructively our technological "anthill" as positive members, replacing their elders as they retire from their jobs.

In earlier times, especially in the archaic mythical days, a youngster took pride in imitating his elders and was full of vigor to become a man like they. Today a youngster detests the ways of his elders and refuses to step into their shoes.

It may very well be that our youngsters are subconsciously aware of the fragility, insecurity, or perhaps, even of the absence of fundamental standards in our lives. Knowing this, they refuse to "under-stand" them and thus they revolt against them. If this is so their protest or rebellion would not have to be considered negatively, if only these youngsters would come up with new, young ideas or principles. Just saying "No!" stubbornly does not make them any better than us. Loudly and thoughtlessly they use the slogans of freedom or peace, without having any worthwhile insights into the meanings of these grand truths.

Hippies, beatniks, "vietniks", "peaceniks", freedomites, and so on fail to understand that freedom is not shallowly understood liberty : freedom does not mean an absence of any regulating order. A cultural life is not accomplished (realized) when everyone goes his own way. Such self-determination, manifested, for instance, by draft card burning in the United States, is a typical example of anarchy. On the other hand, a truly cultural life does not consist of deciding all the major issues by democratically cast votes. True freedom is not achieved by the voice of the majority. Such freedom does not treat man as a *spiritually* living entity in his inner self; rather it treats him as an all around completed entity which has realized in itself its individual fullness or perfection.

We know that a real society, a real cultural world or *Dasein*, or a real individual in such a society has the feature of lack of absolute fullness or perfection. The fullness of man or of his world always stands out beyond mere man or a wholly humanistic world; it points toward superhuman principles. Both — man and his world — undergo a cultural growth or cultural life. In this growth or life true freedom is not liberty (total unrestriction of an individual or the humanistically cultural world), but a being open, being available, or being free towards one's own or one's world's fullness or completedness, even though such fullness is never realizable.

Accordingly, the fullness of being-man is never in man himself as the point of heaviest weight located in him. Man, by being open to this fullness of being-man, being free to it, lives a cultural life, dwells poetically. If man's essence of being-man (his inner self) would belong to, would be in possession or control of man himself, he would then live an immanent, an anthropocentric life, and freedom would be liberty — freedom centralized or rooted in man himself.

Since, however — as we have seen before — man's essence of being-man, his inner self, is beyond man, it is in the hands of guiding, ordering, transcendental powers — considered by Heidegger to be the interplay of earth, sky, gods and mortals — his freedom is not his own self-determination; rather it consists of his openness, availability, "under-standing" or responsiveness to these transcendental powers. In this respect we elders, as well as our youth, fail to grasp the true meaning of freedom. Accordingly, the youngsters, the "freedomites" (fighters for freedom) are just as "democratic" as are their elders.

Is man's cultural mission accomplished by attaining sheer liberty, that is anarchy? No! Is it accomplished by the well organized democratic togetherness of faceless human zeros which rule everything by the will of the majority, that is, by quantity with no regard to quality? No! Man's cultural mission is accomplished by men who humbly, respectfully and carefully search for the lost principles which would lead humanity toward everyone's own self-completion, toward the realization of everyone's responsive "under-standing" to transcendental principles, the gods still unknown.

Every individual cannot open the holy (wholly) ways to human fullness. There are a few — the ones who are chosen or called — who are capable of transmitting the godly *logos* to their people. These few are the priests, poets or leaders of these people. Freedom is *ipso facto* a freedom to society's great men, who have the sight of the ever-elusive hints of gods and who are able to transmit these hints to their people. A lordly or kingly man (gods' serving man) sets his people free.

By their adherence to liberty, the youngsters maintain an anthropocentric attitude rather than one of true freedom. However, by revolting against and rejecting almost all our humanistic values, they display unhumanistic or else unanthropocentric tendencies. This would mean that their godlessness is godlessness without anthropocentricity, without humanism.

By rejecting the humanistic norms of our godless world, rebellious youth *quasi* opens the door for the influx of reality hitherto not understood but already waiting for our response. Through this door the breeze of the future gods is bound to flow into our *Dasein*.

Since these principles are unknown to the rebelling youngsters themselves, they are lost and in a state of disorientation. Dissatisfied with the world of their elders and lacking the sight of the world of tomorrow, they are generally victims of foreign political forces which seek to bring about the disintegration of the sequentially flowing culture of the traditional Western world. These foreign forces are almost exclusively various brands of Communism (Russian, Chinese, Castroist and others). These forces successfully use (or rather abuse) the disorientation of our youth to create disturbances and to undermine the cultural life in our free Western world.

Algirdas Budreckis, who made a careful observation and investigation of student riots on the university or college campuses of North America, finds that these riots are not spontaneous, but that they are an outcome of the careful planning of a comparatively small group of individuals who are the agents of countries seeking the downfall of Western democratic strongholds, in the first place, of course, the downfall of the United States of America.

In all cases of student riots, Budreckis discovers the same pattern or procedure.[52] According to him, these agents get in touch with groups of people who may have some reasons to be dissatisfied with their environment. University or college students are to a certain extent trapped by democratic and technological successes of their elders. This success leaves the younger generation hardly any new unexplored areas to which it can apply its talents and creative energies. The youngsters thus face the dilemma of either following their "brilliant" elders or opposing them by creating chaos or anarchy. The greater part of the world's youth chooses the latter. Budreckis calls this attitude of resignation boredom. Because of boredom, the youngsters are eager to jump to any venture to fill in some way their inner emptiness, the vacuum in their souls.

The enemy agent infiltrates these at first small groups of dissatisfied students and search with them for some injustice, some negligence, some intolerance, some abuse in their society, especially in the administration of their schools. If there is no obvious "evil" on which they can put their finger, these agents, the leaders of revolting eager student groups invent one. It makes no difference what kind of "maltreatment" — real or imaginary — is there to be attacked; the most important thing is to direct the spirit and energy of dissatisfaction against the administration of the school and furthermore against the administration of the ruling offices of the country. Freedom, peace, human rights and the rights of students are effective slogans, so handy for throwing into the faces of the establishment.

---

[52] *The Lights of Homeland*, June 11, 1970.

Agents with their auxiliary squadrons spread their "ideas" by organizing meetings of larger groups of less venturesome students and by performing impressive demonstrations. The next step after the initial demonstrations, is a mass meeting with invited speakers. In every major student riot, a liberally minded professor or some well known popular personality can be found and invited as the principal speaker. Any opposition or even criticism of the rioters "programme" is accused and attacked as being the work of the enemies of freedom, an attitude of the flatterers of the prevailing administrative system, an attitude of those who do not support peace, the mentality of toadies who support the military-industrial complex, or the position of the adversaries of truth and of human rights.

When the gradual agitation of large masses is complete, the final act of destructive rioting is carried out. This gives no other choice to the administrators of the school but to call the police to restore order. This is precisely what is desired by the initiators of these riots, since now the "academic autonomy" is violated and a splendid chance is provided for "undeniable proofs" of "police brutality", since there are always "impartial" reporters at hand who represent the newspapers, television, and other public media. These reporters very ably catch the scenes where an "idealistic" student is mistreated by the police "in a barbarian way".

A cool, unbiased and careful observation would reveal much the same tactics in the procedure of all such student riots. Moreover, more or less the same pattern or programme is maintained in the events of other social disturbances, caused by the fighters for racial freedom and equality, the anti-war movements, in the battle for the legalization of drugs, and even in the women's liberation front.

The enemies of the free Western world (the Communists) are most intensely interested in making it defenceless. They attempt to render it thus by the peace and anti-war demonstrations which they initiate and inspire. It is shocking to see how successful they are in this respect, not only among the students but even among some high-standing political or cultural personalities in our world.

On September 10, 1968, the president of the Student Union of the University of British Columbia in his speech agitating a promotion of peace, demanded that the science of chemical war materials be banned from the curriculum of Canadian universities; and moreover, that all social ideologies in any way supporting war be eliminated from the social sciences. The speaker did not know (or more probably, he did not want to know) that a blind defencelessness will not promote the well-being of Canadians, but much more surely, it will lead to the eventual elimination of the Canadian nation from the map of the world. A vacuum does not long stay a vacuum. In the case of Canada's (or any other country's) total disarmament, the well-armed countries would immediately overrun Canada with their armies and populate it with their own people, making Canadians mere second class citizens or even extincting them totally (in the event of a "liberation" by Mao's China!). Nature teaches even the smallest insect how to defend itself. Just as the peace and equilibrium of the animal world is not attained by making animals defenceless but, on the contrary, by making them capable of protecting themselves and their young, so cultures or nations can provide their people with peace and help them to attain a peaceful harmony or co-operation with other cultures or nations only by acquiring a means of defence.

Youth alone cannot be made responsible for its anti-social, anti-government disorderly, or rebellious attitudes. By trying to gain some insight into the background of the destructive and rebellious attitudes of the young generation, we may better understand the ultimate causes of or reasons for their apathetic attitude towards the ideals of their elders. It may well be that we, the elders, and our anthropocentric, godless principles, more than anything else, take away the healthy enthusiasm of our youth. Our 'prosaic "(non-poetical) way of life with man as the ultimate measure of all truths, already clips the wings of any flight of youth toward the bluish land of Eldorado.

Let us take the example of patriotism. Patriotism, in mythical, and even in comparatively recent times, was an enthusiastic venture of young men and women. Responding with ardent love to the gods of their land, they displayed remarkable endurance and strength in suffering and provided their inner selves with a deep meaning of life. In serving their earth and skies, their gods and fellow men, they lived a "poetical" life of *Mania*.

The schools of yesterday taught the youngsters the love of their own land along with various scientific subjects and arts. Today's history and geography textbooks in our schools are void of any patriotic interludes. Patriotism is banned, just as is religion or any concern for transcendental reality as such. " 'Patriotism', said Docter Johnson, 'is the last refuge of a scoundrel'. In an age like ours it is the sign of the immature and the irresponsible".[53]

Patriotism is only one instance. We could easily find that almost all the major ideals of the old world or the old godly cultures are gone from our godless *Dasein*. With their departure, real enthusism has gone as well. Therefore we should not wonder about the apathetic attitudes of our youth.

[53] George Wordcock, "Patriotism Today is the Sign of the Immature" in *Victoria Daily Times*, May 23, 1970.

Being too busy in constructing our godless world, we ourselves mistook our zeal to build up our anthropocentric technocracy or enthusiasm. Our younger generation is not fully — at least not as yet — absorbed by its inner depthe into the edifice of our anthropocentric world. It may be that subconsciously they are becoming aware that in our world true enthusiasm is a sort of insanity or immaturity.

Why does our youth rebel? To a great extent it does so because we, the older generation, have lost our firm stance amid the cultural principles once unquestionably certain. We no longer know why we do what we do. When we need an opinion about something, we ask the expert on that particular "line' of specialization. Or else we seek a solution to any problem in the opinion of the majority. At times we even ask the opinions of those whom we instruct, guide or educate. Following Dewey's educational philosophy in praxis, we allow the patient to be his own doctor. Often we ask students themselves what their ideals or their outlooks on fundamental cultural values and the meaning of human existence are. Can we, then, be of any authority to or have any prestige among our youngsters? Our confusion and the fact that we are lost amid the structural principles of reality is the true birth-bed and reason for our rebellious younger generation. We do not know what is right, what is great, what is heroic, what is holy! How can our youngsters know it?

All rebellious movements of "peaceniks", "vietniks", "black power", hippies, and so on are nothing but radicalizations of the lack of true principles or ideals of technocratic man. In the technocratic world human freedom is distorted, perverted, twisted, or betrayed. It is so because it does not mean or express a surrender to or a service and "under-standing" of powers which stand above merely human standards. No one can be a great man or hero without a zeal, urge, or an immense desire to submit himself to a higher or divine order, to gods. Can we call anyone who fights or struggles only for his own well-being or for that of his fellow men great or heroic?

If "Peaceniks" and Co. serve only their own well-being in their own way, they walk on the same godless ground as we do without our anthropocentric efficiency and austerity. Rebellious youth, instead of trying to rediscover the lost principles of its aged culture, instead of reviving its dead gods, carries on an orderless, lawless, empty life. In such an atmosphere, in such a spiritual climate, no greatness or heroism is possible.

It is quite conceivable that beyond the apathy of our youth concealed lies enthusiasm. Lacking the sight of the future gods and their "under-standing" great men, our youth projects its concealed enthusiasm toward

the pseudo-great men of today (since genuinely great men are lacking).
Due to the clever psychological manoeuvres of Communist agents who
create slogans and images appealing to rebellious venturesome minds,
our youth has begun to adore men who have no genuine enthusiasm or
greatness, but who, on the contrary, represent an anthropocentric socialistic
system or doctrine controlled in much more detail by the clear-cut regulations according to which all men are driven like cattle into the pastures of
the "earthly paradise". These idols are Castro, "Che", Mao and others,
who seek the downfall of the United States of America, the fortress of the
free world and perhaps the last resort of a chance for the future's cultural
rejuvenation. This fortress — even though anthropocentric itself — leaves
room for "godly" movements when the time will be ripe for them and when
our future enthusiastic or "poetical" men will present us with the images
of future gods.

Every man in the ancient Egyptian world, as we already know, instead
of having his own individual, "democratic" self, had the self, the *Ka*, of his
king, by participating in it — in the *Ka* of his idol. Such a participation,
rather than the maintaining of one's own self as "democratically" equal
to everyone else's, is enthusiastic : a participation in the life of a god (this
is so because having one's own *Ka* meant implication in the being of a god).
The king, permeated by the godly *Ka* (of Osiris) was the presence of the god
(Osiris) in the living world of the Egyptians. The people, participating in
the *Ka* of their king, participated in the being of their god and thus their
existence was enthusiastic.

Our youngsters, imitating their pseudo-idols, display an analogy to the
Egyptian mythical world and manifest their enthusiastic attitudes. Such an
attitude, wrongly oriented, but rightly trusted in their depths, which are
concealed (even to themselves), point beyond the anthropocentric world.
The most effective or most striking manifestation of trans-anthropocentric
attitudes is freely accepted death in search for one's ideal. A man who dies
for his ideal is a hero. He is — to say in the least — selfless in the sense of
his overcoming of his egocentric or peripheral self. Even thought selfless,
however, he may still be anthropocentric. He is so when he dies for his fellow
men, for his nation, for his like-minded pals, or for humanity in general.

We must emphasize here that strictly speaking there cannot be any hero
in a purely anthropocentric world. In other words, no one dies for purely
humanistic ideals. Accordingly, there cannot be any Communist or democratic (American) hero who is a hero in the true sense of the word.

Whenever someone sacrifices his life for others (for his nation, or family,
or for humanity), he sacrifices himself for their well-being. What is man's

well-being? On both sides of the fence in our politically divided world (Communist empires on one side and Western democratic countries on the other) the ideal of man's well-being is a state, wherein all things, all commodities, all values, all "goodies" of any kind are made accessible to all the members of the nation. According to this, it should follow that someone who wants to be a hero should die seeking the plenty of life for his survivors; for instance, seeking the plentitude of champagne, caviar, and other "goodies" for their tables! Is it so? Not quite!

It is true, however, that a member of a family would die defending the possessions needed for his family, or a warrior defending the food storages needed by his fellow combatants to survive. Nevertheless, the provision of his fellow men with food, commodities and things of comfort is not the ultimate aim for the hero's death. The preservation of the lives of one's loved ones or like-minded pals is done principally to let them carry on, to realize or to attain the ideals sought by them and the dying hero. If, however, these ideals are their own well-being, the fact remains principally the same.

Krivis, the highpriest of archaic Lithuanians, at the time of a disaster which brought calamity or hardship to the whole nation, after transmitting the will of gods to his people, following which they would overcome their crisis, he himself would frequently end his life by throwing himself into the holy flames of burning oakwood, the wood of the god Perkunas. This he did during the sacred ceremonial rites in the holy grove. By his death *krivis* commemorated the highlight, the *holy* day, of a certain phase of the Lithuanian *Dasein*. With the message of his gods, signed by his own death, *krivis* helped his people to take a firm stand in their days of disaster by following their gods — mainly their god Perkunas — and by thus overcoming their crisis. The aim of *krivis* was not the well-being of his nation, but the protection of the gods' presence in his nation. A disaster was merely an indication that somewhere his people deviated from the ways of the gods. Their "under-standing" of their gods would return them to their proper holy ways — the ways by which they guarded their gods in their lives. *Krivis'* death, thus, was clearly a venture into the beyond of the purely human milieu.

Anthropocentric heroes — be they technocratic idealists of a Communist or democratic brand — do not die only for the well-being of man, but for humanity's ideals. Peripherally approached, these ideals are humanistic. When seen radically (with recourse to the roots; *radix* — "root"), however, they may be revealed as transcendental. As such they are in the concealed background of the technocratic world, inaccessible and impenetrable rationalistically or theoretically. With an existential inquiry (standing out beyond merely immanent principles) from a "poetical", enthusiastic viewpoint anthropocentric heroes may be revealed as dying for the gods of tomorrow, of whom they are not aware peripherally, but sure of in their inner selves.

Death, just as Nature in her concealedness, is not only improperly understood, but it is bound to remain so. "One cannot gaze for long either at the sun or at death", says F. La Rochefoucauld.

Our youth is skeptical and apathetic as regards our humanistic ideals. That they have this mistrust is understandable as well as justifiable. It is so because we, the older generation, do not dwell in a harmonious wholy or holy world. Instead, we live in cultural ruins amid heaps of cultural debris. Our technological success outshines everything else; in addition, it overshadows and makes unnoticeable the disunity in contemporary man's innermost self and the shortcomings of present-day (humanistic) *logos*. Being confused and lost on our cultural cross-roads, we do not impress our youth and fail to be pillars of strength in their eyes.

Our youth is out on a search. A search for what? They do not know this themselves yet. The youngsters refuse to step into our shoes and carry on our enterprises. By this mere refusal or denial of our shattered cultural values or ideals, our youth does not enter a true cultural world. Youth must, however, find and discover its true cultural way, rooted in its inner self. A study of the great cultures of the past during their heights or times of greatest flourishing is very helpful for the laying out of the ways for the cultural ventures of the future. This study must be crowned by finding one's own cultural standing, one's own stead in the trans-humanistic milieu of our *Dasein*.

Every true culture in history is godly. There is, however, no culture absolutely valid to all men and all times. There is no one and exhaustive culture of humanity! A wolf has brilliant traits or qualities. Yet these traits or qualities are not the ideals of all species of animals. An eagle has characteristics or features totally different from those of a wolf, and yet they are just as brilliant as those of the wolf. An animal does not have to be wolf-like or eagle-like in order to be brilliant, however, he must possess *some* brilliant qualities to survive in Nature's play and to manifest (to assemble) this play by his way of life. Analogically, we can say much the same about our youth : a young man today does not necessarily have to serve certain cultural ideals, nevertheless, he must serve *some* ideals — *he must serve some gods* or else he will betray the mission of his being-man. By being merely a sign carrier protesting the ills of the adult world and creating disorder on city streets, he is more a nuisance, an absurdity, than a constructive participant in a cultural world.

Only when a young man, instead of merely protesting and throwing bricks into the windows of public buildings, sincerely goes out on a search for a truer ideal in man's life — on a search for future gods — only then can he help the ailing and shallow contemporary world by steering the boat of the cultural life of his co-travellers into deeper and mistier, but more grand and godly waters glittering under the dawn of future gods.

The first step in a youth's search for gods is his becoming loyal once again to his own family and elders in general, and then becoming a sincere searcher for the new horizons, the dawn of new gods. Co-playing with the gods of the future — not rioting and throwing bricks — may upset the hitherto shallow values of the technocratic world and will provide humanity with a milieu for a greater life. Godlessness will then be succeeded by the ultra-modern — by the "bluish" — godliness.

CHAPTER II

THE EVENT OF CULTURE

Culture is the milieu within which Nature's pristine, ever-concealed powers break through into openness. Such a break-through, as we have already seen, is Nature's mode of self-concealment. When the ever-concealed transcendental powers break into openness or disclose themselves — when the dark *physis* becomes the lit-up *logos* — they perform a cosmic guilt, which they immediately reconcile by prevailing as concealed in the light of disclosure. *Physis* comes into the light of *logos* in such a way that it is present there as concealed : it withdraws itself from this light.

Nietzsche's Will to Power is an impressive dynamic image of the event of *physis-logos-physis* in its everlasting fluctuation — the image of Nature's play. We know that Nature's play, chaos, is older than and anterior to our earth, our Mother Earth, and we also know that Nature's play will outlast our earth. Only in a fraction of the earth's life, between two dots — one indicating the beginning of our earth in the cosmic fires, and the other indicating its end or extinction in these fires — does Nature manage to bring herself into openness or disclosure. The various human cultures (not only our own Western culture) can be considered a window, a screen, into which Nature's play brings itself at the rainbows of our cults and in which it simultaneously conceals itself. This means that there is no absolute or perfect culture, nor that there can ever be such a culture.

A search for gods formulates man's way of being. It formulates his primordial dwelling in his cultural milieu, his *Dasein*. The search for gods, the backbone of cultural life, does not and cannot reach its end or accomplishment. Man for ever travels searching for his gods. Even in godless times he is merely in a situation of having lost, or of having been thrown out from, the trails of his search. There is no ultimate end, no fulfillment, no harbour for man's errings, where all man's insecurities, troubles, problems and strivings — where his search — comes to an end.

1. *Philosophy and Things*

The cultural world has, as its ultimate ground, an abyss — the abyss of Nature in her concealment. Even though an abyss, Nature is the utmost firm ground for any immanent reality — for things. Things would never be disclosed — could neither be meaningful nor meaningless — if not for a cultural world.

Philosophy is the cultural field concerned with gaining an insight into or comprehension of the ultimate principles of reality. In the era of its beginning, philosophy — the early Greek philosophy — was concerned with these principles under the viewpoint of their transcendency or their being trans-entitative.

Ironically, the so-called Greek classical philosophy — the philosophy of Plato and Aristotle — gradually lost sight of transcendental reality and began to be concerned with immanent or entitative reality, the reality of things. The abysmal grounds were left unconsidered, while things (entities or beings), well founded in these grounds, gradually became the sole reality. Generally speaking, things in the classical philosophy of Greece were understood and interpreted by a mighty pair of concepts which have dominated Western philosophies for roughly two thousand years. These concepts were spirit and matter or form and matter.

In Plato's philosophy form was still a transcendental reality due to its being anterior to things, that is, due to its being unentitative. Forms or ideas were extraneous realities as regards things. Plato understood ideas as being static, that is, as indestructible, eternal, unchangeable, perfect. A philosopher, the man of wisdom, to him was the one who had the knowledge of ideas in their harmonious hierarchic interbelonging. Accordingly, the meaning of culture for Plato consisted of becoming acquainted with the world of ideas. By knowledge of this kind the understanding of things in their true nature is rendered possible. Since the time of Plato, this aspect of perfect knowledgeability of the ultimate reality, and along with it, of the true, eternal, and perfect meanings of all things was thought of as possible in our Western world, and it was merely a matter of time before the perfect or absolute knowledge of things would be gained. If today we look forward to total and exhaustive understanding, interpretation, and domination of our world, we are the true progeny of Plato.

Plato eliminates the obscurity or concealment which in the pre-classical philosophies and in mythical thought was seen as integrally implied in the very event of fundamental reality. He eliminates *physis*. With this elimination he, instead of seeing the fundamental reality as abysmal or chaotic, begins to see it as well founded or solidly supported by itself. Now, since — as we have seen — things, the immanent reality, are well-founded, while Nature's play, the *physis*-is-*logos*, — even though founding all things and serving as their ground — itself remains unfounded or groundless, Plato's consideration of transcendental reality's being well-founded moves it closer to things — to what is founded or has grounds or causes for its being.

Aristotle makes a large stride in the direction of the "entitativisation" of the ultimate grounds of realities by understanding things as having implied in themselves the static (ideal) forms to a certain degree. According to Aristotle, there is no transcendental reality — no ideas in their own separate world. There are things only. Whatever is not a thing *is not* at all!

Even though Aristotle eliminates transcendental reality from the philosophically understood Western cultural world, he maintains firm forms or essences of things as "ideal" in the sense that they are eternally true to everybody's intellect at all times as long as one rightly (rationally, logically) uses his mind.

St. Thomas, and medieval philosophies in general, secures the permanency and unswerving truth of all things in the being or essence of God, the supreme being which founds and establishes all things. St. Thomas modifies the essentialistic or thing-centered world of Aristotle by making it theocentric — founded and maintained by the supreme thing or supreme being.

Kant shatters the "firmness' of the idealistic and essentialistic cultural world by seeing it as subjective. Kant rejects the thing-centered as well as the God-centered world by centering it in man : by making its anthropocentric.

With this shift Kant presents to us objects which are marked by the aspect of clarity, as what is found in man's mind — in the subject. The subject, unlike objects, lacks clarity even though it is anterior, more fundamental and thus more real, than the objects. The subject is pre-entitative and thus transcendental. Immanent reality — closed and self-sufficient, ideal and absolutely true for everybody at all times — is shaken up by the breaking into it of transcendental principles. With his inquiry into and investigation of the *a priori* subjective principles of reality, Kant puts the theme of Nothingness *qua* concealment into things (their foundations) themselves. He does so most strikingly, perhaps, by presenting the subjectivity of space and time.

With the dependability of objects on the human mind, they lose the unswerving firmness, which they had in the Greek idealistic-essentialistic and medieval theocentric periods of philosophical development. However, since to Kant the structure of the subject is lasting, firm, and "ideal", objects too, can be thought of as being so.

Husserl, who sees the mind as "perspectivistic", that is as being able to maintain various angles of subjective approaches, forsakes the Kantian understanding of the human subject as statically or stably firm. Like Kant, he maintains that there are no absolute objects, that is, no "mindless" objects, but unlike Kant, however, he maintains that the mind (consciousness or subject) can have various approaches, various systems of viewing objects and therefore it (the mind, subject) as well fluctuates or is dynamic; it lacks monotonic uniformity and absolute or perfect firmness or stability. With Husserl's thought the anthropocentric standing of contemporary man already undergoes a shake-up.

Heidegger, from the very beginning of his thought (already in *Sein und Zeit*) makes a careful study of subjectivity, the "perfect" axle of Kantian reality, according to which all things or all objects are firmly set in their meanings. He finds that the grounds of subjectivity, or being-man, lie in *Dasein*. *Dasein* for him is the world of man, rather than man's essence, as it was understood to be at first. *Dasein* does not belong to man, but *vice versa* : man belongs to *Dasein*. The meaning of *Dasein* is well expressed by Heidegger's word : "*Dasein* is the being-held-in;-Nothingness".[54]

Here Nothingness, just as in the mythical or pre-philosophical and early philosophical thought of the Western world, means concealedness. On the abysmal ground of Nothingness, in chaos (*Abgrund*), all the colorful array of things with their clarity and splendor finds its supporting firm ground (*Grund*). Nothingness, Being in its concealment, sways everything in any cultural world. Such a sway marks culture as having a shortcoming. This trait is not really a trait, as it is not accidental and thus avoidable, but is essential. This shortcoming means precisely the imperfection, or rather unabsoluteness of culture at its very roots.

Since things are founded in Nothingness, they and their meanings are also not disclosed or set absolutely. Accordingly, no philosophical or scientific theory — no matter how precisely and logically it is worked out or built up — can reveal things with an absolute, one-sided, perfect meaning and thus present them as absolutely true and real.

The non-absoluteness of disclosed cultural principles and the meanings of things in Heidegger's philosophy does not indicate its being realtivistic or nihilistic, as it has often been assumed. It rather means that every culture maintains firm, well founded, and holy principles in its *Dasein*

[54] Martin Heidegger, *Was ist Metaphysik*? (Frankfurt a. M. : Vittorio Klostermann, 1949), p. 32.

with clearly set meaning for everything in it and with clearly marked out ways in it for men who live godly lives by respecting the swaying powers of their cultural world. This firmness and clarity is, however, restricted to a certain culture, or rather to a certain phase of it. This firmness or clarity can in no wise be extended to the culture in the whole of its development and least of all to the whole of humanity — over all other cultures.

In man's life in his world, he cannot guide himself solely by the transcendental principles which are disconnected from things and from living situations. This is so because these principles are essentially concealed; they hold themselves in withdrawal. They come to light only in things and on man's ways, on which man finds himself together with other men. By handling or making things with respect and by entering the ways of his world with the others (with his fellow men), he becomes aware of the flash-ups of the transcendental light which orders, arranges, articulates, and sways everything; he becomes aware of the powers of gods, present in the things of his living world and in his ways in it. He thus guards the godly powers, guards his ways and guards things in their meanings by his cultural — that is responsive — living : by his standing in the abyss of Nothingness and by holding his stead rooted there.

2. *Rational and Existential Things*

Immanent philosophies — philosophies according to which things, beings, or entities alone are real, and according to which any unobjective, unentitative, or non-being reality is no reality at all or *is* not — see a thing as always founded in another thing. They see a group of things with a lesser degree of "beingness" or entitativeness as owing itself to a smaller group or (in medieval times) to a singular thing, which founds itself and thus has the highest or most intense degree of entitativeness or realness. All things, whatever degree of realness they have, are rooted or founded in the supreme being, the realness as such.

Immanent philosophies, even though they admit manysided mutual interrelations of things, tend to investigate the essences of things in their initial mutual isolation. With this they try to say that things or objects are well rounded and philosophically determinable in their essences before they can be treated as mutually interrelated. Relation, or rather relatedness, is merely an accident.

The feet of a mountain goat, for instance, are well adapted "for travel in rugged mountainous terrain. Their hoofs have sharp edges and the undersides are concave, enabling them to adhere somewhat like suction cups as these agile creatures make their way up and down seemingly impassable cliffs. Caribou have huge rounded hoofs to support their weight on snow or spongy tundra, and the edges of their hoofs are sharp to prevent skidding on ice. The camel's cloven hoofs are very broad and cushoned with thick soles — adaptations for travel over yielding desert ground".[55] In the above description of the hoofs of some animals we can see examples of *necessary* interrelations of things or objects. Thus, the hoofs of mountain goats clearly are interrelated with the rocky cliffs of mountains, the hoofs of caribous clearly refer themselves to their own weight, to winter snow and ice and to summer's soft spongy northern grasslands, and the camel's cloven hooofs belong to desert sands.

Are these accidents — unessential traits of qualities — or animal hoofs truly "unessential"? Is it not for these traits or "accidental" qualities the very core of the respective animals stands or falls?

We know that an approaching dark cloud indicates rain. A dog, hearing the rattle of his dish, becomes instantly aware of his meal, even though it may not yet be his supper-time. An ice cube in a glass of ginger ale produces a gentle, somewhat dull sound when bumping onto the sides of the glass. It, along with the ginger ale, is really and *essentially* interrelated with heat, thirst, sweating, with a modern household with commodities of refrigeration, and so on.

With the methods of immanent or entitative philosophies, along with the scientific interpretations of reality founded in these philosophies, all the above mentioned qualities, characteristics, or accidents of things can yet be thought of as certain traits of the things. These traits, however, are here separable from the substances of the things, or they can be conveniently substituted by some others. For instance, a white house can be painted pink. In this example the house as a substantial entity is fundamentally real, while its color (white or pink) inheres in the real entity of the house and thereby it acquires its realness which, being non-substantial, is of a lesser intensity.

Scientific interpretations of things can go considerably farther than just denying realness in its full extent to "accidental" realities. Sciences frequently not only degrade the accidents of *real* entities (substances), considering them as real in a subordinate sense, but they go so far as to shatter the realness of the substances of things — they shatter their substances. For instance, an ice-cube in a glass of ginger ale really is not an ice-cube. It is rather a combination of a few *true* or *real* elements of reality. These are hydrogen and oxygen in certain proportions under a certain condition of temperature.

[55] Richard Carrington, *The Mammals* (New York : Life Books , 1963), p. 58.

Only a "dreamy", "poetical" person may think he is drinking ginger ale with an ice cube in it. A sober-minded scientific man would know that he is placing into himself a certain quantity (a glass-volume) of a certain chemical compound. He may even think that he places into himself a certain cluster of tiny, dynamically moving particles charged with positive and negative loads of electricity. In his well-known example of a blossoming tree faced by a "sober"scientific observer, Heidegger emphasizes that there is really no tree in the perspective of a scientific eye. Instead, there are immense clusters of dynamically moving and variously circling electrons around their protons in richly diversified organizations.[56] Anyone who thinks he is facing a beautiful, blossoming tree, according to the above "sober", scientific approach, is naive, is "poetical", is unrealistic.

An attempt to restrict realness to substances or to the "elements" pushes the problem of fundamental realness farther away instead of solving it. Existentialistic philosophies, by trying to stress the *essential* interbelonging of things, are principally stressing that the essences of things or their substantiality are not a sufficient or adequate foundation for their realness. Things are not self-supporting. What we are trying to stress here is not that things involve other things, but that they principally involve transcendental realities. Only these constitute the foundation which makes things real and thinkable.

A mountain goat's hoof refers to the mountains of its habitat and also to the clear skies often situated above the layers of clouds in high moutains. A caribou's hoof, by its very make-up "recalls" northern grass plains, murky in summer and covered with snow under wintry skies. A camel's hoofs "speak" of desert sands burned red by a hot sun in cloudless skies. The hoofs of all these animals refer to Nature's working powers, which throughout the ages model and creatively shape them rendering the lives of the animals concerned here fit for their habitats.

These working powers of Nature become disclosed in the human *Dasein,* in man's cultural world. They are disclosed in a different way in different cultures. Mythical man saw these powers of Nature, which creatively model animal and human lives, as gods. In our godless times we interpret the formation of the hoofs as a result of various entitative factors, refusing to see any transentitative play of Nature in it. A little closer to this comes the theory of the selective development of individuals or whole breeds of animals in the milieu of Nature's terrain. Some individuals or some breeds are more

---

[56] Martin Heidegger, *Was Heisst Denken?* (Tübingen : Max Niemeyer Verlag, 1954), pp. 17-18.

capable of adapting themselves to their circumstances — especially during drastic changes — than are the others. We can state here only briefly that things — in this case the hoofs of some animals — necessarily refer to earth, sky, and to man's cultural world which always involves gods or their lack, their absence.

It is needless to say that earth and sky (not even mentioning men and gods) cannot be seen here overhastily as clear-cut entities, or a group of these. Earth as a planet and the sky as a huge space of ether filled with a multitude of celestial bodies are understood totally entitatively. Just as anything whatsoever, they presuppose or are preceded or preconditioned by our "under-standing" of the openness in which reality, Nature, or Being, *is* or comes to light, to disclosure. In this openness we *are* and, in a different way, things *are*. The openness (*Dasein*) renders possible any encounter of any thing or any object by the subject. Things are always somewhere and always necessarily at some time, and this "somewhere" or "sometime" is not a thing. Primordial or transcendental space and time constitute an ordering-diversifying movement in the sense of *Be-wëgung*, or play. Openness is always spatio-temporal play, and it does not come to us as some abstract cluster, but befalls us colorfully in our living cultural world as the interplay of earth, sky, gods, and our inner selves — as the cluster of transcendental powers, assembled by the things of our living world. The latter are rendered possible by the former.

An ice cube in a glass of ginger ale would be meaningless if not for *Dasein* wherein it is rooted. Without the foursome — transcendental powers of earth, sky, gods, and mortals — any logically formulated description (such as the chemical formula of H_2O or theory of electrons-protons) would say nothing or would be mere tautology, if not for the "under-standing" (awareness or unawareness) of the four transcendental realities which are reflected or assembled by the ice cube.

An ice cube can be thought of only as frozen water, drawn from a spring or received from a faucet. Even when it comes from the faucet, water nevertheless originates from a spring, a well, a creek, a lake, or some such body of water; furthermore, — it comes from clouds in the sky. In all these cases water is rooted in the openness between earth and sky.

An ice cube floating in a glass of refreshing beverage would have no meaning if not for a man's thirst, especially during the days of summer heat. An ice cube in ginger ale is a part of the modern man's household along with the well-functioning freezing department with which a modern kitchen is necessarily equipped. Kitchens are a significant part of well-planned modern homes along with the picnic benches alongside swimming pools surrounded by well-kept green lawns and other similar features.

An ice cube in a glass of ginger ale is well known to one who knows modern man's environment in detail — who knows his *Dasein*. Such a *Dasein*, on the other hand, can be properly understood by understanding basic principles or standards which govern modern man's life. In modern *Dasein*, unlike in that of mythical man, man thunders through his living days in the midst of his powerful technological devices, like Zeus or Odin in the days of yore. Such thundering is not merely a manifestation of man's brilliance; it principally means man's procedure toward his aim of self-accomplishment; it is realized by his total conquest or control of everything in Nature. Modern man, *by his very trait of godlessness*, involves the presence of gods *in the mode of their absence* from all things of his technocratic world, including the ice cube.

Theoretical or rational interpretation of things usually refers or relates them to others which make them understandable. Thus, by considering a glass of ginger ale with an ice cube in it as a beverage or by understanding water as being H_2O, we simply formulate a tautology seen from the perspectives of the ultimate (transentitative) ground. This tautology consists of treating one kind of entitative or objective reality as another such reality.

According to an existentialistic approach, a thing can be understood by a break-through from entitative to transcentitative reality, which founds or renders thinkable any entitative reality. According to existentialistic philosophy, whose principal theme is the explanation or illucidation of subjectivity by posing it as *Dasein*, a thing is grasped or understood by "understanding" the interrelation or interplay of *Dasein*'s four principles : earth, sky, gods, and mortals, which are reflected and thus assembled by the thing understood. If entitative explanation (although logical) is a tautology, the existential interpretation presents the thing understood as standing under unentitative (neither objective nor subjective) principles of reality. With this explanation the meanings of things are liberated from the yoke of essentialism as well as anthropocentric idealism, which in technocratic times orders, rules, and classifies all things. The break-through into the transcendental milieu of reality is a break-through into a godly and thus mythical grasp of the things of man's living world.

The transcendental principles of culture, unlike the immanent ones, lack one-sided clarity. A man of a certain culture *under-stands* earth, sky, gods, and his own life's mission in a different way than does a man of a different culture. Instead of trying to arrive at absolute, clearly and encyclopedically defined meanings of things which would be valid to everyone at all times, he should seek their truth in his own world *existentially*. Often — as it is today — these meanings are no longer known to us consciously. They, however, are still known subconsciously, in our inner selves. If not for this knowledge, we would truly live in a totally confused world, where everything is explained *tautologically* by everything else and where there would be no hope of our ever knowing what is good, what evil, what is right, what wrong, what is holy, what is profane, what is beautiful and what is ugly, what is great and what is miserable, and so on.

In our confused, godless world we can gain godly standards for tomorrow by letting things appear as they are in themselves, that is, by making a step back into our inner selves and ceasing to violate things by the clear-cut rational systems which we throw upon the things in the way that a fisherman throws his net, and enslave them. After things are in the control of our system, we dictate them and set them in their meanings, providing them with their objectivity. We determine the objectivity of our things by our *a priori* subjective, godless tables of values. When we let things themselves shine with their meanings, gods, rather than our subjective *a priori* principles, begin to shine along with the things.

Things outside the openness of man's cultural *Dasein* remain concealed or hidden. They step out into the open light of truth with man's participation in Nature's play : in her creative works. Such a participation affects the "natural" and "man-made" things equally. We never find ready-made things. They become things, that is, they become the assemblers of the transcendental powers of reality, by our responsive reception of them from Nature as her gifts. A man who finds a cool, pure spring on some hillside amid trees receives it as a gift of earth, sky, and gods. By his receiving it as a holy and vital "thing" from Nature's inexhaustible horn of plenty, he makes it meaningful. This spring compels him to make a halt there, build his cabin, and start his homestead. The cool, pure water from the spring provides him, his family, and his animals with their daily needs of water to thus carry on, and perhaps to accomplish, the mission of his life placed upon his shoulders by the gods of his destiny. Gods themselves are immortal. They do not depend on water for their survival, and if it was only for them, the water of this spring would remain obscure and so would they as the givers of gifts to men. Man's responsive attitude to water as the element of life is his responsive attitude *as a mortal* (immortals do not respond to the elements which grant life). Man in his mortality is a participator in founding the meaning and thus the being of a spring within the openness of his world.

Man, although a significant participant in founding the meanings and being of things, is in no wise the sole giver of meanings to things, unlike the rationalistic, subjectivistic philosophies are inclined to see him. Man *discovers*, rather than makes, the spring. His acute awareness of this aspect, in mythical times was accomplished by the cult of his gods. The first drops of a new spring then were to be poured on the altars of the gods, as a sign indicating that this water was theirs. Man's responsive participation in the disclosure of things as founded in gods was demonstrated by a man himself drinking the water of the spring. All this indicates man to be the co-player with the gods, in which play the meanings of things are set or determined. By his responsive-submissive standing under his gods (their under-standing), he became their partner and thereby a participant in the ruling and swaying over things by the gods. Mythical man was involved in the play of his gods, and things owed their being to him as the co-player with the gods or with Nature.

Man's understanding of things is anchored in his "under-standing" of his gods. Man's responsive or "under-standing" attitude is revealed by the similarity of structure in "natural" and "man-made" things . Often, going to Salt Spring Island from the ferry terminal at Crofton, at low tide I used to see a "skeleton" of a fisherman's boat, partially covered by the ocean's sandy floor. This boat must have been sunk long ago and was deteriorating by being incessantly washed by the sea waves. I noticed how remarkable was the resemblance of the shape or structure of this boat skeleton to that of a fish. Since the sideboards of this boat had fallen off, its frame structure (skeleton) was clearly exposed and it vividly "recalled" the structure of a fish skeleton with its heavy front part and gradually slimming tail section. The working powers in Nature which construct things, are principally the same ones active in the "natural" things as they are in man-made things. A bear is provided with a heavy fur and a man provides himself with a heavy wool coat for the cold seasons. It is Nature who does both : provides the bear with his fur and the man with his coat.

In godless times things, instead of being transcendentally founded and grasped, are understood and explained by the entitative or peripheral means. To get to the truth of things, one would have to be guided by gods. His responsiveness to them would help him to restore a firm world with well established manings for things and well outlined ways for human life in it. We are in need of gods in our godless world.

Language provides the guidelines for the search of the gods of the future. By a humble and respectful attitude toward things and words in "poetical" relay or genuine thought, man can enter his way of a search for gods in our godless world. By not overpowering things with our mighty dominating systems, but instead letting them appear to us in their own light, we can gain the sight of the transcendental powers in them owing to the fact that things are the assemblers of transcendental realities. By dominating and controlling things with our anthropocentric standards, we keep the transcendental realities in them supressed. A responsive and respectful attitude to things can liberate these forces again.

Subconscious psychology states that deep inside us, in our inner selves, there are mythical-symbolic images still alive from the time of the dawn of our culture. These mythical images are called archetypes. They are principally unentitative and are loaded with or permeated by transcendental powers. Archetypes — archaic words sounding inside us — can be "recalled" by patient, submissive, waiting. Men who wait thus are genuine thinkers and are, above all, poets. A true poet does not fabricate a piece of poetical work by responding to the rationally elaborated rules or aesthetic regulations or to the tastes of the crowds, but by his availing himself of his inspiration, which enables him to speak enthusiastically. A poet, prior to any thinker, is bound to name the gods of the future and present or introduce them in his works of art vividly and colorfully. The way of the search for future gods is (or will be) led by our enthusiastic poets, who are simultaneously bound to be our first priests of the dawning gods.

We indicated earlier that a *realistic* understanding of reality is "poetical" principally because it is the *under-standing* (the standing under) of the gods. Logical or scientific understanding of reality, even though it claims absolute truth, is principally an ignorance of the transcendental powers of reality which found all things; it is the ignorance of gods. Such an understanding is godless.

Due to the renewal of insights into the foundations of reality, lost since mythical times, by "poetical" or *realistic* means, godless shallowness is overcome. In spite of this, no system which absolutely explains everything is attained. Even though the poetical-existential insights into the transcendental criteria of reality are not universally applicable to all humanity or to all phases of the cultural *Dasein*, they, nevertheless, are most high, holy, and worthy of devoting or even sacrificing one's own life to. A hero dies for *his* and his community's truth — the truth of his living *Dasein*. There is no universal, cosmopolitan hero of humanity because there is no absolute culture for all humanity.

3. *Man and Animals*

Heidegger considers man to be the shepherd or guardian of things in the light of Being — of Nature. This quality of man makes him distinct from the animals. Things in their meanings and being are in need of the human *Dasein* — are in need of a cultural milieu — wherein they can have their places assigned to them by the ordering and arranging powers of *Dasein* and wherein thay can shine by being disclosed in harmony with all other things in this milieu.

Man can be the shepherd or guardian of things or beings by virtue of his understanding (which simultaneously is his "under-standing") of Nature's all-ordering, all-organizing powers, her *logos*.

To grasp or understand a thing necessarily means to hold a standpoint beyond it. If we would bore a hole in a thing and plant in it a sensitive artificial eye, we would not see anything. For an understanding sight it is necessary to first of all grasp a wide horizon with a multitude of other things on it, in order to gain a sight of, or rather an insight into, a particular thing.

The trilobite, an aquatic animal long extinct, had a long triumphant span of life as the most excellent creature of Nature. Trilobites dominated the primaeval waters from 600 million years to about 230 million years ago. This animal was well equipped to live in the lukewarm, shallow waters which covered almost the entire earth at that time for there was little land above the water. Its bodily structure and the mode of its life was a successful response to its living environment. If we would try to understand the organic build and the ways of life of this strange animal without simultaneously considering its living environment, we could not make any well founded insight into its essence and features.

We are well aware of the widely differing features of animal feet. Only by a broad, retrospective survey of the habitats, food, enemies, and so on of these animals, can we better understand the structures of their feet. "Such rather slow mammals as bears and primates have feet with large, flat bearing surfaces extending from toes to heel, the whole of which are normally in contact with the ground during part of the walk. This stance is known as "plantigrade", derived from the Latin *planta*, meaning "the sole of the foot", and *gradior* "to walk". The faster dog and cat, on the other hand, are "digitigrade" — they stand and walk on their "fingers", with the heel, or hock, being permanently raised. A third category of mammals, including horses, antelopes and gazelles, is "unguligrade" progressing on the very tips of "fingernails", which have become protected by the enlarged nails we know as hoofs".[57]

The above passage illustrates well that a knowledge or understanding of a thing necessarily implies the knowledge of many other things or — which

[57] Carrington, *op. cit.*, pp. 57-58.

is more correct — implies the knowledge of the whole milieu. A short-sighted logical-scientific method does not really see any milieu (*Dasein*); it merely sees other things or their features, qualities, traits and such like.

To one with the "sober" or scientific viewpoint, the creative powers present in Nature's works, her play, are thought of as simply a result of "natural selection", according to which individuals better adapted to their environment survive while those not so well adaptad fail to do so. "One race of pocket mice, which lives on the gypsum sand dunes of New Mexico's Tularosa Basin, is almost white. Another race, a closely related species, inhabits dark lava flows in the same area and is almost totally black".[58]

"Natural selection" is a principle of biological sciences, which reduces all creative procedures in animal life to mere chance or accidental events. Perhaps it is truer to say that Nature's aspect as a chaotic cluster of events in the inorganic world maintained by the evolutionists, is applied here to the world of animals under the name of "natural selection".

Rationalistic interpretation, which is anchored in things and their interrelations and is blind to any transcendental reality, elucidates the development of animal species with an obvious tendency to reduce the "natural selection" to mere chance or an accidental occurrence. With this tendency the rationalistic grasp of reality seems to disprove any unentitative event of Being — disprove Nature's play.

It is important to stress here that all by itself, there cannot be anything accidental nor any chance occurrence. A cabbage seed which happens to fall in a tomato garden grows up there as a thing of chance. The same cabbage would be fully meaningful in a cabbage patch and not accidental. This illustrates that the extraneous point determines whether a thing is meaningful or accidental. This extraneous point principly is not another thing, but the whole, a system. We must have a system (a "trans-data" whole) before we can orderly arrange our data in a orderly fashion to form an overseeable whole. Only within a system can we clearly see what is meaningful and what meaningless. A thing all by itself can be neither meaningful nor meaningless.

Into a parking meter we can deposit a penny, a nickel or a dime. If instead, we would deposit some coin of the ancient Roman Empire, different in its weight and size from any of the above mentioned coins, the meter would not "work". In the "world" of the parking meter, a Roman coin is meaningless, unordinary, accidental, or a non-classifiable reality. Is such a coin really meaningless? Let us take a different viewpoint : in a numismatic shop a

---

[58] *Ibid.*, p. 102.

Roman coin is highly valued, while the contemporary currency is ignored or treated as valueless or meaningless in the numismatical "world".

Analogically to rational systems, in the milieu of Nature's play, her *logos*, a chance or accidental reality or event can be seen as positive or negative. If there was no sway of Nature which holds all things in a harmonious order or *logos*, there could be no deviation, exception, irregularity, or anything unorderly or accidental.

The accidental work of "natural selection" precisely indicates Nature's creativeness. Nature carries over more or less all features of the elders of some breed into their progeny. In addition, she presents them with a whole array of new characteristics. Because of some of these new characteristics, individuals of a new generation may prove themselves better and more capable of coping with their environmental conditions than are those who do not possess these characteristics. It also is possible that the new characteristics may cause the ruin of the species.

Natural selection is Nature's creativeness, by which she originates new species or subspecies of animals. In the mythical world, things, plants, or animals were regarded as drawing their meanings from transcendental or godly backgrounds. The dynamic play of Nature was seen then to be the variously interrelated activities of gods. In this play, some of the gods kept a close companionship with others and, on the other hand, had an opposing or hostile attitude toward others. This, of course, is more obvious in the sway of gods in human lives than in those of animals. For instance, between Hera and Athena prevailed a bond mostly of mutual friendship. In the Greek *Dasein* this friendship was clearly manifested by the well known hero Odysseus, favored by both of these goddesses. Aphrodite, however, almost always opposed Hera and Athena in their dominances. Helena, the wife of King Menelaus, was Aphrodite's favourite, while in the eyes of Hera she maintained very low esteem.

In spite of frequent clashes between the gods, they maintained, generally speaking, a harmonious creative activity in their transcendental milieu. The interrelations of gods, whether friendly or hostile, constitute a well-balanced dance, a play within the whole of Nature's play. All that is accidental, the entitative, triggers transentitative forces which, by counterbalancing the accidental make it less "accidental". Natural selection belongs in Nature's harmony.

Nature's play always has many novel, or even revolutionary upsetting traits along with the conservative ones. Renovating forces or forces of revolt, bring something new and manifest creative works — be it very insignificant at first — which, under certain circumstances, may become widely dominant and spread into various breeds or species.

The first living beings were aquatic. They thrived when the seas were shallow and the waters lukewarm, with an abundance of nutritious water plants. These first animals were egg-laying. Eggs (spawn) hatched well in water because its temperature was the same as that of the fish.

In spite of various innovations and many new features in the animals of later eons, the egg-laying trait was preserved in reptiles and still later in birds. Nature provided the eggs of land animals with a hard shell to equip them better for their harsh conditions. This, of course, she evolved by "natural selection". Moreover, the material holding the spawn together, which prevented their being scattered by moving waters, was substituted by nests built by terrestrial animals : eggs were covered up with soil or surrounded by cozy structures of various nest materials.

Even the non-egg-laying types of animals truthfully represented basically the same procedure of egg-hatching, in an irrecognizably changed or modified manner, however. In mammals Nature preserved the egg-laying and hatching device by letting the embryo develop in an enclosure (more similar to that of spawn than to hard-shelled eggs) which contains water and other materials to satisfy its needs which remain located inside the animal, unlike in fishes or terrestrial egg-laying living beings. Bodily temperature here is relatively the same as it was in the ancestral waters or in nests warmed by the heat of the parental body. The final process, the mammalian way of "hatching", is the moment of giving birth.

Mammalian birth-giving may be considered advanced, complicated, and different when compared with the hatching of eggs in the primaeval waters. It, however, undoubtedly has the same character when looked at from a more fundamental viewpoint. Much the same thing must be said of any innovation in Nature's play. All changes or revolutionary intrusions into age-old ways of animal life maintain the basic sameness.

Nature, when developing a new breed, new species, or a new mode of procedure in animal life, makes, in a manner of speaking, a dip into her primaeval source — anterior to all things from where she comes back with a novelty. This was the way Nature solved the egg-laying and hatching problem in reptiles, birds, and mammals. Adverse climatic and other circumstantial condition have made the egg-laying and hatching inadequate for the survival of mammals in their changed environmental conditions. Nature made a "dip" into her creative source — wherefrom she once brought forward the egg-laying and hatching device — and wherefrom she now came up with the strongly modified, above-mentioned device.

In Nature's ever-concealed source (her womb) all the characteristics of things and animals lay stored. Every new species, new breed, or subspecies, or even a modification of a species or subspecies is a procedure of Nature's *creative* work. A complex animal is not a patched-together, more advanced organism determined by merely mechanical chance causes : it is a whole (holy) creation set out by ever-creative Nature. Moreover, every individual in Nature is a new creation; it hardly ever is a "mass product".

Nature changes everything and simultaneously preserves the same in everything. A new creation is a preservation of the old by a relapse into the early and original phase of play. Deeply in its roots everything remains the same. *Nature plays.*

Sameness, first of all of course, means the sameness of Nature's transcendental powers or the sameness of the gods who govern their whole (holy) areas in Nature's totality or wholeness (holiness). Besides, this sameness also refers to the immanent realities — to animals themselves. In spite of widely different characteristics among the animals, starting with a tiny insect and ending with the mighty grizzly bear, the king of the northern forests, they are all same as animals.

Observing animals, we often see some of them as blindly stupid, while the others appear clever and able to learn new things. Such is the difference between the animals whose lives are governed purely by instincts and those who are called intelligent animals. A wasp would fly toward a burning candle dozens of times, each time burning itself a little until it is finally burned to death. It would never *learn* to stay away from the candle thus saving its life. A hungry dog, on the contrary, would grab a bone taken out of boiling soup and after burning his tongue, would restrain himself from grabbing again. Moreover, by remembering previous experiences, he most likely would wait patiently until the bone cooled, before consuming it.

There are birds and wild animals of the forests who are notorious for their cunning in eluding traps set for them or in finding new, *clever* ways of catching their prey in a peasant's barnyard. All this manifests the intelligence of some animals. Some scientists quite rightly define the intelligence as "the organism's ability to adjust successfully to its environment".[59]

Instinctive knowledge, or rather an instinctive way of living, is an animal's blind following of Nature's guidance, which is planted deeply in it. At times when circumstances were changed and the instinct-guided animals ran into a danger of extinction because of their rigid adherence to the ways they followed under the old circumstances, Nature made a "dip" into her "wholly" (holy) source, from where she surged up with a new device of intelligence. Animal intelligence, being a novelty, is simultaneously meant

[59] *Ibid.*, p. 182.

to serve the same purpose as instinctive knowledge. Instead of following a rigid instinctive operation which proceeds in a definite way, the intelligent animal is marked by its ability to turn in new directions and open new ways of animal life. These new ways actually are not totally new; they are merely the by-passes along the old ways. Here we face very much the same activity in the world of animal life as we do by observing a river delta. When the river bed is dammed or blocked by sediments or other obstructions, it breaks open into a new arm and thus the *same* river flows on.

Animal intelligence is a modification of instinct. Activities of intelligence are most noticeable in the animals whose young must undergo a period of education in order to be capable of facing the situations of adult life. The offspring of instinct-guided animals "know" with precision how and when to act. "Mammalian young are not ready to face the world alone a few hours after birth, as young snakes are. They need care and protection. And as animals, they need childhood. As one goes up the evolutionary scale, instinct plays a smaller, and intellect and training a larger role in the life of the individual".[60]

Against the widely accepted asumption that the intellect means a further advancement on "the evolutionary scale" and instinct points to primitivity, we must say the opposite : the intelligent way of life is more primitive than is the instinctive one. However, we must quickly insert that here, "primitive" means "pristine" or "primordial"; it means a being closer to Nature, who is primitivity *qua* pristinity as such.

Things are finite while Nature is infinite. This means that things are set on certain paths on Nature's map, and move on their paths according to Nature's guiding principles (which — as we have seen — may clash or conflict). In other words things always have their ways on Nature's map. Instinctive animals follow these ways rigidly, while intelligent animals follow them in a "vibrating" manner. Man alone differs from all the animals — be they instinctive or intelligent — by not having a definite path given to him — neither rigid nor flexible.

While any breed of animals is totally taken out from Nature's infinite creative source and is placed on its way, man is "primitive" or pristine to such an extent that he is caught in the whirlpool of Nature's play. Being rooted in Nature's pristine source, where dancing gods dwell, man is pathless and chaotic. However, he cannot remain so : he must again and again enter a way. Man's entering involves his own creative co-operation in the works of gods, who alone are the principal powers of Nature which

[60] *Ibid.*, p. 154.

break open in ways (*be-wegen* — Heidegger) in Nature's openness, in the cultural *Dasein*.

Instinctive animals are firmly chained to their ways of life. Intelligent animals are set much more loosely on them. Man, *homo sapiens*, is wise, rather than merely intelligent. His wisdom or "under-standing" is his being located in Nature's creative source itself, which is anterior to any ways. Interestingly, Nature chose primates — the most intelligent animals — instead of biologically more advanced and more developed mammals, to introduce the most "primitive", principal or godly being — man.

Since both instinctive and intelligent animals maintain their ways, their actions are calculable and predictable. Other animals can build up escape or defense strategy against them or find ways of preying on them. A defense against man is not so easily calculable, because he, unlike the animals, does not have a definite pattern by which he acts or manoeuvers. Because of this, in the eyes of animals (or other men) man's actions are erratic. Animals stay out of man's ways. A Lithuanian proverbe says : "Beware of a horse from behind, — of a cow from in front, and — of an evil man from all sides".

In man, in his inner self, there is necessarily the feature of all-sidedness. Because of it, man is the co-player of the gods. The gods are Nature's powers which open the ways for animals *without* their co-operation, and for man — *with* his co-operation. "Man is the only animal to have made the transition of this new phase, where he can now, if he wishes, largely determine the lines which his physical, mental, and social development should follow. It lies within his powers, if he uses them wisely, not simply to record his history as if it consisted of predetermined events, but to shape it with a good understanding of the laws which govern change".[61]

Being a "pathless animal", man always feels an existential pressure to find his way. Unlike an animal, he lacks a way, and in this sense he is incomplete or, as Nietzsche puts it "a sick" animal. Man's self-awareness is due to his not having a way or his being a pathless animal, or rather it is due to his very inner self (his peripheral self is the inner self restricted to a certain way entered by him).

We do not feel our lungs, our heart, or any other organ as long as this organ functions properly. As soon as it stops functioning so, as during some illness, we become aware of the organ, and along with it — of ourselves. When we get bronchitis, we know that we have lungs or rather that we

---

[61] *Ibid.*, p. 168.

lack healthy lungs, and we become acutely aware of our own existence in the malfunctioning of our health.

Animals have no awareness of themselves in the sense that they do not really know that they *are*. An animal lives by blindly following Nature's guidance, while man does not really live *biologically*, for he does not *blindly* follow any firm biological pattern. He exists in the sense that Heidegger understands this term as meaning a standing out from his path of life and thus standing in the transcendental Event of Being. By his "ex-sistence" man guides and models his own life responding to the harmoniously playing powers of Nature. By his "ex-sistence", his standing-out into Nature's play, man serves this play : he allows it to break through into his living world, his *Dasein*.

Man's failure to perform his mission of being-man, his "ex-sistence", is his openness, his freedom, to Nature's transcendental movement which founds all things and all immanent events. Such an openness or freedom ultimately taken is a cult — it is a response to gods. Hence, culture is what makes man distinct from any animal.

An animal is not cultural, because he is set by Nature on a definite path reserved for him. An animal does not partake in the creatively dynamic, boiling, all-founding kettle of Nature, the Horn of Plenty. Only the cultic being, man, does so : he partakes in Nature's play, in her disturbance, brought to him by Nature's rising to disclosure (*logos*) and her falling back into the shrouds of concealment (*physis*). Man's cultic — and therefore his cultural — trait is displayed more penetratingly and more diversely by the favoring and frustrating works of his gods who never leave man alone even in the phase of their withdrawal or silence during the godless eras.

Throughout millennia man was considered the most advanced being when compared with the animals. Man was regarded as gifted with features or characteristics which were absent in animal life. He was thought of as exceeding all the animals by his altruism, love, nobility or dignity, by his fidelity, heroism, and so on. Behaviouristic biologists of recent times have plentiful data which show that most of the above "humanistic" traits are had by many animals. On the other hand, if we try to be unprejudiced, we will find plentiful "negative" features in man, such as avarice, ingobility, envy, infidelity, bloodthirstiness, and so on.

In spite of all this, man is godly; however, his godliness does not consist — as traditional ethics is inclined to see — of man's goodness or his "positive" characteristics. It rather consists of his primitivity *qua* pristinity by which he stands at the roots of all things or by which he is anterior to all things just as are gods or Nature. Transcendental powers, responded to by man, may mark man with negative traits no less than with positive ones. Even a "sinful" man may be godly (Helena during the Trojan war). Man's pristinity — his participation in Nature's play, his dwelling close to Nature — is the nursery of his cultural activities. In man's cultural world, in his living days as man, the ultimate transcendental powers, which sway and order everything, break through and find their stead.

To consider man as good or evil is to consider him as in the animal milieu. Some animals are good, such as a watchdog or a milking cow, and some are evil, such as a wolf or a fox. The criteria of being-man, — "ex-sistential" criteria — are cults; these are beyond good and evil.

Since technological man is godless and thus cultless, his way of living, too, stands under the criteria of good and evil. These criteria are increasingly being determined *democratically*, where good is what is beneficial — mainly in the way of commodities — to the majority of the people and evil is that which is disadvantageous to the majority of people.

Technological man very effectively stresses his superiority over everything else by technological means, and he has gradually taken over the habitats of all other animals, preserving only those which are beneficial to him.

All animals seek to survive, and they tend to outdo or overshadow all other animals, especially those which depend on more or less the same means of survival as they do. Accordingly, technological man is very animal-like. The difference between the two is that an animal struggles for survival and superiority depending upon the natural means with which he is provided by Nature, while technological man in his struggle for survival depends largely on the means with which he provides himself. Technological man, being godless, lacks cult, the essential feature of humanness (of being-man). Therefore, due to his cultlessness, modern man is merely a mighty technological animal.

4. *The Community*

The archaic ways of life were preserved in the log huts of Lithuanian peasants almost until the Second World War. These huts used to be filled with things of the pre-technological era. They were various odors, such as that of cucumber pickling, jelly making, bread baking. wine making, ham curing or smoking, and so on; — these things also were various utensils or furniture : heavy oak benches and tables, large brick baking ovens, maple wood spinning wheels, or weaving looms, casks, troughs, wooden spoons, and various baskets.

All these things of the Lithuanian *Dasein* have been considered the gifts of gods — even though they were mostly made by men. Bread, berries, cucumbers, and so on — all were considered the gifts of Mother Earth (of Zemyna). Almost all materials for the utensils were the gifts of Medeine, Zemyna's daughter. The capable womanly hands making jellies, baking bread, making sauerkraut were such because of the teaching of the godess Dimste, Medeine's sister. Men, making the spinning wheels, casks, wagon wheels, and other implements, were taught by Dimstpatis, Dimste's husband.

All through the last century or two, the awareness of the above deities has faded away. The things of a Lituanian household, acquired by man's responsive activities, principally were considered the gifts of God (if no longer of gods), and the Lithuanian peasants' existence still preserved godly or cultural aspects. In no wise was their *Dasein* governed by purely anthropocentric principles.

The mythical or godly world is Nature-related. Dwelling in it, man "under-stands" (stands under) Nature's sway. Contemporary man ignores, does not respect or respond to Nature's all-swaying principles — he does not stand under Nature's *logos*. Instead, he overcomes or overpowers every thing by systems established purely by him. By means of these systems man controls the things of his world. Moreover, he places himself under the sway or control of his systems. His machines, institutions, plans, projects or programmes hold sway over him no less than they do over the things. Technological man "under-stands" (stands under) his machines just as he "under-stands" the "almighty" clock dominating his days.

Contemporary man dominates his social life in much the same way as he dominates or rules the things of his world. The community of ancient days was anchored in the cult of its gods. This was most manifest during the days of festivity. Men stood together exposed to blessings and disfavor of the gods of Nature, trying by their own surrendering responses to improve their lot. Dalia, the goddess of destiny in the ancient Lithuanian world, held every individual open — and thus free — to the gods. And she did so with the whole community; it was exposed to the favoring and damaging sway of the gods.

Until the end of the XIXth and early part of the XXth centuries Lithuanian peasants used to gather together during the long autumn and winter evenings in one of the village peasant homes — each evening in a different one, until the whole village was thus visited by everyone — in order to be together under Dalia's sway. They used to come with their work : women with their spinning wheels and men with the materials for making ropes, lashes, harnesses, and other things. During these get-togethers under the sway of Dalia and the gods in general, beside accomplishing their work, they cultivated the "spiritual" part of their *Dasein* : they sang together, related ancient sagas, legends, or fairy tales. These evening get-togethers (*vakarionys*) were the remnants of the community's cult, mainly "understanding" the goddess Dalia. This cult was the community's co-participation in the works of the gods.

Contemporary man is individualistic. The modern society or community is established by men themselves for their economic or entertainment benefits. Both of these benefits are totally anthropocentric. Professional unions and social clubs are totally "humanistic" : they lack cult and are godless.

The rare crimes in the ancient Lithuanian world were handled by the community itself. Anyone who would steal a horse or in any way transgress on his neighbour's rights, used to be punished by the decision of the community's elders. There were no written laws, and, in spite of this, the social life was relatively secure, firm, and orderly. Crime consisted principally in the lawbreaker's offense of the gods, and only secondarily in his offense of his fellow man. A young man who would mislead and harm a girl by false promises of intending to marry her, was punished by the "senate" of the village (the couincil of elders) as the breaker of Milda's, goddess of love, norms, and only in addition because of the harm done to the girl.

Contemporary man himself establishes the laws of his world. He does not receive them from the gods. Laws are based on the will of the majority. The wrong-doer is punished because he harms his fellow man. Offense against gods is no crime today. The weight of moral laws is in our time rooted in the individuals of the peripheral selves and not in the transcendental or godly powers which sway over wide areas of men in their inner selves and make them feel as belonging together under the domination of gods. Modern individualistic man is not a man of community. This is so because the community "under-stands" him; he does not "under-stand" the community, swayed by the gods.

A man driving to work today meets other drivers going in the opposite direction to their jobs. They pass each other in sour moods, total strangers. In our artificially held together society man bypasses man coldly, indifferently, with no trace of love. It is so because our society does not "understand" any gods. In a godless world there cannot be any real enthusiasm — no devotion, sacrifice, love, patriotism, or heroism. If, however, these things still occur, they indicate the presence of godliness deep in the hidden layers of modern man's souls — in their inner selves.

Man cannot be blamed for his lack of enthusiasm, for his godlessness. His world makes him so, and the revival of his enthusiasm can come only from gods — the gods of the future. Anyone who would purely by his own rigorous will, stubbornly and resolutely, try to be patriotic, to love his fellow man, devotedly work for his community, and so on, would only fool himself and others rather than constructively re-establishing an enthusiastic world. Before anything else, he must go out on the serach for gods, and only then, responding to and "under-standing" them can he co-play with the new gods in opening a new cultural *Dasein*, the world of tomorrow.

Just as man is punished because of his crimes against his gods, so can he be loved, respected, and adored as standing in the service of the gods. Serving them, man can properly become a compatriot in a real or "godly" community.

A real or enthusiastic community is yet possible today — in these essentially unenthusiastic times. It is possible in the occasions originating in our inner selves which are mostly not manifest and not easy to grasp. During my doctroral graduation ceremonies, in which the relatives and friends of the graduates were participating, there was a stand-up to honor those who helped the graduates in attaining their academic degrees. During this minute I was clearly aware of Lione-Bernice's (my wife's) devotion and the enthusiastic support which she gave me during my work leading to this graduation.

Due to our difficult economic situation, I was several times about to drop the effort of working for the degree. She kept encouraging me to persevere. She worked full time in order to provide me with the time needed for preparation studies.

After my graduation I experienced many rejections by various universities or colleges where I applied for a teaching position. Because of this, many a time we were penniless and I was unable to get any job. Even during the time of writing the present study I do not know from where the money for next month's expenses will come. In all of these severe situations Lione-Bernice stood by, undergoing along with me all the agonies of the collapse of our dreams to gain a modest environment for my creative work. My triumphs and failures were also hers. This community of mine with her is not an individualistic bond between two peripheral selves, but a bond of our mission rooted in our inner selves and standing under the obscure or concealed principles which bind the inner selves of men. This mission is ultimately not of our planning; rather it is placed upon us by our Dalia, goddess of destiny, who steers our ways and makes them enthusiastic even though they are often filled with daily agonies.

Each individual in the Lithuanian society felt that his destiny was guided by *his* Dalia, and he called her "my Dalia". Also the society or the whole nation had its Dalia in the days of mythical culture. Dalia burdens the individual,society, and nation with their ways of life. By responding to these ways, the individual, society and nation either accomplish their missions or — being irresponsible — fail to do so.

Dalia, Moira, Fortuna or any other goddess of destiny does not assign the individual's or community's way all in the same way or according to the very same pattern. There is no supercultural Dalia and therefore no super-cultural, universal, or absolute moral laws or an absolute ethical doctrine.

Even the historical flow of cultural determinants through *Dasein*'s terrain does not remain the same. This means that the forces of destiny may bind different communities to the same culture in its different phases. History tells us of very fruitful encounters of highly different cultures and their merging solidly into one phase of bloom or flourishing. The well-known Olympian Greek culture of the Homeric and post-Homeric phase of the Greek *Dasein* reached its splendid acme due to its merging or blending with the conquered Mycenian culture of Mother Earth and her daughters — Night, Moiras, Eumenides, and others. Less well-known is the analogical merging of the ancient Lithuanians' god Perkunas, the ruler of thunder, lightening, and justice, with Zemyna, the goddess of Earth. Incidentally, before this merging the dead of the Lithuanian society used to be buried, while after it they began to be burned with impressive cult ceremonies.

History knows cases where various cults failed to blend into a unique congenial culture and remained in a state of confusion, followed by cultural disintegration. Such cases are typical of late phases of culture's lives, where various cultural elements constitute a cultural conglomerate instead of result-ing in a homogenous blending. Thus mighty empires often reach their ends by degenerating into clusters of disunified fragments of religious cults or rites which fail to grow together into a genuine monolithic phase of culture.

Our modern community is godless. Man and man's planning alone deter-mine the codes of moral life "democratically". Today, it is true, for instance that in the continent of North America, we have various religious commun-ities, mostly of one or another brand of Christianity, which seem to clearly speak for the "godliness" of people. None of these religions, however, has any over-all dominance. They run parallel. State laws even prevent any of them to become dominant. Therefore, teaching religion is banned from the public educational institutions. This clearly confirms that we live in a purely anthropocentric world, in which man, and no god, directs the ways of life — be they individual or social.

A godless life — flattened or peripheral — leads to or opens up an inquiry into our cultural ground. This inquiry may be an initial phase of the search for the future gods, with which a firm and enthusiastic cultural community life, involving the inner selves of men, may get its start.

The life of the inner self — existential life — unlike that of the peripheral self, is involved in the transcendental event of the gods' dance or Nature's play, and only in this way can a true human community be founded. The existential life of the inner self is the life of openness toward the transcendental cultural principles. Such an openness is always man's co-openness with the others — with his society. "Indeed! As far as man exists socially, he exists by being open to the world".[62]

Cult ceremonies or the celebrations of festivities are always social, and in these ceremonies or festivities the community's and the individual's inner selves are rooted. The community is never a sum-total of the individuals. It consists of the togetherness or interbelonging of men with transcendental powers or gods. A crowd is no community, until it "under-stands" the community's gods.

Accordingly, a neighborhood is not determined by spatial nearness between two next-door families, but in their belonging together, in their "under-standing" of their gods. "Two solitary peasant homesteads — if these still exist — which may lie apart an hour's walk over fields, can be most beautifully neighbourly, while, on the contrary, two town houses which stand *vis-à-vis* on the same street or which may even be constructed together, may know no neighbourness".[63] The true neighbourhood does not consist only of the togetherness of two or more persons or families, but their togetherness *under* their culture's gods.

5. *Culture's Finitude*

Our rioting youth and the fighters for racial freedom — instead of constructively searching for new gods in whom alone the true cultural society or community can be founded — come up with slogans denying our present cultural system and promote actions which destructively manifest their dissatisfaction with the prevailing order. Broken windows, burned cars, injured people, looted stores — all this is sheer destructiveness with no trace of culture of any kind. Is this the right way to delete our cultral wrongs and establish a new and *better* society? Not at all!

[62] Fink, *Spiel*, p. 227.
[63] Heidegger, *Unterwegs zur Sprache*, p. 210.

The Assyrian culture replaced the Sumerian, the Dorian replaced the Mycenian, the Christian replaced the Roman cultures, and so on. All these cases were followed by a cultural development and renewed flourishing. The older cultures here were replaced by younger ones — principally by a constructive-creative introduction of new gods who — in most cases — amalgamated, merged, or blended with the old ones.

Thus it does not mean that the Assyrian, Dorian, or Christian cultures were better ones than those which they overshadowed. It only means that a breaking or stepping in of new transcendental powers, new gods, into human *Dasein* occurred. Under the pre-human sway of Nature one breed or species of animals often outdid the others, becoming dominant. Such a new bread or species did not necessarily have higher perfection or supremacy. It was merely the outcome of a new phase or new segment in Nature's play, sparkling with her self-disclosure-concealment.

Today's humanity lives under the codes of Western culture. It is not the best of cultures and thus it can always be substituted with a different or better one. However, any out-break of a new culture or a new phase of Western culture can arrive into our world constructively and creatively with its own light and its own ordering principles — with the swaying gods of the future. The destructive deeds of an anarchic mob are never the carriers of culture.

No gods — be they of most prominent cultures — are absolute. They live out their lives in our cultural worlds, even though they are immortal. Their death is their withdrawal into the twilight of our *Dasein.* Even though gods are not absolute, they nevertheless are the *ultimate* of a respective cultural *Dasein.* Man must surrender himself, his deeds and his life to these principles; he must allow his gods to shine into his world, his living days : he must "under-stand" them, in order to be great or cultural. The non-absoluteness of gods in any culture, including the most prominent cultures of our Earth, means the prevalence of anti-godly — yet transcendental — powers in it. Such were the Titans in the Greek world, conquered and banned from the Greek *Dasein* by Zeus during a certain cultural phase; or such was Loki, who started the downfall of the Teutonic gods — their Twilight. A proverb says : "The devil hides himself even behind the Cross". Here, the presence of ungodly — although transcendental — powers in the godly world of Christianity is emphasized.

The above passages indicate that it is not man who destroys cultures, but rather that the transcendental powers present in cultures themselves — responded to, however, by man — do so. Precisely, cultural birth, development, and decay best express Nature's play. They indicate Nature's life, her beating heart with its pulsating sequences of disclosure and concealment.

In pre-cultural times, Nature spoke or disclosed herself by introducing plant life in addition to the already existing mechanically originated and formed things. She did the same with animal life, governed at first by instincts. Instinct directs living beings in a different way than, for instance, does the sunshine directing the branching out of a tree southward or toward the light. The intellectual animals modify the instinct guided-ones, and thereby they bring in a new phase or facet of Nature's play.

Wisdom, man's openness to Nature's playing powers, is his implication in these powers as their co-laborer. By his wisdom (which is originally a cult in which man's "under-standing" to beauty — Nature's appearance in human *Dasein* — occurs), man is held in the midst of Nature's self-disclosure-concealment.

In man's cultural world not only one or another facet of Nature's play comes to disclosure, but with this facet the whole play of Nature breaks into openness. This means that in a certain twinkle or facet of Nature in a cultural world, the whole shine, the whole jewel of Nature's play, her everlasting life has its stead (*Da*) in the human *Dasein*. Thus, the stead is never absolute, because by a twinkle of a certain facet all other facets (or the whole jewel) *are disclosed as concealed*. This, nevertheless, means disclosure.

Nature's play with its twinkling disclosure-concealment is mirrored in the human cultural world by the interplay of earth, sky, gods, and men. These transcendental or unentitative powers in which the meanings and being of things are rooted too, appear in the mode of disclosure-concealment. We always know what earth or sky is. Nevertheless, we can never know what earth or sky is with clarity. The earth on which we walk and on which we live is not merely a planet. A planet is an astronomical object, but not an unentiative living milieu. We find many things — inanimate and animate — on our earth, but we never encounter earth as earth. Is earth soil, clustors of rock, groups of continents with oceans between them? No! All these things are or can be found on earth. By boring into a rock or by digging into the deep layers of earth we may discover various earthly things, but never earth as such. The very same must be said about the sky. It sends us warmth or withholds it; it sends us light and withholds it. Rain, showers, snow, winds, breezes, and storms come to us from the sky, The sun and moon "travel" over the vault of heaven, and the stars twinkle in the sky, but where is the sky? We cannot answer this question. The sky holds itself in withdrawal. In spite of this, it constitutes ,along with earth, our living milieu.

Gods are present at every step in the life in the living world of a mythical or "poetical" man. Simultaneously, they conceal or withdraw themselves by their very approaches toward man. "God is present by concealing himself".[64] The absence of gods in godless times is not the same as their absence in the mythical world. In godless times not only the presence of the gods is not felt or experienced, but even their absence or concealment. In these times gods are silent : they announce neither their presence not their absence. In these times, the search for gods is inactive.

Man, the fourth transcendental "partner" of the foursome, also manifests himself by his great and "immortal" deeds. His works "disappear like smoke" as the poet Maironis says : not only the great men but also their "godly" creations sooner or later fall into oblivion. Even their *Dasein* fades away as if it never had been — disappears like smoke. The "eternal" Egyptian pyramids crumble and the sands cover them up. Likewise the grandiose temples and majestic obelisks sink into the sands. What is man in his deep inner self? Who knows? Man is obvious and obscure at the same time. He steps forward as one of the mightiest powers in Nature and, as they all do, he withdraws himself into shrouds.

Man is distinguishable from the other three transcendental powers because he, unlike they, is also a thing, an entity. Man is a being. He differs from all other beings or things by the characteristic, essential to him, of standing-out into the movement of the interplay of transcendental powers. Moreover, being a thing, he is *quasi* a spot (*Da*), where transcendental powers — including man's own responsiveness or availability to them — break through into the openness of man's cultural world, of his living days.

In this sense man is a thing against which the transcendental powers of his *Dasein* collide and burst into openness due to his response to them. By his responsiveness to the movement of transcendental powers, man becomes essentially what he is : he becomes man. Man's responsiveness is viewed by Heidegger as his responsiveness to the language (*logos*) of reality (Being). As we already know, language in this sense is not a labelling of already present or available things with names. On the contrary, by their names, things are disclosed and thus they come into being. Language is anterior to encyclopedian language. Language means man's founding of his *Dasein* by his responsiveness to transcendental powers or his being a co-founder of things with them — with the realities anterior to things.

Dasein, perhaps, can be visualized as a map crisscrossed with a multitude of paths. These finite (non-absolute) paths of a finite (non-absolute)

---

[64] Heidegger, *Erde und Himmel.*

cultural milieu bring to disclosure, to *logos*, the ever-concealed background of reality (*physis*). By responsively walking these paths in the territory of *logos*, man participates in the Event of reality's disclosure, which, by disclosing immanent or entitative realities, discloses transcendental powers as well. By walking these ways, man accomplishes his mission of being-man and thus he discloses himself as the co-player with the other playing transcendental powers. The importance of the problem here compels us to quote Heidegger's words : "To break open a way, for instance, through a snow-covered field, in the Allemanian-Schwabian dialect even today means *wëgen*. This transitively used verb means "to build a way" and, while building it, to hold it open. *Be-wëgen* (*Bewëgung*) — thought of in this way — no longer means "to take something back and forth on an already available way", but first of all, to bring the way forward and to be this way".[65]

"Movement" in German is *Bewegen* or *Bewegung*, while "way" is *Weg*. The uncommon German word *Be-wëgen* or *Be-wëgung* serves Heidegger to indicate man as the co-opener of the ways in his cultural *Dasein*, in the *logos* or reality, along with the principal opening transcendental powers of earth, sky, and gods which found everything.

Be-wëgen occurs or realizes itself through the human language which principally is soundless. Such a language is the language of living in the sense of guarding things in their own meanings (founded in *Dasein*) instead of overpowering or violating them by our absolute, logical, scientific, or other anthropocentric means.

Pristine language is "poetical"; it discloses gods — utters their names — by naming things. Philosophical language is the thinker's attempt to regain the pristine or godly roots of "worn out" or profanized words. True, or cultural, dwelling — the guarding of gods (and other transcendental powers), while guarding things in their pristine meanings, is "poetical" dwelling. As soon as man becomes the master of his language and uses words by strictly controlling them logically according to definitions given in his established dictionaries and encyclopedias, he becomes irresponsive to gods and to his own "poetical" inner self.

Early man, because of his involvement with superior realities, the gods, must be considered as more cultural than contemporary man, in spite of the latter's majestic technological achievements. The centre of a caveman's home (the cave) was the fireplace, which was merely a pit in the middle of the cave. Instead of rooms, there were niches in the sides of the cave remotely resembling the rooms in a house. The central part of the cave — the fire-

---

[65] Heidegger, *Unterwegs zur Sprache*, p. 261.

place — was devoted to the gods. The family's sacrificial donations (*duonia*) were performed here with certain rites. These donations marked man as the co-player, and thus the partner, of the gods. Because of this, man, too, was allowed to sit at the fire on the edge of the pit, and eat his meals *with the gods* who were as present here. Daily meals were always meals with the togetherness or participation of gods.

At the cave fires stories of godly works were told or hymns sung. Also, dances or magic were performed by which man attempted to turn the favours of some of his benevolent gods toward himself or turn away from himself the harmful acts of other gods. Respect for both was maintained.

Mythical "stories" were born at the fireplaces of early man's caves. These "stories " were poetical and thoughtful at one and the same time. The caveman was a man of culture. If, however, instead of cult, we consider the capacity for manufacturing technological goods or products as the true measure of culture, then, of course, technocratic man is a man of culture, while the caveman lacks culture altogether.

In the present study we maintain cult as being the true measure of culture. The highlights of various cultures in history are those which are noteworthy for various great creations of man. These creations are not merely mythical tales of gods and heroes, but the temples, monuments, songs, thoughts, and other manifestations of man's responsive language to the language of Nature.

Accordingly, we would like to stress here the high cultures as the eras of cult peaks. This is so because cults during these eras acquire impressive, "immortal" or "classical" manifestations of the ultimate principles of reality. All high cultures crumbled after a comparatively short, brilliant span of flourishing. The crumbling indicates precisely that any grand disclosure of the ultimate majestic pillars of reality — of the mightily swaying gods — is simultaneously their misrepresentation. This misrepresentation is the revelation of gods which falls short of what gods really are; it is a guilt against or disruption of the very character of the concealment of the gods. Only when crumbling, does a majestic temple of a god tell the complete story of the god — it discloses him as retreating, thus inviting a renewed search.

This casts a sad "bluish" hue upon human existence. Why *are* we, if we get nowhere? "Merciless" is the word used by Otto Zierer when he speaks of the collapse of the supercultures of the pre-Greek and pre-Roman era. "Unable to apprehend this, ask the conquered of their silent gods why the noble and the great had to sink down under the raw force of barbarians.

"Because of endless beauty and everlasting seemed the empires on the Nile, Euphrates and Tigris...".[66]

---

[66] Zierer, *op. cit.*, Band I, p. 40.

The sad outcome of a culture (any culture!) should not make sceptics of us. Not at all! Man must hold onto his cultural principles. He must try to re-discover them, for they have the tendency to fall into oblivion. He must view them as his ideals and arrange the mission of his life so that it is oriented and directed toward, or according to, these principles. He must surrender himself, his creativeness, and talents for their sake — for the sake of his gods — rather than for his own well-being.

History must teach modern man not to try to absolutize his own cultural phase. If he does so, he inevitably ends up with culturelessness, because within an absolute culture man is no longer on the way of the search for his gods, but he becomes merely a tiny wheel in his absolute world which functions like a brilliant, mighty robot — totally completed and having reached the acme of its civilization.

History teaches us to always wander on the ways of gods, on the search of gods.

CHAPTER III

CHRISTIANITY

In spite of the sometimes seemingly unrealistic problems within the present study, it is basically an inquiry into the realities close to earth; it is concerned with things, real or earthly walks of man, and it treats of the communications between men in their social or family living days or living situations. It is a study of man's experiences of his world tending to its ultimate principles or criteria.

In accordance with this, Christianity is approached here from the standpoint of man in his living world and from the perspectives of his natural (*qua* transcendental) experiences. In no wise is any attempt made here to discuss specifically Christian problems by weighing their validity or criticizing them on Christianity's own supernatural level. The main question here is a consideration of Christianity's interrelation with cultures. Is Christianity a culture or is it supercultural? Does Christianity substitute culture or some of its areas? Does it modify cultures? change them? If it does so, has it a right to? These questions should become more or less elucidated in the progress of this chapter. Our initial standpoint here is that the meaning of our Western culture cannot be exhaustively treated without some insights into the meaning of Christianity and its interbelonging with culture.

1. *Christianity in General*

All genuine cultures in their origins are mythical. The basic theme in the mythical world is Nature. In Christianity the basic theme is God as the supernatural reality and man as involved in God's supernatural works. We must note here that the mythical world is never "manless" : it always views man as standing in Nature's play, or rather in the play of various powers or principles of Nature, in the play of gods. Due to this, in the mythical world man constistutes an uncircumventable factor in Nature's transcendental movement.

Christianity stands above Nature's Event, above her play, and therefore it is basically not concerned with man in Nature, but rather with man as involved in the supernatural event. Accordingly, man does not constitute the main theme either in the mythical world or in Christianity. The main theme of the mythical world is Nature and her play, and of Christianity — God and His creation.

According to the Holy Scriptures, God created man complete (a super-man) in the complete (that is, supernatural) milieu of Paradise — of God's world. Because of his guilt, the first man, Adam, lost his superhuman completedness and simultaneously he lost the perfect world of God, Paradise. Adam's sin implanted in man a desire for Christ — for that through whom man's completeness can be restored.

Adam's sin gave the beginning to Nature and to *natural* man, that is, to mortal man. By his own *natural* powers, man can in no wise do good or redeem his guilt. His desire for Christ is a desire for a redeemer. Redemption is an act of God's mercy, His Grace. Man, however, must actively participate in this act of God's mercy, in His Grace — in the act of man's redemption. "Infinite offence requires infinite retribution : after Adam a redeemer had to be found whose merits or payment could equal the gravity of Adam's sin : a second Adam had to make infinite retribution".[67]

For man's redemption God sends His son, Christ. Christ, like Adam, is of God's world. He, however, is born into man's natural world in order that with his sufferings and death he would redeem man's original and all subsequent sins and would make man worthy again of the citizenship of God's world.

By becoming a Christian, a follower of Christ, man reacquires his supernatural "citizenship". This means that redemption is principally a gift. This gift calls for man's acceptance of it and his surrendering of himself to it. The gift of redemption is realized by several supernatural gifts, called sacraments. The most noteworthy of them are baptism, the Eucharist, and penance. On the grounds of these sacraments man lives a supernatural life, and in this way he enjoys *quasi* supernatural powers, the graces ,such as faith, hope, and love. By faith man has knowledge of supernatural events; mainly, he knows God. By hope he hopes for the ideal, complete, and eternal life — the supernatural life, the kind Adam had lived in Paradise. This complete life is realizable after man's (natural) death. By love man loves supernatural reality, principally God. Christianity, thus, is the story of man which starts with Adam's fall and ends with Christ's second coming,

[67] ed. George Brantl, *Catholicism* (New York : George Braziller, 1962), p. 62.

which puts an end to natural man, and thus to Nature as well — the play-ground of natural man.

Christianity, concerned with man in the supernatural event of original sin and redemption, tends to degrade man in Nature, Nature herself, and also natural things. "Those things withheld me from Thee", says St. Augustine, "which yet, if they had not their being in Thee, would not be at all".[68]

This shows that Nature and natural things, and of course, most of all, natural man, are, nevertheless, significant in the Christian world or the Christian evaluation of reality. Christianity thus cannot totally oppose or degrade Nature and therewith culture. This is one of the major points which interest us here in this chapter.

Throughout the centuries, Christian thinkers maintained a relatively high esteem for Nature, for the natural powers in man, and for natural things. Even though faith was placed above reason, the importance of the latter was emphasized and often brought into harmony with the former. "The act of faith which is supernatural is grown in the soil of nature and is strengthened by natural belief".[69]

This harmony most of the time overlooks the gap between the natural and supernatural, thereby washing out the essential difference between Christianity and cultures. Such overlooking, for instance, took place with the philosophy of St. Thomas. According to him, the whole of natural reality can be explained in its full elucidation, leaving no room, no dark corners, for Nature's essential aspects of concealedness, mystery, or hiddenness. Such an elucidation is carried further by man's power of faith. In this way, reality, explored by ontology and completed by theology, constitutes one solid and clear totality where everything from dust to God is exposed to the light of intellect+faith beyond a shadow of a doubt — exposed with all possible interrelations between whatever is real. St. Thomas' philosophy is especially famous for its five proofs of God's existence.

It is needless to say that the approach we maintain in this study opposes any interpretation of Nature, of man, and of the meanings of things with absolute and definite clarity, not even mentioning raelity, which lies beyond the natural.

Christian thinkers, who are more acutely aware of drastic differences between the natural and supernatural, are also well aware of the difference between man as standing in Nature and man as the citizen of the world of

---

[68] *Ibid.*, p. 18.
[69] *Ibid.*, p. 21.

God (*civitas Dei*). This difference hints of a supernatural self in man along with his natural self. This deeper self is, of course, even more concealed than the natural inner self. "Do not you believe that there is in man a deep so profound as to be hidden even to him in whom it is", says St. Augustine.[70]

Since we maintain the difference between man's peripheral self and his inner or lordly self in his living world, in *Dasein*, the Christian self on the supernatural milieu would then mean a self of the third rank in man.

Between fall and redemption, Christian man struggles for his Christian self — for his immortal soul. This means that he does not have it, but seeks it; that he is on the way toward it. The tension of the supernatural event, the event of fall redemption, marks Christian man and his world as highly dynamic.

The Catholic Church finds in the history of the Jewish people before Christ the drama of the consequences of sin and the intensity of longing for redemption. The Prophecies foreshadow the coming redemption; the texts are laden with symbols of the Messiah. The world stood in need of Christ, the new Adam, the God-Man whose supreme vision and infinite love would restore to man the power to see and to love.[71]

With this power man re-acquires his supernatural self. The theme of the Christian drama is man's search for his lost supernatural self. Man is not the main actor in this drama. However, it is not without man. Man, the way he is known in the mythical or natural world is not the real participant in the supernatural drama. In his fallenness he lacks his supernatural self. Adam, man of the supernatural self, was the participant in the drama of Christianity. His guilt, ultimately traced down to its roots, exposes the guilt of natural (supernaturally self-less) man — the man of fallenness. Thus far, the natural man is noteworthy for his passivity as regards the supernatural drama.

Christ is man with a supernatural self. Simultaneously he is God himself, who steps out into fallen man's world to do good or to repair the original guilt and thereby to bring man back to his original or supernatural fullness. Christ thus — and not man — is the real actor in the drama of Christianity. "The Incarnation — the tremendous fact of God becoming man by the union of a divine and a human nature in the Person of Christ — is the mystery which lies at the heart of all Catholic belief".[72]

Man's participation in the supernatural drama is enabled by virtue of the Graces granted to him by Christ. "I live, now not I; but Christ liveth in me" (Gal. 2:20). Even though he has a subordinate role in the drama of

[70] *Ibid.*, p. 12.
[71] *Ibid.*, p. 64.
[72] *Ibid.*, p. 67.

Christianity, man has rather a heavy burden laid upon him, demanding from him often strenuous efforts to carry it.

We have no intention to analyze here this burden and man's complex undergoing of various supernatural requirements or obligations — the supernatural criteria or norms of Christian dwelling. These problems belong specifically to Christian doctrine, concerned with various areas of Christianity, such as moral, educational, social, historical, and so on. They all go under the title of "Christian culture".

What interests us is not so much the above mentioned specific problems within Christian doctrine, but rather Christianity or Christian culture as such in its alignment or belonging together with or diverging from culture as such. We are also concerned with the comparison of mythical man with Christian man. These interests of ours call for an inquiry into the meaning of the supernatural as compared with the natural. A decisive aspect in the latter intricate problem points to a question : does the supernatural life substitute the natural or cultural life or does it only complement it? Can Christianity be properly called culture? Man under supernatural laws or norms, does he necessarily or only circumstantially stand under the cultural criteria or norms? Can he be cultureless at all?

2. *Judaism*

Before making any hasty conclusions, we must briefly make some preliminary remarks concerning the character of religion in the natural (or mythical) milieu and that in the Christian. The supernatural character of Christianity clearly marks it as principally not implied in Nature and her event, but rather as standing above her and being — at least to a great extent — independent of her. All mythical religions stand close to Nature's rhythmics; they are founded in it. Because of this, they are religions of *natural* experiences. Gods are encountered by mythical man in the milieu of Nature — not in the same way, however, as are things or other men (encountered), but as mighty transcendental powers which found all things and outline man's ways. Even though transcendental, these powers — being the background of the immanent realities — can be and are known to man by his own natural powers.

Christ and the basic or fundamental Christian truths are not found in the world of man or in Nature. Their revelation is the outcome of the supernatural message of Christ and of the prophecies of supernaturally *gifted* or inspired men, originating in their inner experiences. It is not the world or Nature, but man's inner self that is the source of Christian teachings. Is this inner self the same as that of mythical man? Of course not!

To gain a somewhat better insight into the above mentioned intricacies, it is worthwhile to make a brief inquiry into Judaism, which constitutes the background of Christianity's origin. Judaism, generally speaking, is more earthbound than is Christianity. This is obviously due to one of the basic elements in Judaism, namely, the consideration of the Jews as a chosen people, and also due to God's granting to them their promised land. Moreover, the historical aspects are much more concrete in Judaism than they are in Christianity : God redeems the Jews from slavery in Egypt, leads them to their promised land and assures them of His care in all the situations of Jewish life. While Christianity speaks of the superearthly kingdom of God, Judaism emphasizes the earth as God's. "... no people could claim ultimate ownership in any land, for the earth is the Lord's".[73] Curiously, even the "Hebrew word for 'place' is also used, in rabbinic literature, as a synonym for 'God' ".[74] This can be the remains of the early times of Jewish beliefs, when earth — the living milieu in the sense of the Jewish *Dasein* — was thought of as ultimately holy or as holiness as such : it was thought of as divine, as godly, as God.

A Jew is bound to his land. In spite of all his wandering in various foreign lands, he must seek a return to his holy land. Such is God's law and his will.

For Israel is called God's heritage, and the land is his heritage, and the Torah (Law) is connected with both, with the people of God and the heritage of God, and whoever leaves the one has also abandoned the other.[75]

The earthbound character of Judaism is noteworthy here in order to gain a better insight into the interbelonging between the supernatural and natural. The Jewish bible, being well concerned with men, especially with the Jewish nation, guides the Jew on the ways of his *Dasein* with hardly any reference to a beyond-the-world milieu. "In the Bible itself the arena of man's life is this world. There is no doctrine of heaven and hell".[76] Moreover, the world here must be considered as the proper milieu of God's presence (Shekhinah). In Genesis, Rabbah 19:7, it is stated that because of the sins of the Jewish people, God retreated from earth into further and further firmaments and that only the great Jewish men or prophets — Abraham, Isaac, Jacob, Levi, Kehat, Amram, and finally Moses — brought

---

[73] ed. Arthur Hertzberg, *Judasim* (New York : George Braziller, 1962), p. 148.
[74] *Ibid.*, p. 228.
[75] *Ibid.*, p. 171.
[76] *Ibid.*, p. 207.

Him back to His proper place of presence — brought Him from heaven to earth again.[77]

The sins and virtues of men, thus seen, considerably affect God. This, unlike in Christianity, presents God and men (rather, God's nation) as strongly interdependent. The Jewish God stands much closer to His children than does the Christian God. He participates in Jewish exiles. "Whenever Israel is enslaved, the Shekhinah /the presence of God/, as it were, is enslaved with them".[78] This latter aspect underlines the historicity of the Jewish God; his intense involvement in Jewish living days, in their *Dasein*.

The central theme of Judaism is the nearness of God to his chosen people, the people of Israel. This nearness is felt in various historical epochs of Jewish life. A Jewish prophet explaining to his people why God is so near to them said :

... because He loved your fathers, and chose their seed after them, and brought you out of Egypt with His presence, with his great power, to drive out nations greater and mightier than you from before you, to bring you in, to give you their land for an inheritance, as it is this day.[79]

The Chosen People are not so well cared for by God. On the contrary, God often exposes them to greater sufferings and harder tasks than any other nation. However, he never totally abandons his people and keeps his promise to them.

God's constant nearness to his people is maintained by the Torah, the holy Law of the Jews. "Obedience to the Law is therefore not slavery to a divine despot; it is the way of regular encounter with God".[80] As the giver of the Law to his chosen people (and not to humanity in general!), God is acutely present in the world of the Jews. Faithful obedience to the divine Law is demanded of the Jewish people. "... for I have given you good doctrine; do not forsake My Torah..." (Prov. 4:2) [81] By their obedient response to the Torah, Jewish people re-emphasize God's presence in their world; they serve his presence.

Instead of having the generalized omnipresence or ubiquity of the Christian God, the Jewish God is noteworthy for his presence in the world of the Jews and in their history only. The Torah's presence in the Jewish world — its upholding by the Jews — makes God intensely present in their world. The

---

[77] Cf. *Ibid.*, p. 49.
[78] *Ibid.*, p. 156.
[79] *Ibid.*, p. 23.
[80] *Ibid.*, p. 27.
[81] *Ibid.*, p. 29.

Torah is given to every member of the Jewish nation and every person in this nation is a person by his fidelity to the holy Law.

Martin Buber, the leading Jewish existentialist theologian, profoundly believes in the fact of the encounter between God and the Jewish people. For him it is an event which recurs in the personal experience of each Jew, so long as he chooses to be a Jew and to hear the voice of God addressing him.[82]

With God present in his world, and with his own encounter with God in his living days, a Jew dwells in a holy milieu. In his everyday environment a Jew works for God's persence in his days. He contributes to the establishment of the kingdom of God and the brotherhood of men on earth.[83] It is not only prayer, worship, or other religious rites that serve God's presence in the Jewish world, but almost anything or any action of a Jew. Love of his nation, "... personal friendships and kindness, intellectual pursuits, artistic creation, the preservation of health and the care of diet..." [84] — all are religious acts. Due to this, "... the Jewish home became a sanctuary in miniature, its table an altar, its furnishings instruments for sanctity".[85] Every step in the life of a Jew is permeated by his encounter with God. All human works, if not serving God, are hollow and substanceless. "Unless the Lord builds the house those who build it labor in vain". (Ps. 127:1) [86]

The Torah, seen from a certain angle, is much like the *logos* in the Greek *natural* world. It can be compared to a godly blueprint which outlines man's ways in his world. A life may seem filled with great deeds or enterprises; however, as long as it is not guided by Torah, it is a meaningless erring in a vacuum. On the other hand, life could seem grey, dull and eventless; if, however, it follows Torah, it is divinely colorful. "And what was the first request of our pious mothers", says a Hebrew poet, Hayyim Nahman Bialik,

over the Sabbath candles? "May it be Your will that the eyes of my children may shine with Torah". Nor do I doubt that if God had appeared to one of these mothers in a dream, as He did once to Solomon, and said, "Ask, what shall I give unto you?" she would have replied even as Solomon did, "I ask not for myself either riches or honor, but O Lord of the universe, may I please you to give unto my sons a heart to understand Torah and wisdom to distinguish good from evil".[87]

---

[82] *Ibid.*, p. 40.
[83] Cf. *Ibid.*, p. 73.
[84] *Ibid.*, p. 74.
[85] *Ibid.*, p. 75.
[86] *Ibid.*, p. 78.
[87] *Ibid.*, p. 86.

The Jew's upkeep of Torah makes him God's partner in the course of the sanctification of the world. "To be like God in the Jewish view means to be his partner in ruling the world and carrying forward the work of making order, i.e. just order in the world".[88] Man's partnership with God, according to Jewish faith, will be sealed by the Messiah, who will restore peace and harmony in the world and who will establish a permanent and just order in it — the order which was thrown out of balance by the original sin of man, by Adam's guilt.

3. *The Ecumenical Spirit*

Adam's sin threw God's primaeval perfect world (the supernatural world in the Christian understanding) out of order. God was aware of such a possibility when He created man. Nevertheless, he went ahead to do so, depending on His own strength, upon which the order of the world rests and thus will necessarily be re-established.

"Consider the work of God; who can make straight what he has made crooked" (Eccles. 7:13). When the Holy One, praised be He, created Adam, he showed him all of the trees in the Garden of Eden, telling him, "Behold, My works are beautiful and glorious; yet everything which I have created is for your sake. Take care that you do not corrupt or destroy My world".[89]

Restoration requires man's co-operation in God's own works : in Christ's redemption, in Christianity, and in paving the way for the Messiah's coming in Judaism. The event of fall-redemption, as we have seen, is clearly supernatural, while the disturbance of the primaeval order of the Garden of Eden and its restoration by men, following Torah, whose work will be completed by the still awaited Messiah, is not so obviously supernatural. Nevertheless, we must admit that Jewish religion has little manifestly pronounced *Event of Nature*. It clearly is concerned with man in his historical events, and not — at least manifestly — with man as entangled in the sway of Nature, in the rhythmics of the seasons, growth and the development of plants and animals.

Because of this we must consider Judaism, as well as Christianity, as a supernatural religion. Christianity's supernaturality throughout the centuries of the Church's development in medieval and modern times maintained as though its own life, severed from the living situations of secular lay people. Due to this, a gap gradually developed between the "bloody" vital problems of man alive in the nations and cities of modern Western

[88] *Ibid.*, p. 178.
[89] *Ibid.*, p. 180.

humanity, on the one hand, and the complex mechanism of the Church's hierarchy geared by various clearly pronounced regulations, dogmas, or any other stiff truths with little, if any, living breeze from the world of man, between his native earth and sky, struggling with his fundamental problems. The Church maintained a cool and indifferent attitude toward living man's earthbound principles; it ignored his often helpless search for the ultimate meaning of his *natural* life, for the ways of realizing it — for realizing his naturally-cultural mission of life. Catholicism, more than any other Christian denomination, displayed the most rigid remoteness from man's living roads, and kept itself in an estranged isolation.

The Second Vatican Council broke the age-old dams and let free the stored up "perennial" criteria, which burst, one after another, and thus opened up new vistas for the revitalization of the Church of tomorrow.

The Church of yesterday stood firmly and was mighty and dominant. The spreading of "good tidings" to all nations and cultures simultaneously meant the surrender of these cultures to Christian truths. They were forced to abandon their own world outlooks. This, of course, was most dramatically carried out by the medieval crusades and, in later times (including our own), by missionary work, where the principles of other cultures were mishandled by re-interpreting them to suit the Christian "unquestionably true" standards.

With the Second Vatican Council, Christianity is adopting a listening attitude and is becoming willing to adjust to the other faiths and other social units or groups. It no longer maintains a commanding attitude.

To a great extent, this significant change in the life of the Church, initiated by Pope John XXIII, is interpreted as the Church's entering a democratic course. This is indicated by the lessening of the authority of the Pope, who is now more frequently referred to as the "Bishop of Rome", by the increase in the power of bishops and more initiative given to priests, and by even allowing parishioners, the "Christian nation", to have their say-so concerning almost any Christian problem. Brotherhood is stressed now, rather than paternity.

A brotherly attitude and love is expected now not only toward all other denominations of Christianity, but even toward the peoples of non-Christian religions. Moreover, a similar attitude is maintained even toward the irreligious communities, including Communism.

In spite of all these obvious "democratic" features, it is a rather shallow or superficial interpretation of the new spirit of the Church which began with the Second Vatican Council. Shallow is the consideration of the basic motive in this movement of the Church by seeing it as taking a democratic

course and thus following the "most perfect" social form of humanity —
that of Western democracy of recent times.

The truth lies in that the Church has gradually realized that Christian
culture alone in itself is neither possible nor realizable. Christian culture is
in need of "natural" culture. Only in the element of the natural can supernatural Christianity pose its own way of life. Man cannot stand only under
the supernatural criteria and guide his life according to them. He necessarily
is involved in natural events not only of the immanent kind, such as the things
which surround him, but also of the transcendental kind, such as the unentitative, yet natural, principles which dominate things and man himself;
for instance, the transcendental powers of Nature, which in the mythical
world were thought of as gods.

Since today's "natural" world is marked by the powerful sway of democratic principles, the Church today must become democratic in order not to
bar itself off from the living world. We must quickly insert here that the
Church's becoming democratic is in no wise its ultimate aim. Democracy
is the living milieu of the contemporary world, and the Church must step
into it to remain culturally alive.

There are tendencies in some areas of the interpreters of the ecumenical
spirit which seek to "modernize" Christianity in accordance with the pattern
of American democracy. Here the hierarchy of the Church, instead of being
Christ's representatives, become the representatives of the "Christian
nation".

A "natural", or rather, cultural state can be democratic in the sense that
every individual in a nation, society, or in humanity is equal to everyone
else as regards his being-man. A Christian, on the contrary, is the one who
stands under the supernatural Grace (first of all, under the sacrament of
baptism, which elevates him above mere natural — pagan — man). The
priesthood in general is marked off from the above by a special sacrament
which elevates it above the ordinary members of the Christian community.
In no wise can the priesthood be decided by the will of the majority of the
nation.

Contemporary democracy is anthropocentric. Accordingly, man here is
the highest being. Everything else in reality is inferior to him. Today there
is nothing holy in the contemporary world, unless it is man himself. The
advocates of the Church's becoming democratic rapidly proceed toward her
profanization. This can be considered as symbolized by the custom now of
participants in Holy Mass not kneeling down during the Consecration.
According to Antanas Maceina, "the difference between the sacral and profane is disappearing for the sake of profanity. The Lord's appeal to Moses

'take your shoes off, for the place where you stand is sacred' (Ex. 3:5) today loses its meaning more and more".[90]

The advocates of democratization of the Christian Church should not forget her basic mission of the sanctification of humanity. She must do this by joining the frontiers of cultural life. In the chapter concerning godlessness we have seen that the contemporary anthropocentric godlessness inevitably and sequentially leads or points to new dawns of godliness which are bound to follow the overcoming of anthropocentricity — it leads or points to a search for gods. The cultural function of today's Church is not an admiration of anthropocentric democracy and its imitation as the best of all possible forms of worldly life. Today's function of the Church is a co-search for the absent *natural* cult, of the deeply concealed cultural principles in today's anthropocentric world. Only with this cultural function can the Church properly accomplish her own supernatural, and thus supercultural, mission.

The supernatural culture or supernatural life — be it that of the Church or of individual Christians — is not "self-sufficient" : it presupposes cultural (in a true sense!) or natural life. In fact, there is no supernatural culture, as culture is always "natural" in the sense of its occuring in the milieu of Nature's transcendental principles, on Nature's playground.

This would mean that Christianity, remaining the same as far as its supernatural principles are concerned, may be highly different as far as various *cultural* principles of cultural milieus, where Christianity realizes itself, are concerned.

The discovery that Christianity stands above cultures is very important : it shows that it — itself being no culture in the true sense of the word — cannot interfere with, or even less, destroy cultural principles of those cultures in whose milieus it steps into. Instead of interfering with or destroying the cultural principles, Christianity, according to the ecumenical spirit, must complement them by orienting them toward the supercultural standards or criteria.

According to some contemporary Christian theologians, the early phase of Christianity was "down to earth", and therefore *natural*. It had permeated the lives of the early Christians in all their living tissues. It may have been so, and in addition, it is quite possible that still recent Hebrew traditions in that time, along with the usage of the living language of that time (Latin and ancient Greek), held Christianity in the whirlpool of the living days of the

---

[90] Antanas Maceina, "The Tragedy of the Church" in *The Lights of Homeland*, March 5, 1970, Nr. 10.

society which had existed up to that time. Only in later ages, when Christianity held its own empire, its own language (Latin), administration, laws, rules or regulations, and especially, its own interpretation of reality and human conduct on the ground of its own "perennial" philosophy, it closed itself off from the living communities of various countries of Europe, and later, of the whole world.

The Second Vatican Council thus not only shows tendencies of drifting back to the attitudes of the early Church, but it re-acquires the Jewish kind of religiousness which strongly permeated the daily lives of the Jews.

We have mentioned that Judaism, when compared with Christianity, gives an impression of being "natural" or "worldly". However, the truth beyond this impression is that the Jewish God, and the event of Adam's sin which finally is absolved by the Messiah, are supernatural. What is important here is the fact that the Jewish holy writings do not speak of these supernatural realities apart from the Jewish living world. God steps right into the Jewish world by presenting his Torah and thereby by making Himself present in their world. Jews, by respecting the Torah in their daily works and actions, hold the supernatural realities present and alive in the midst of their days. This does not mean that the Jewish religion is "natural", that is, cultural; nevertheless, it means that the Jewish attachment to their supernatural realities (God and his Torah) are imbedded right in the midst of their culture.

Christianity did not have its own culture. Instead of permeating various cultures without distorting or destorying their principles, it has built up its own *quasi* Christian culture. It did what principally is impossible, just as, for instance, the supernatural naturalness is impossible! Because of this, Christianity generally was hostile to any culture. In its long history it committed more theocides than any other religion in the world, contributing thereby to the augmentation and cultivation of the godlessness of Western culture.

Christianity, just as any other supernatural religion, must become cultural in the sense of its permeating one or more cultures without destructive or hostile attitudes toward their fundamental principles, or else it eventually will become dead. Nietzsche's "God is dead" precisely expresses Christianity's — and therefore God's — death for the reasons given here.

The prophet Isaiah's word nicely expresses the *natural* mode of the Saviour's supernatural coming : "Drop down dew, ye heavens, from above : and let the clouds rain the just. Let the earth be opened and bud forth a saviour : and let justice spring up together". (Isa. 45:8) [91]

---

[91] Brantl, *op. cit.*, p. 65.

Even though cultural, the Jewish religion is not cultural to the degree of mythical religions. This may be so because the Jewish religion has not sprung from Earth or Nature. It was brought to the Jewish nation by its prophets — from the depths of their souls.

There are reasons to believe that in the dawn of the Jewish religion there was a true mythical phase. This is testified by some great Jewish holidays in their original meanings.

Judaism, the way it is known, possibly was a result of nomadic life in deserts. Surrounded by sands with hardly any vegetation or animal life, the Jewish world was man's world, and the major events here were the historical events of the Hebrew nation.

Judaism is a religion not of nature, but of history. There are many passages in the Bible which sing the praises of God in nature, but the characteristic Jewish experience of God is the awareness of His presence in human events. Every aspect of the Jewish tradition is pervaded by the memory of His redemptive act in the exodus from Egypt. Almost the whole of the religious calendar is an act of recalling the past experience of the Jewish people as the record of God's relationship to it.[92]

A cautious and cool approach to the meaning of some holidays in the Jewish calendar would disclose that they preceded the historical events which they are supposed to represent. Jewish holidays are more ancient than Judaism the way we know it. They are of mythical origin.

The holiday of Sukkoth, for instance, "is a way of remembering the forty years of wandering by the Jews in the desert on their way to the Promised Land".[93] This holiday occurs in the autumn after the time of harvest. A characteristic feature of this holiday is the practice of living in temporary shelters with the boughs of trees for a roof. During the harvest days, the "pre-Judaistic", mythical Jews moved out into the fields and lived there until the end of the harvest. Before returning to permanent quarters, they celebrated religious rites honoring the gods of the harvest, thanking them for the season's gifts and sacrificing to them the best lambs of their herds or best ears of their field crops.

After the shift from settled agrarian life to nomadic desert life on the way to the Promised Land, Jewish prophets re-interpreted the ancient mythical holidays to suit their nation's historical events. They introduced one mighty God, exceeding any deity of the agrarian world. The God of the prophets was the guide and kind, loving protector of the Jews in their wanderings. The holiday of thanksgiving gradually lost its original meaning

[92] Hertzberg, *op. cit.*, p. 19.
[93] *Ibid.*, p. 130.

and became merely a commemoration of the wandering Jews in search of their Promised Land.

Likewise, in the background of Rosh Hashanah, the Jewish New Year, Nature's rhythmics prevail, rather than historical events in the life of the Jews. Perhaps the most noteworthy Jewish holiday is Passover. This holiday commemorates the freeing of the Jews from the "house of bondage" of Egypt. The eating of unleavened bread is significant of this holiday. "They left Egypt so quickly at the moment of redemption that the Jews had no time to allow their dough to leaven".[94] Accordingly, unleavened bread has a reference to the great supernatural event of God's freeing the Jews from their bondage in Egypt.

A more original, and very possibly truer, meaning of Passover refers to the spring festivity after the winter season. Each spring of the year brings new blessings of the gods. The overflow of life is then abundant. A true respect of or response to the powers of the returning vitality of the year, which invigorates everything alive — plants, animals and men — can be presented to the gods of vitality, vigor, fertility, abundance and riches by temporarily restraining oneself from all the wealth of gifts. Such restraint is a response to the meager months of the year, arranged by the sway of the gods.

Before the holiday of Passover Jews had to search their houses by candlelight for any food which contained some leaven or which had undergone the process of fermentation. Fermentation indicated the origin of life and vigor by Nature's godly creativeness. All such food had to be eaten before the holidays; the surplus may have had to be given to neighbours, to passersby, or fed to animals. After a certain hour of the day before the Passover holiday the past year's leavened foods still present had to be burned. With this burning, the time of dark, frozen and lifeless duration had its beginning. Only after being acutely aware of the phase in Nature's rhythmics when Earth and her gods tarry passively without yielding any gifts, granting no life to anything, by himself abstaining from the invigorating gifts of gods, man can overwhelmingly experience the mighty re-entry of the life-supporting powers of Nature in the spring.

Only an analogous resemblance between the dormant state of nature and the endurance of bondage by the Jews under Egyptian rule, and furthermore between the bursting out of vitality of everything alive in the spring and the Jews regaining their life of freedom by setting foot on the way home makes the mythical Passover a supernatural holiday of the Jewish nation.

[94] *Ibid.*, p. 123.

The mythical significance of the Jewish unleavened bread can be well compared to the rites of the annual "rejuvenation" of household fires in the mythical Lithuanian culture. Each year, before the holiday of the Sun (the longest day of the year), the fires in every household had to be put out. Holy fires of oak wood were burned to the glory of Perkunas, the god of thunder and fire, presided over by the high priests (*krivis*) with the participation of the whole Lithuanian community. The housewives of every household carried home burning tinder from the holy fire of Perkunas and started the new fire of the year.

There are many Jewish prayers which still retain mythical, and thus natural, elements in themselves. These vestiges of the "pre-prophetic" (natural or mythical) phase in the Jewish supernatural religion can, for instance, be seen in the following prayers :

Praised are You, O Lord our God, King of the universe, who brings forth bread from the earth...
Praised are You, O Lord our God, King of the universe, Creator of the fruit of the vine...
Praised are You, O Lord our God, King of the universe, who has fashioned such beauty in His world.[95]

In Christianity's conquest of mythical cultures, some grand natural holidays were re-interpreted by the Christian missionaries, in much the same way as the mythical holidays of the Jews were by their prophets, to suit the commemoration of the basic Christian supernatural events. In this way, the main Christian holidays, Christmas and Easter, were fixed to coincide with the ancient mythical holidays of the birth of new light (Christmas) and the awakening of Nature's vigorous vitality in the spring of the year (Easter).

We can conclude from what was said above that Judaism and Christianity (and we can add here — any other supernatural kind of religion, such as Islam and Buddhism) presupposes the mythical, that is natural or cultural, world, in which their supernatural sway alone can livingly go on. As soon as mythical cultures are eradicated, suppressed, or destroyed, instead of living and spiritually growing and developing supernatural cultures, we end up with lifeless, monotonous, mechanical ceremonies, estranged from "bloody" events of cultural vitality, in which nothing constantly new, enthusiastically captivating and surprisingly electrifying ever occurs. A supernatural culture without the natural-mythical undergrounds may be a complex and gigantic, yet formalistically dead, robot-like structure which

[95] *Ibid.*, p. 244.

inevitably is bound to remain outside of the ways of living, searching, working, "poetic" and thinking humanity.

The Second Vatican Council steers the contemporary Church not toward the phase of democratization, but rather toward, or perhaps into, cultural or natural waters. By such steering — if they co-operate — both sides (sacral and secular) may benefit.

Pope John XXIII obviously meant that all real cultures (pre-Christian or non-Christian) are welcome in the family of Christianity. Christianity is supercultural, but in no wise is it contra or anticultural. It is, however, in need of a cultural milieu (man's living *Dasein*) in order to be itself culturally alive. Even though supercultural, it must become cultural, or else it will run a risk of becoming closed in itself, a dead tick-tock functioning outside of cultural rhythmics. Christianity can have cultural significance only in a cultural milieu. Without the cultural play (which is never absolute!) Christianity is meaningless; it is then a dead abstraction.

Early Christianity used Judaism for its cultural milieu, which again was nourished by the pre-Judaistic mythical culture. Medieval Christianity drew its living juice from the cultural aspects of pre-Christian European nations. According to Friedrich Schlosser, a noted German historian, Christianity has borrowed the idea of world fire (*Weltbrand*), in which the world sinks into its twilight and from where the dawn of a new world arises, by expressing it in the combat between the prophet Elias and the Antichrist.[96] Moreover, we know well that the medieval principles of chivalry, military courage, fidelity to land and king, heroic battling for faith and Christ, respect for elders, highly elaborated, chaste and faithful love, along with high esteem, for women, and so on — all originated from the pre-Christian, mythical principles of the morality of European nations. It is wrong to consider medieval virtues as solely originated in the Christian supernatural norms. On the other hand, some negative aspects concerning the cruel (and definitely non-Christian) mistreatment of pagan nations by the Christians principly is due to the cultural standards or principles of the European nations after their Christianization. The idea of the Devil, for instance, which varies from one European nation to another, to a great extent owes itself to the Christianization of the negative, hostile, or vicious spirits of different mythical origins.

The preceding considerations point out that, just as there is no absolutely and universally valid culture, so there cannot be any form of Christianity

---

[96] Cf. Friedrich Christoph Schlosser, *Weltgeschichte* (Stuttgart und Leipzig : Deutsche Verlags'Anstalt, 1900), Band IV, pp. 591-592.

absolutely and universally realized for all time. Due to this, Christianity does not solve cultural problems (which essentially are incomplete, indefinite or non-absolute!). It merely penetrates these cultures with mysterious clarity which goes hand in hand with equally mysterious obscurity. This so-called "night of sainthood" stresses that the supernatural life or enthusiasm of a Christian does not remove obscurities typical of any culture. On the contrary, increased divine supernatural light is flanked by the increased darkness of the unknown.

A guide in these burdened ways of supernatural obscurities is one's own supernatural self — the Christian consciousness. We have already made a distinction between the peripheral or conscious self, which lacks the transcendental qualities of true culture, and the inner or lordly self, which weighs all things according to transentitative or transcendental, that is, cultural, standards.

The peripheral self is one of many such selves, who in one or another way are equal. The peripheral self is "democratic" and because of this, today in our anthropocentric modern world such a self stands above the inner self, who, because of his uniqueness, is considered unadjusted as regards accepted "normal" ways, a drop-out, a misfit.

The Church in our democratic times inevitably tends to become "cultural" in the anthropocentrically democratic sense. Because of this, the ecumenical spirit is interpreted as tending toward democracy. A more proper approach would reveal that the ecumenical spirit, with more farsightedness tends, or should tend, toward a search for democratic man's deeper self. Such a search inseparably is a search for transcendental properly cultural principles — for gods.

Heidegger considers the inner self (*Dasein*) of man as his "being-held in Nothingness".[97] The inner self is not an individual self (even though it is the basis for any individuality) — it is not one of many equal selves — but is the unique self which constitutes man's selfhood or "personalness". Antanas Maceina, a prominent European theologian, interestingly stresses that man has his origin in Nothingness. Animals, unlike man, originate not from Nothingness, but from a certain species. This means that man, properly understood, is not a member of a human species, but that each human is a species of his own. "If man originates in Nothingness, it means that he does not originate in something: he has nothing behind himself — totally nothing which he could call his beginning or his source".[98] Obviously, man's origins are in the holy Abyss, in Nature.

[97] Heidegger, *Was ist Metaphysik?*, p. 32.
[98] Antanas Maceina, "Religija ir Evoliucija" in *Aidai* (*Echoes*). (A cultural magazine published by the Franciscan Fathers in Brooklyn, N. Y.), 1968, Nr. 10.

The inner or cultural self means man's openness to transcendental reality (to Nature and her gods). We know that the supernatural self, as man's openness to the supernatural reality, to God, is not an openness based on his own *natural* strength, but openness on the grounds of his supernatural gifts.

Just as the supernatural culture is an impossibility without a culture, so is the supernatural self impossible without the cultural inner self — without *natural* selfhood. A person in the Christian sense is a cultural person or self with all his cultural powers and qualities, who in addition stands under the supernatural norms or standards which gain an upper hand or a superior sway over strictly cultural problems.

The Church's turn to the "democratic" self would mean her flattening and degeneration, while her turn to deepened cultural inwardness would place a Christian on the way of a search for higher natural or cultural principles, in the play or to whirlpool of which a deepened Christian supernatural life can be attained.

The pre-ecumenical Church stood much closer to the peripheral self than to the cultural inner self.

The former era is known as the epoch of Christian humanism at its fullest where... man is defined by his "nature", an abstraction made from particular individuals, race, geography, and education : man is absolutely the same everywhere. All this is a far cry from biblical anthropology, which stresses the direct personal call (vocation) to each sacred human person by the personal Lord of history.[99]

A peripheral self, a self in the anthropocentric world, deems to be the ruler of all things and a guide of himself. The cultural self is responsive : instead of dominating things, the man of the inner self guards them in their meanings, arranged by the godly *logos* of Nature. Such a man, instead of guiding himself totally by humanistic principles, guides himself by responsively co-operating with the all-ordering or all-guiding transcendental powers of Nature. The cultural self, man's very being-man — concealedly if not overtly — is possessed by everyone. Unlike this, the supernatural self of a Christian is present only in those who are in grace, who are gifted by God. "By grace are ye saved through faith; and that not of yourselves : it is the gift of God". (Eph. 11:8). Just as no one dwells in a supernatural milieu, but always in a natural-cultural one, so no one has a supernatural self. As we just noted, the men of the peripheral self — culturally self-less — are men of the era of godlessness. In spite of this, these men

---

[99] Rev. Peter J. Riga, *The Church and Revolution (Some Reflections on the Relationships of the Church to the Modern World)* (Milwaukee : The Bruce Publishing Co., 1967), pp. 31-32.

are not absolutely self-less. Their inner self is veiled or concealed; it is in a dormant state within them.

4. *Prayer*

Prayer belongs in the very grounds of a cultural life. In no way is it properly man's communication with the supernatural powers of reality. Prayer is man's invasion into divine order — into the play of gods, into the drama of Nature.

We have seen that by the acts of cult, the acts imbedded in the very heart of culture, during his holy days or festivities man partakes in the banquet of the gods. The mythical high priest, "medicine man", *krivis*, invades the community of the gods, and by magical means or with appropriate prayers tries to turn the blessing powers of the gods toward men or turn the hostile or harmful works of unfriendly gods away from his people or community.

Christian prayer is prayer of one in grace or of a group in grace for God's mercy at various occasions. Here man does not become a partner of God or God's co-player — as he does in the mythical or natural world. By the acts of his inner self, man partakes in Nature's creativeness; even thaugn responsively, he is Nature's companion in her creative works. The best that a Christian prayer can do is humbly ask.

A mythical man is great or heroic by doing godly things. The greatest Christian virtue, on the contrary, is man's humble submission to God. Humility, as man's supernatural greatness, is manifest in the Jewish Bible.

The Holy One praised be He said to Israel : I set My love upon you because even when I grant you greatness you make yourselves small before Me. I gave greatness to Abraham, and he said, "Behold, I am dust and ashes" (Gen. 18:27); to Moses and Aaron, and they said "But what are we?" (Ex. 16:7); to David, and he said "I am a worm, not a man" (Ps. 22:7).[100]

In the mythical world man, too, is a nothing, "a shadow of a dream" (Pindar) without the gods. However, when he is favored by the gods, he acquires grand positive qualities and virtues. In the Christian world, the virtue of virtues is humility, and all other virtues are but modes of humility. In the Jewish liturgy of Rosh Hashanah it is said :

Man's origin is dust and he returns to dust. By the peril of his life he obtains his bread. He is like a fragile potsherd, like grass that withers and a flower that fades, like a fleeting shadow, a passing cloud, like the blowing wind and the floating dust, like a dream that vanishes.[101]

[100] Hertzberg, *op. cit.*, pp. 29-30.
[101] *Ibid.*, p. 139.

Prayer, or rather cult, on the cultural or mythical level is the mark of man's distinction from the animals. There are many traits or qualities, such as dignity, chastity, fidelity, tender love, and so on, which had been wrongly considered as exclusively human virtues, which in recent times have been recorded in animal lives by ethologists or animal behaviorists. Even the capacity for intelligence is not restricted to man, as there are intelligent animals. Prayer, or rather cult, is a trait of man — or we should say the very core of that which constitutes the very being-man — it is possessed by no animal and therefore it makes up the difference between man and animals. *Properly* human intelligence, wisdom, is cultural, it is man's thinking response to the *logos* of gods.

We know that everything cultural — often called spiritual! — is found in Nature. Nature is her majestic play (*physis*-is-*logos*), and with this play she grants grounds to all beings by setting them on definite ways she outlines for them. Nature also gives grounds to man's being-man by throwing (*Geworfenheit* — Heidegger) him into pathless chaos, anterior to the ways of things, throws him into shapeless or formless pristinity, into the still boiling source of her creativeness. On the grounds of this abyss, this chaos, man makes his own venture, his own outlines (*Entwurf* — Heidegger) — he becomes Nature's partner in her work of creativeness.

By virtue of his creativeness, responsive to Nature's creativeness, man brings to light or to disclosure the very play of Nature as a cluster of unentitative or transcendental working powers, mythically thought of as the family of gods. Man serves Nature much like an eye. In the perspectives of this eye (in man's cultural world, his *Dasein*) Nature displays herself : she unveils herself or brings herself into sight.

Christianity, or any supernatural culture in general, does not set man free from his cultural function. It rather brings along with itself trans-natural, that is, "trans-transcendental" principles into the whirlpool of cultural life.

It is a grave mistake to consider man as an exclusive child of God, who, after being baptized (having become a Christian), becomes a stranger or often hostile to the natural, that is, cultural, world. Only by maintaining his cultural pledge and allegiance to the cultural principles of his world, can man become a worthy child of God. Without his cultural allegiance man would remain a pusillanimous, faint-hearted, substanceless entity. Lacking his inner core (as is typical of contemporary technocratic man!) he would be as though transparent. The cultureless man, because of his transparency, cannot gather, assemble, reflect, or bring to sight the supernatural light properly into his living days. Cultureless simultaneously is supercultureless or un-Christian.

5. *Christianity and Culture*

The Church of yesterday seemed to maintain a "cultureless" position, or perhaps we should say she seemed to maintain her own culture which she tended to consider absolutely valid. Truthfully, she was "stuck" or was caught in a certain cultural phase in the development of Western culture, and because of this, she stood away from or was not participating in the living growth or development of this culture. As an outward mark which symbolized the Church's cultural stagnation along with this culture's being disconnected from the natural fleeting growth and development of culture, was her adherence to the Latin language — a dead language.

By breaking this cultural freeze-up, Pope John XXIII anticipated the freeing of Christianity toward a renewed cultural life.

This decision of the apostolic Church incarnated the principle of a continuous *metanoia aggiornamento*, or reform which will permit the Church for all time to be free of any particular sociological or cultural context, while allowing it the continuous freedom to seek out and incarnate itself in various cultures in order to achieve its mission of proclaiming Christ as the Savior of mankind.[102]

Christianity exists not for the sake of God. Christ became man in order to help mankind, and his teachings are oriented to such helping. Christianity belongs to the living days of humanity. Since man by his very essence is a cultural being, Christianity necessarily refers to culture. "Religion, for man, cannot be disincarnate or unrelated to this culture in which he lives".[103]

This in no way means that Christianity *in itself* is incomplete without culture. It, however, is incomplete as regards man. Man is "thrown" into Nature's dynamic creative-destructive play, in which he participates or co-operates. It is wholly *human* for him to be aware of Nature's transcendental play and of her transcendental principles (the gods). As far as the supernatural reality is concerned, it cannot affect man unless through the medium of the natural-cultural. It is not *human* to be aware of the supernatural principles. God's word, the supernatural *logos*, can only be presented to man by the language of his living world by cultural or natural language, the *logos*.

When God reveals himself, he must do so in the forms and realities which man can understand and in that sense the infinite is limited by the finitude of his finite creatures. Consequently, unless this is recast into such finite but real representations of man's experience today, the eternal verities are in grave danger of making no sense

---

[102] Riga, *op. cit.*, pp. 2-3.
[103] *Ibid.*, p. 25.

to man today... It is true that God's word is above and beyond the fluctuations of cultures and expressions; yet it can become meaningful to man *hic et nunc* only by a sort of continuous incarnation into new forms expressing new experiences so that true divine truths can be captured and increased, as it were, in robes of another culture and experience.[104]

When things are understood as rooted in their meanings (as Heidegger maintains), language then ceases to be merely the sum total of labels given to things already there. Language (*logos*) rather is the ground or the source of all meanings. Language or *logos* is the transcendental articulating or organizing power of pristine words (archetypes) which found and thus disclose beings. Language or *logos* is never static, even though it is the language of the same ultimate truth, the ever-concealed Nature or *physis*. The Holy Scriptures were given to mankind in a cultural language. The cultural languages of various cultures and of various phases of these cultures require constantly new Christianization of one's own life — cultural life.

As we already know, there is no absolute culture valid to all humanity and for all time of humanity's existence. Christianity cannot be cast into or enveloped in certain, as it were, absolute cultural robes for once and for all. Such absolute robes would fail to make Christianity a living power in man's world. On the contrary, they would mummify it or put it into a cultural grave.

Unless the Christian man can dynamically re-orient himself to this world and adapt to it, then, to use a favorite phrase of our day, God is indeed dead to modern man. If it is true that the Word became flesh, communicating thereby the effects of his divinity to the culture and world about him, then the Church can and must become incarnate within the temporal structures of men.[105]

Christianity in its mysterious supernatural milieu, of course remains unchangeably the same, but due to man's cultural dynamics — his ever twinkling participation in Nature's play — Christianity must be re-acquired constantly anew and captured thus, brought into the midst of man's living days. Any carry-over of cultural, rather than supercultural, norms of a previous cultural phase or milieu builds a barrier between man and God rather than helping man to be near Him.

Unless the Church can shake off the cultural experience of a former age and adapt God's eternal word ("which remains forever") to this new experience, then God must continue to remain "dead" to the man outside the Church.[106]

---

[104] *Ibid.*
[105] *Ibid.*, p. 5.
[106] *Ibid.*, pp. 21-22.

With this in mind, we can see that any expectation to get a blueprint for Christian man's daily work and for his guiding of himself on the ways of his life means a misunderstanding of Christianity by considering it the "true" culture, rather than seeing it as a crowning of culture superculutrally. Holy Scriptures are not a reference book for man's natural-cultural life as, for instance, the Jehova's Witnesses are inclined to maintain. "The Gospel does not offer a ready-made blueprint to the good life. It does not solve all man's problems in advance".[107]

By inviting man to the supernatural life, God simultaneously invites him to live his cultural life with its diversified activities or works. According to Riga, Pope John XXIII in his *Mater et Magistra* "emphatically declared that the material universe and material labor of mankind are willed by God".[108]

The misconception of Christianity as a solid doctrine worked out in detail and absolutely valid principally was due to "absolute" and exhaustively worked out philosophical systems. These systems and the Christian theology built upon them mainly were resting on the two "unshakeable" poles of the material and spritual. According to such an approach, not only things but also Nature were proclaimed "material", and principly only the supernatural reality was "spiritual".

The mythical world and some of the existential philosophies consider Nature as holiness and things as holy in their "essentiation". Material-spiritual is an outcome of philosophy at a certain phase of its historical development. It belongs mainly in the systems of so-called immanent philosophies, that is, philosophies, which — ignoring transcendental reality — consider things or beings as real, while unentitative for them is as much as unreal.

"Spiritualists" generally invite mankind to reject the world and worldly things on the ground of their "materiality" and to be occupied only with what truly *is*, what is "spiritual". According to them, the latter is the supernatural reality — mainly God and his word. the Holy Scriptures. Spiritual also is the human soul as created according to the image of God. Rejection of the world and worldly things amounts to rejection of culture as such. Man as a spiritual being, accordingly, is a stranger in Nature and in culture. "Spiritualists" totally ignore that man as man is a cultural being as well as a natural being. By his own human powers man can have no awareness,

[107] *Ibid.*, p. 35.
[108] *Ibid.*, p. 31.

no comprehension, no love or faith regarding that which is beyond Nature. To reject things and Nature and start solely with God would mean the same as, for instance, the uttering of God's name without first taking a breath. We must take a breath before we can say "God". Moreover, we know God as our guide in our living days in our world amid our things which we cherish and to which we are attached or those whch we hate or oppose. We know God as our provider with what we need in order to live and to enjoy our days. In a world without bread and butter, without green grass and blue sky, without falling rains and the warmth of the sun — without anything whatsoever — moreover, without a world, the openness of our cultural *Dasein*, where we stand surrounded by things — how can we or how do we encounter God? In the absence of all the above mentioned things does the word "God" still mean anythings to us? Can a man taken out of his cultural milieu still encounter anything? Can he *be* at all?

We are planted in a *natural* (Nature's) environment like a bush, and only with all our reachings into black soil, into wind and rays of sunshine, do we get to know gods, and perhaps, God.

God is the Creator; He is guide and protector. Man of today, just as much as man of the past, stands amid more or less clear things or entitative events in his world (his *Dasein*). The well established cultural (natural) world grants all the clarity to things and their events, and, while in itself it is always veiled, it nevertheless is always understood. Comprehension of the world is different from and is presupposed by the comprehension of things.

Man is in need, among many other things, of a shelter to protect him from adverse climatic conditions and from hostile animals or humans. According to the way of thinking of St. Thomas, the concept of shelter is arrived at by the rational work of abstract thinking applied to the data of perceptual experiences. In God, the idea of shelter is anterior to things or entities called "shelters" and it renders these possible. In God the idea of shelter, just as any other idea, has the best clarity.

Whether it is so or not, we can neither affirm nor deny, since we are men and not God! We are "thrown" on earth for earthly life. Being in need of a shelter, we are companions of many animals. These dig burrows, build nests, find a hollow in a tree, and so on. Even plants thrive better in sheltered areas, as if they were at home there.

Mythical man observed the presence of a sheltering power in his world. In the Lithuanian myths Dimste, the goddess of settlement or homestead, was also the goddess, Nature's transcendental power, which had granted to animals the ability to establish their "homes", to shelter themselves. The knowledge of sheltering — be it instinctive or rational — precedes any shelter or windbreak in the world. The sheltering reality as imbedded in Nature as such, is anterior to sheltering things. The former renders the latter meaningful. All by itself, a shelter would be meaningless.

The Christian God, as protector or shelterer, is not God in his supernatural milieu. He rather is God Who is present in our world as One who cares for us. We have nothing to say about God in his supernatural milieu, impenetrable and inaccessible through our purely human powers. When we speak of God, we speak of Him as present in our vital situations. Thus we call Him our guide, provider, orderer, shelterer, and so on. All these qualities obviously are "earthly" or "worldly". The goddess Dimste of the mythical world can be thought of by a Christian as a certain presence of God in his world — in the way of His protective, sheltering care of humans and of animals. God, without such "earthly" modes of being present in our world, is colorless and transparent. He becomes colorful, meaningful and real as one or another swaying power — or rather, all swaying powers — of our world, of our *Dasein*, of our culture. The mythical man understood these powers as his gods and saw them as harmoniously belonging together. If a Christian man thinks of this harmoniously belonging together of the transcendental principles of his cultural world as present in God, he then would have much more realistically livingly experiencing God in his living days.

Transcendental powers (gods) in the mythical world, even though they were the ground of all meanings and all realness in man's world, were themselves elusive. Periodically occuring festivities, in which everyone participated, gathered men from their attachments to narrow every-day immanent occurrences and brought them to a renewed confrontation with their gods. During the grand days of festivity the people of the community re-experienced the dramas of the gods in their lives and thereby they acquired their inner solidity of being persons. A person is unique due to his very own response to or his "under-standing" of his gods. By his response man acquired his true inner self, which makes him a companion or a co-player of his gods. The inner self is attained through gods. Experience of gods is man's existential quality, on the grounds of which he is distinct from any animal, moreover from anything whatsoever. Things or animals, unlike men, are not persons.

Man — even though a person, a man of the inner self — does not possess a capacity for supernatural response as far as his knowledge or dwelling is concerned. Such a capacity is only had by extraordinary gifts or graces of God, which elevate man over and above his cultural being-man. The supernatural gifts or graces must acquire cultural or natural qualities in order to be understood or comprehended by man. This is why Christ was born a man. To God — even as the giver of supernatural gifts or graces — man would remain deaf and blind. Only Christ, with his teachings robed in cultural robes and with his gifts of bread and wine in an earthly way, only he can affect man : he can be understood and responded to by man.

When God permeates realities which, in mythical times, have been thought of as gods and which now, in the late philosophical era, can be interpreted as transcendental or transentitative principles of reality which hold a sway in man's cultural world, He then is encounterable and is apt to be responded to by man. Just as during the *natural* (mythical or cultural) festivities man's companionship with gods is renewed or restored, so Christian festivities are days of restoration of man's supernatural companionship with God. These are the days to receive God's graces, necessary for man's supernatural life — for his mission in the search for his supernatural self, for the eternal happiness of his soul. Holy Mass radiates with graces upon the Christian community.

Man's inner self is every cultural man's cultural target. An animal has the "heavyweight" of his essence in himself, given to him by Nature. Nature ascribes to man some of her own function : she provides him with an ability to form his own self in accordance with her principles or deviating from them. In this way, man's "heavyweight", his inner self, is the aim he must seek. Man is an "out-standing" or "ex-sistential" being, while an animal is immanent.

Christianity appeals to man, asking him to exceed his very being-man, that is, to exceed his inner self. For doing this, Christ and his Church provide man with the supernatural powers, with graces. On the ground of these gifts man must acquire his supernatural self. The acquiring of one's supernatural self is not a rejection of one's natural self. The inner self here becomes permeated by the supernatural self, and they both become man's mission of realization; they become inseparably one. The procedure of accomplishing man's Christian or supernatural mission merges with his mission of acquiring his natural self — his lordly self of greatness.

Culture is man's existential burden which is not had by non-existential beings (for instance, by animals). Christianity is an additional burden which is not placed as separate on man's shoulders. The supernatural burden of man penetrates his natural burden and drives him to a life greater than greatness.

Christianity, because it reaches us through our culture, cannot become a rationalistically built up doctrine which points out man's way with absolute and infallible sureness. My friend in Prince George, Milt McKernan, during our discussions emphatically opposed the existential, that is, cultural, standpoint in man's encounter of God, as well as man's culturally or existentially insecure way of being a Christian. According to McKernan, God guides and protects His Church. Moreover, He provides man with a firm book of codes which determines the Christian's actions with total sureness in all of his living situations.

McKernan overlooks that man is meant (thrown) to live or to dwell in insecurities. Man is man only when he is floating on a barge tossed around by a stormy sea. The barge alone does not guide man on the high seas. He must depend on his barge, but no less on his own steering which responds to the movements of the barge and even more to the movements of the stormy sea. By his response man constantly makes adjustments in the course of his floating.

If God would not secure Christian man's way by His established, totally dependable, guidance of the Church who provides man with a definitely formulated book of codes, McKernan would cease to be a member of the Church. He compares such a situation with a traveller in a plane. If he was this traveller and would not have confidence in the pilot, he would parachute from the plane. Due to the insecurities of cultural dwelling, which are not removed by the supernatural Christian principles, man is never a secure and passive passenger in a plane piloted by a dependable pilot. This man himself is the co-pilot, and he depends on the pilot no less than on his own hand co-operating with the hand of the pilot.

Nature throws man, as it were, into a boiling kettle, where he does not have any absolute "up" and "down". He must co-determine the "up" and "down" of his "thrownness" (*Geworfenheit*) by his own projection (*Entwurf*) founded on the grounds of his "thrownness". This is so because man, being a cultural being, is always barred off from absolute security and absolute orientation. Since Christianity, as we have pointed out, is experienced by man in the medium of culture, it, too, is such that man partakes in the course of elucidating its "ups" and "downs" in his particular cultural living situations.

No judge can direct us absolutely in our living stituations by his book of codes. He cannot determine which of our acts in the Christian, as well as cultural, milieu are absolutely wrong or absolutely right. We ourselves, in our storm-battered barge are the best "measuring stick". Instead of a book of codes. we have the compass of our inner selves in ourselves. Of course, we do not try to deny here that there can be a firm, unswerving knowledge of God's guidance; or also that there can be a sure knowledge of right and wrong according to the supernatural criteria of right and wrong. This knowledge, however, is based on faith, and it always implies man's inner self, elevated to a supernatural self by Grace. Knowledge of the inner self is not made obsolete here; instead it is only modified.

A man with a book of codes — be he cultural or Christian — resembles a switchboard operator, who presses precisely this or that button for each right decision or right action. Thus, a cultural or Christian man can live out his life totally mechanically and find his road to ideal humanity or to Heaven conveniently paved. He can live out his life totally self-lessly. He does not struggle through often abruptly ending forest trails; erring, suffering, despairing, hoping, finding and losing again; following the rising sun or the twinkling North Star, often covered by clouds; briefly — he does not live a "bloody" life with love, joys, sufferings, expectations, enlightening visions, depressing blows of destiny, always facing the unknown, always hoping and always venturing into great deeds.

To live blindly according to a book of codes, does it mean to be a perfect man or a perfect Christian? On the contrary, it means to cease to be a human who walks on dark earth under a sky full of light but never penetrable, following the guidings or misguidings (misleading) of the gods who may be loving, protective, helpful, but just as often are hating, forsaking, playing tricks. To live according to the book of codes means to betray one's "stormy" mission — to betray one's own self. We cannot live like gods or angels, because we are not gods or angels. And if God, the Saviour, would secure our life with an absolutely clear and valid book of codes He would betray the mission of being-man given to man by God the Creator. Christianity does not absolve man from culture; instead it penetrates his culture with supercultural might.

6. The Relativity of Christianity

In his historical cultural world, man encountered God as Christ, the God-man. Only as man, a godly man, was God apt to be encountered by man. Throughout all the history of Christianity, Christ is encounterable through the Bread and Wine. The Bread and Wine are earthly, and simultaneously they are superearthly or supernatural. Man himself is an earthling. However, he is such in a transcendental, and not in an immanent way — the way in which things and animals are. Only through the supernatural power of Christ, of the Bread and Wine, that is, through Grace, can man become a Christian — a superearthling, yet still an earthling.

Man encounters Nature and her gods on the way of his mission of being-man. He does not encounter Christ on this way, unless it is by the power of Grace, given to him on and above his being-man. Christ is an invasion of Earth. He is an earthly vehicle of God, just as the Bread and Wine are vehicles of Grace.

A vehicle obviously is inferior to that of which it is a vehicle. It is merely a means, a way, and, to some extent, a barrier, a separating medium between Heaven and Earth, between the supernatural and the cultural. Because of this latter point, Christianity in some phases of past history, and often even today, considered earth and earthly happiness rejectable for the sake of Heaven and heavenly happiness. Must it be so? No! The means or a way should not be rejected but fully maintained. Without the way, there is no destination, no ultimate home. Not to reject, but to cultivate and to transcend means to love Earth and the earthly life. To be a Christian presupposes being a culturalist.

The Church is the representative and place-holder of Christ. So is the Pope and the priesthood. Some theologians or religious thinkers were pondering a question — is the Church Christ? or is the Pope Christ? Without answering these questions, we can ask further : is Christ God?

Christ had a certain growth, appearance, strength. He lived in a certain place at a certain time. He fell under the cross. He sweated and bled. He got tired and thirsty. Christ was a man.

According to Bultmann's theology, the Holy Scriptures are not God's words, period! They are God's words *as they mean to the human ear*. The human ear is deaf to God's words. Therefore, the Holy Scriptures are given in human language; they are made suitable for the human ear. Man as man cannot confront God. Therefore God approaches man in a limited way. Christ is not God in His own milieu. He is God in our world. He is God's son. Christ is God as God can be apprehended by or known to man. Christ is God in the way He appears in human sight. We adore Christ and respect the Church, the Pope, and the priesthood, and thus we please God, our Lord.

Man does not know the supernatural, therefore God sends Christ, His son, to reveal it to us. God as God is unapprehensible to us, men. God must dilute Himself in human cultural waters (become Christ) in order to be apprehended by man. Human knowledge exhausts itself by Nature. Only God as Christ can grant supernatural knowledge or gifts to men. Christ is a paradox : He is God and he is man.

The modern man, including today's Christian, must become aware that there is no absolute "table of values" or codes of morality. There are various cultures with their binding holy laws, their often uncrossable borderlines or unbreakable barriers. Man *as man* never is above culture; he is always a child of one or another culture; even when he breaks away from it as though becoming cultureless. None of the cultures are absolute in the sense that their laws or demands would be made binding to everyone, to all humanity.

In spite of culture's finitude, into which man finds himself thrown, he must live in it with total unswerving surrender : man must serve his cultural principles, his gods. He knows that his ultimate cultural principles are divine even though not absolute.

Our Christian theology tended (and still does) to *perfect* standards or codes applicable *absolutely* to every situation of every man's life. Today, with the ecumenical spirit we must realize that divine standards come down to us in the medium of our cultural waters. Even Christ had to become *very human* and a participant in the pre-Christian Jewish cultural world before he could bring forward to us his supercultural message.

A sincere and impartial investigation or exploration of any culture in the world would find basically positive values in all of them. Dignity, nobility, concern, love, sacrifice, and so on, in one or another way, are present in any genuine or mythical culture. Adoration of superhuman powers, respect for the community's sages or elders, hospitality, love of one's neighbor or countryman, and many other qualities or values are, generally speaking, present in any of the earth's cultures.

Just as any thing, any plant, or any animal never is totally negative in Nature (Nature never abandons or never is a stepmother to anything in its milieu), so every culture is willed and cared for by Nature.

The specific values of Christianity are other than culture or cultural values. However, they can attain or affect man only through a cultural medium — through man's living world or *Dasein*. Christianity made its first steps in the medium of the Jewish cultural world, which, especially in original phase, was mythical or natural. In principle, Christianity can permeate any culture — be it one highly different from Judaism or not.

A culture may combat another culture, just as one species of animals may combat another, and accordingly, one Christian culture may combat another Christian culture. This does not means that Christianity combats Christianity, but that the two vehicles of Christianity combat each other. This point of view — when fully apprehended, may drastically change the "errors" of Christianity in history, where many cultures were made extinct by the killing of their gods rather than the penetration of them by the supernatural light. All these extinctions or theocides, of course, were not committed by Christianity as such, but by a certain Christian *culture*.

The history of Christianity frequently testifies that the Christian enthusiasm has not always been a supernatural one. It necessarily was simultaneously a cultural enthusiasm, and doubtlessly it still is so.

Mythical man lived in a joyful and horrifying drama, where each year the superhuman powers of Nature combatted each other, keeping man breathless in a tension to survive or to be crushed, to be or not to be. Perhaps the most intense moment of survival of men, likewise of animals, took place during the intense moment of the combat of the gods of darkness and light. This drama took place during the holiday of the shortest day of the year, when the young son Light makes his first move, like a newborn baby. After this moment he grows and becomes stronger and mightier. This festivity is preceded by a period of waiting (Advent). The messenger of the gods, a holy man of the community, comes to his people and announces the birth of the god Light, the Sun god. This joyful guest, according to the Nordic myths, rides on slim-legged and fast running reindeer, whose nine-branched antlers symbolize the sun and its rays. This guest from the gods brings with him green branches of the evergreen, symbolizing the rebirth or rejuvenation of Nature. In the more archaic — pre-Perkunian — phase of the Lithuanian mythical religion, the community was visited by a *vaidilute*, a holy priestess of Gabija, goddess of fire and care, daughter of Zemyna, Mother Earth. In Scandinavian nations, *vaidilute*'s counterpart was Lucie, goddess of Light (the Latin *lux, lucis* is probably a translation of the originally Nordic word for the goddess of light). *Vaidilute*, as well as Lucie, with a green wreath on her head, held a burning candle in her hands, symbolizing the birth of light, sun, warmth, and life.

The holiday of Christmas contains overwhelming and enthusiastic mythical elements along with the supernatural event of Christ's birth. A careful approach of many other Christian holidays would disclose pre-Christian or mythical elements carried over into specifically Christian commemorations. These holidays present an outburst of enthusiasm which is no less cultural than supernatural.

These few occasions of harmony between the cultural and the supernatural throughout the course of Christian and Judaistic histories have been far outdone by the occasions of disharmony. As a rule, a culture should not combat or destroy any other culture. Instead, cultures should maintain mutual respect (as there is no absolute culture with the right of predominance). This concerns the Christian culture no less than it does any other. This does not mean that any culture or Christianity should shy away from any other. Cultural intercourse or intercommunication can be mutually constructive. What is important here is the maintaining of respect for the principles or for the gods of other cultures. A culture, by a respectful communication with other cultures, may find a new flash up of its own cultural life in its own *Dasein*, thereby enriching or intensifying it. Likewise, Christianity may step forward with a new power as a supercultural reality thanks to its respectful penetration of until then alien elements of the non-Christian cultures.

In recent decades we have often heard of genocide, that is, of the killing or destroying of a whole nation, which often means of a culture. A nation or culture can endure much and survive. However, it dies — even though its members may physically still vegetate — whenever its principles or its gods are eradicated. Accordingly, a genocide principly is a theocide. When the gods of a nation or a culture die, the nation has no higher aims left, no invigorating enthusiasm, no splendid virtues, no multicolored ways of greatness, no meaningul daily tasks, no festivities, no great examples set by heroic men, no sages, no poets or prophets.

Often in history, a culture, being convinced of its absolute validity and superiority over any other cultures, committed one theocide after another. Such repeated misdeeds are typical of historical Christianity which distorted and destroyed many a great and dignified culture by proclaiming its gods untrue or even as satanic forces. Christ's motto, according to which He did not come to destroy the ancient laws, but to improve them, was totally ignored and disregarded by His heirs.

A cultural man's adherence to his own culture, cults, and gods is marked by his intense faithfulness to them. Any denial, degrading, or adverse treatment of his cults and gods automatically sets such a man against those who mistreat his culture. This attitude of his is an outcome of or flows out from deep conviction rooted in his inner self. Mistreatment of his culture is a mistreatment of his inner self. Dr. Martynas Anysas held a lecture to a local Lithuanian society in Chicago, January 1, 1966, where he introduced the major points of his forthcoming book on the ancient Prussians. Among many other points he indicated then that in the Xth Century, Adalbert, Bishop of Praha, and Brother Bonifacius were killed by the Prussians while they were trying to introduce Christianity to them, simultaneously degrading the Prussian gods and their cults. Because of this, "the Holy Seat" (of Rome) sent well armed crusaders who mercilessly crushed the Prusssian nation for its refusal to abandon its cultural ways and gods. According to Anysas, the conquering crusaders "did not allow to the pagans any right to fight for their freedom". Moreover, Dusburg, the writer of chronicles for the crusaders" wars,

does not praise, even with one word, the Prussians' love of freedom and their heroism. According to his opinion, they are all devils' instruments, Belial's children, who must be forced to Christianization or be destroyed. He views these matters with the eyes of a medieval Christian fanatic.

Dusburg was not an odd fanatic of his time. Almost all unruly and militant Christians, with comparatively little exception, maintained basically the same attitude toward all pagans. They served their master (Christ), not by proclaiming his gospel (that is, not constructively), but by destroying the holy cultural treasures of nations to whom they were introducing Christianity.

According to Dr. Jonas Balys, the missionaries of Christianity chopped with axes the holy trees adored by the ancient Lithuanians. They persisted in extinguishing the holy fires, which were kindled and guarded incessantly by the *vaidilutes*, the priestesses of the ancient gods. They identified the gods of the Lithuanians with devils or witches.[109] These missionaries used to tear off the animal skulls, attached to the walls of the homes. These skulls had religious significance to Lithuanian society. The missionaries crushed them on the floor with the heels of their boots. Moreover, they did the same with the holy serpents adored by the Lithuanians and kept in their homes as important animal deities.[110]

The conquest and destruction of Prussia, a nation related to Lithuania, by the "holy" crusaders, blessed by the pope-emperor, is a historical fact which in brutality, mercilessness, cruelty and inhumanness equals, if not surpasses, the deeds of the Spanish general Cortez. In both cases, noble, culturally high standing, nations were massacred with unequaled cruelty.

In these or similar historical events, it is not the massacre of people (genocide) which constitutes the crucial point, but the crushing of the nations' cultures — of their cults and their gods. When men die, there may still be some survivors who then may carry on their service to their gods and thus keep their culture alive. However, when the gods die, or rather, when they become absent from or silent in man's living world, the survivors of the nation live a meaningless life, become mere shadows, unless they join the culture of the conquerors and thus acquire a new cultural life.

Englishmen or Britons are known as cultural missionaries throughout the world. They are proud of the numerous cultural planatations they have started all around the globe. These plantations, however, were preceded by the graves of the conquered peoples' gods. This procedure can be compared with a "primitive" native village, which, after being burned, smashed, and bulldozed, becomes a site for a modern British-style town with an administration building, schools, Anglican churches, branches of businesses with main offices in London, and residential areas resembling those in England.

Some nations — for instance, the American Indians — failed to adjust themselves to the English brand of culture, and thus they became culturally

---

[109] Cf. Balys *op. cit.*, p. 109.
[110] Cf. *Ibid.*, p. 116.

useless, in a sense, drop-outs. They seemed to constitute a need for special treatment assisting them in their "culturalization". Many other nations or countries under the English flag succeeded in adjusting themselves to the "true" English culture and became thriving British provinces.

American democracy has much the same attitude as the Britons. Expressively or not, it considers the ideal of any nation or any culture the attainment or realization of the true replica of the American way of life.

Communism — or rather the two major Communistic countries, Russia and China — expressively stress and, wherever possible, carry out by military force their brands of humanity's ideal. Besides the military invasions and violent eradication of native cultures of any undefended area, by much the same means, the Communistic party or its rulers impose their doctrine upon each individual under their command. They use all available means, including the forced labour camps or methods of brainwashing to indoctrinate individuals and to make them Communist fanatics. If these means fail, the individual has to be eliminated from society either by "liquidation", imprisonment, or confinement in an insane asylum.

The result of all such mistreatment of cultures by other ones lies in considering the culture of the latter as ultimately true. Principly there are no negative aspects in any genuine culture. Negative aspects are an outcome of a certain culture's treatment or weighing under the criteria of another. A culture — whatever kind it is — as long as it is a genuine culture, maintains its standards and criteria as ultimately valid for its own people. These standards or criteria can never be extended over all cultures or all humanity as universally valid.

Just as a note, we would like to state here that neither the British culture, nor American democracy, nor Communism are genuine cultures, since they all are "godless" by orienting themselves according to anthropocentric standards. However, even they — if not in their façades, certainly in their concealed depths — are an outcome, and thus a mode, of a godly or genuine culture.

Humanity, in recent ages, has been striving for realization of an anthropocentric, democratic way of life. Various revolutionary disruptions, a shaking up of age-old anthropocentric ideals, are but symptoms that tomorrow may be all other than what is maintained today. Evolutionary development started since the beginning of the modern era may sink into oblivion, and anthropocentrism along with it. This change may take place with humanity's becoming aware that instead of subduing all cultures under one "true" culture, it (humanity) must acquire a respectful attitude toward the various cultures of the world, without attempting to enslave

them under a certain one. When culture thus is placed above man, it simultaneously will mean a rediscovery of superhuman *cultural* (and that means
natural) princ:ples. These principles are the gods of the future.

A respect for cultures in the times to come is expected of Christianity
as well. This does not mean that Christianity is another culture, but that it
can be alive only by entering man's world and penetrating or permeating
his culture. Christianity has not come to subdue cultures. It has come to
radiate as supercultural in the milieu of the cultural. By annihilating a
culture — killing its gods — Christianity annihilates the milieu (*Dasein*)
wherein it can radiate in its sublime, supernatural light. Christianity should
not combat gods nor merge with them; it should use them as transcendental
natural principles in which it can shine and become alive. In this way it
maintains its supercultural standing without destroying the cultural milieu.
Christianity is a supernatural play which is in need of the living medium of
Nature's play.

There is no cultureless Christianity. Anyone who envisions such Christianity fails to be aware of man's existential mission. As long as man is,
until the last day of his being-man, he is bound to be on the way of a search
for his own inner self. Such a search simultaneously is a search for the
criteria or principles — for the gods — which determine the essence, or
rather the "essentiation" of his innermost self. Theoretical formulations
of Christianity in some theologies expose Christianity as freed from the
cultural. This, for instance, is the case in Hegel's Absolute's self-realization
in the final state. Christianity, understood in this way, is a lifeless abstraction, totally static, bracketed off from the dynamic, living, natural world.
Any elimination of the cultural leaves Christianity a dead doctrine. Pope
John XXIII's deed was the steering away of the Church from abstract
Christianity and heading her toward cultural Christianity.

7. *Christianity's Incarnation in Culture*

In spite of repeated acclamations of contemporary man's world for all
its achievements in scientific or social fields, any sincere inquiry into this
"great" world would discover a lack of firm principles in it — the principles
explaining Nature in her wholeness, the utmost roots of the meanings of
things and most of all, the meaning of man's life, including his ultimate
mission.

This does not mean that we lack theories or philosophies explaining all
this. What is most troublesome is the emptiness of these explanations when
trying to synthesize them. All these explanations are heading in totally

different directions, often contradicting each other. In our world there is no "heavyweight" common point in which all these explanations merge. Because of this disharmonious multitude, contemporary man is much more lost and much more confused than any man of previous cultural phases in spite of his "primitive" stance. Western humanity, triumphing today over all other cultures, simultaneously is wandering in the wildernesses of its thriving multitude of theories, treated as a multitude of opinions. This is so because they all are valued "democratically" without any need to test their validity against any firm principles. Opinions triumph today precisely because in the modern man's world there no longer are any unshakable principles.

Today we do not have any holy or kingly men, in whom the knowledge of the principles — the gods — of the living world (*Dasein*) is seated. Wisdom — if we can find it — today is just another opinion. Instead of a few fixed holy or kingly "dots" on the world-wide map of modern life, today we have a market where everyone shouts his own opinion. Only totalitarian societies (of which all but a few are Communistic) maintain a misleading impression of a solidly unified world-outlook. If ever or whenever these societies will become free to express their own opinions, they will be no different from the so-called free, non-Communistic world.

The contemporary cultural crisis, which consists of the lack of principles, silently outshouts all the noisy proclamations of the firm modern world. There are times in the day or night when an individual makes an inquiry into his own inner self and finds nothing but emptiness there. Perhaps the inner vacuum of modern man tosses him into the noisy market of opinions which help him to cover up his inner vacuum.

To an extent modern man's lack of principles makes him a cultural cripple. From this we can see that his religious crisis — against the firm conviction of theologians of almost any brand of supernatural religion — consists of the milieu of the cultural or natural rather than in the supercultural or supernatural. From this it would be wrong to draw a conclusion that we here consider Nature as such more important than Christianity. Instead, our position here should be seen as maintaining that without a renewed grasp of Nature as the context of all transcendental principles which explain the world around us and which guide our dwelling in it, the Christian way of dwelling is not realizable.

Only when man "under-stands" the principles of his cultural world (not only knows them, but lives according to them — *stands under them*), can he adapt himself to the supernatural or supercultural principles of Christianity. This shows that Christianity can never be statically explained once and for all; it must necessarily be growing, developing — be dynamical. This is so because in the ever continuous changes, modifications and growth of the cultural world, Christianity must necessarily be agile, fluctuating, flickering, and with constantly new flashes radiating within the cultural world — with ever new youth and dynamics.

Medieval philosophies, especially the philosophy of St. Thomas, explain the whole of reality from dust to God : from the least significant entity in the natural world to the peak of the supernatural world (to God). Such an absolute and static doctrine not only thwarts a proper grasp of Christian truths in a living manner, but simultaneously it does the same with the grasp of Nature's transcendental principles — with cultural dwelling. Moreover, we would get closer to the real issue of this doctrine if we say that it completely overlooks or circumvents the transcendental region of natural reality — overlooks the very event of culture.

Such an overlooking is due to metaphysical interpretation of reality. Metaphysical intepreation is concerned with beings (things or objects) alone; it has nothing to say about reality's transcendental principles which render beings meaningful and real. St. Thomas' metaphysics investigates beings in the natural world by gradating them according to their intensity of realness (actuality). Such a gradation is carried on by him across the limit of the natural into the supernatural in such a way that the highest entities in the natural world are followed by the lowest ones in the supernatural world. The gradation of supernatural entities (pure spirits) is crowned by the supreme spiritual entity, God. Such an interpretation of all beings from dust to God constitutes the basic framework of theological metaphysics.

Modern philosophies, less and less concerned with the spiritual or supernatural realities, maintained the entitative gradation of natural realities with man crowning them all. The crisis of modern man's cultural world, generally speaking, is owing to the metaphysical interpretation of reality which began with the classical Greek philosophers. The overcoming or remedying of this crisis — which is a cultural as well as a Christian crisis — calls for a reconsideration of pre-metaphysical thought, while carrying on the latest outcomes of contemporary thought.

The theological character of metaphysics has increasingly obscured and concealed humanity's relatedness to its world. Would not then a reconsideration of the most early dawn of Western thought be a way or perhaps a narrow and fragmental trail for attaining the original thought of the world?[111]

[111] Fink, *Spiel*, pp. 25-26.

The firm world (or rather, firm worlds) consists in man's standing breathtakingly near to and simultaneously always far from his gods. Gods are right in the midst of man's living situations and yet they are always elusive as though they were absent from these situations. Their elusiveness obviously consists of their transentitative character.

Mythical man felt his gods in the marvel of Nature's breakthrough into his living situations. A Greek felt the nearness (and distance) or Artemis in the mountain forests, flooded by moonlight. He felt Apollo in the glare of the sunshine. In the foaming, breaking ocean waves he encountered Poseidon in his mighty realness. The Christian God, however, is not encounterable or experienceable in man's living natural world directly. Principly God is absent from the world. "His absence is attainable only to Faith and never to the natural knowledge of finite man".[112]

Even though absent from the world, God can be attainable to man — be it with faith alone — only in the world, that is, only as Christ. If God would not break into man's living world, He would ever remain a stranger to him. This is so because man principly or essentially is an earthling — a being openly standing in the world, a cultural being. The supercultural can disclose itself only in the milieu of the cultural. A supercultural crisis simultaneously is a cultural crisis; not always, however, *vice versa*.

In his poem "Hymn" (*Giesme*), the poet Baltrusaitis experiences God in the event of Nature, in "the cradle and abyss of everything alive". He speaks of God in terms of the natural. Natural images, apparently under his supernatural enthusiasm, manifest God to him. Thus he feels God in the "patient steer and silent bee" and in "a maid spinning threads early in the morning"; "in seeded fertile soil which supports weeds as well"; "in sowing time and in the time of harvest"; "in clear blue skies and in stormy days", and so on. These fragments of Nature's sway, the backgrounds of which are constituted of gods, have the glare of the supernatural upon them, a hue of God Creator. Experience of such a hue is rendered possible by the supernatural gifts. The Christian culture in the ecumenical spirit, rather than rejecting culture, sees it as the vehicle on which the supernatural light can be caught. In such an approach, the natural retains its genuineness and godliness and, in addition, it serves the supernatural by lending to it a cultural — that is, experienceable — basis.

A short time after my arrival in the United States of America from Germany I had a simple dream, the meaning of which touches upon the theme of the mythical (or cultural) and Christian. I dreamt that Professor

[112] *Ibid.*, p. 133.

Fink, under whom I studied philosophy and through whom I became more intensely interested in mythical problems, had sent me a book. In this book there was a picture of an old Lithuanian hut amid trees and tall grass. It struck me as strange that in the hut there was an altar with burning candles upon it. While I was meditating as to whether this altar should be there or that perhaps it did not belong there, I awoke.

The Lithuanian hut obviously means the ancient mythical world. The altar with burning candles stands for Christianity. At the time of dreaming, unlike today, I possibly was not aware of the potential reconciliation or complementation of the mythical and Christian worlds in myself. The hut is realistic and natural. The altar with the candles likewise becomes realistic and as though natural by having broken into the living ancient or firmly standing mythical world.

At this occasion we can ask a question : are the mythical (and thus cultural) and the Christian, in the living situations of human lives in any way, in their ultimate roots, the same or are they essentially and necessarily of heterogenous origin?

The first thing we can say in answering the above question is that we, to a certain extent, can explore and gain insights into the natural or cultural, while we have no say-so regarding whatever is beyond the natural or cultural.

In spite of this, we would like to mention very briefly two cases — both of the cultural, that is, experienceable, kind. One of these cases is concerned with the Ever-hidden (Atum) of the Egyptian mythical world, and the other has the aspect of reincarnationism, especially when linked to Adam's myth in Hebrew religion. Both of these cases — as we will see — can be seen as closely related.

As we know, the highest or supreme deity in the Egyptian mythical world was Ra, the god of the sun. His very presence, the brilliance of his revelation, was that wherein the most fundamental reality remained concealed. We, on several occasions, have compared the Ever-hidden with Mother Earth, ever dark, obscure, or lightless, who, nevertheless, comes forward through ever lightful gods, her children; with Greek *physis*, the ever concealed, which steps forward in *logos*; or with Nothingness in Heidegger's philosophy, which prevails as Being.

The Ever-hidden, the nameless as such (Atum) can only be disclosed as unknowable. All the manners or ways in which the Ever-hidden (Mother Earth, *physis*, Nothingness) sways as the source of the ultimate, transcendental powers, are best indicated by Nature, who gives birth or a start to or who "essentiates" everything that is, including, first of all, all the transcendental powers, the gods. Nature as the ground of all natural transentitative principles and of everything natural in the entitative sense, is ground-less in herself, is the abyss. Nature ever steps into man's living cultural world, ever withholding herself, and thus she never steps into any cultural world. This stepping-in of Nature or disclosing of herself as concealed — that is, as not disclosing herself — constitutes what we call Nature's play — the abyss which constitutes the ultimately firm ground for everything that is or can be — for everything that is naturally or culturally founded or disclosed.

Is it possible that Christianity, that supernatural God, steps into men's cultural worlds, their *Daseins*, in other than natural ways? Is it possible that the Ever-hidden reveals itself not just as Ra? Is it possible that the Mother Goddess announces herself not only through Nature's gods? Is it possible that *physis* comes forward not just as *logos*? Or finally, is it possible that Nothingness "essentiates" itself not just as Being?

We, of course, can only hint or mention this and have no justified power to answer these questions. Whatever it may be, if the Abyss or the holy Chaos, which grounds everything, really can disclose itself circumventing the natural, it nevertheless can be encountered, understood, or known only within the natural, within man's living situations, his *Dasein*. The supernatural or transnatural, yet, can shine or glare only in the natural.

Adam's myth can be understood as the portrayal of man's ultimate origins as rooted in the Ever-hidden or in Nature herself, rather than in the already founded or created world which properly is called the natural and thus cultural world. The milieu of the Ever-hidden, as chaotic or abysmal, *to an extent* can be considered as transnatural.

The Bible — Jewish as well as Christian — would seem to treat of man in the pre-natural (Paradise) milieu. "Adam was created in this supernatural state of divine favor over and above the extraordinary natural gifts which were his. Never would man, Adam or his heirs, be in the state of pure nature".[113] Because of his original sin, Adam, and with him man in general, became an "earthling", that is, a dweller in the natural world. This calls for an interpretation that man really is man only as guilty or sinful, that is, as natural (an earthling). The man of Paradise is, in the true sense, not as yet a man. In other words, man can be an object of natural consideration only in the milieu of the natural. The man of paradise, man prior to his sin, can only be viewed from the perspective of the natural, that is, in the terms of the natural, even though he is not natural. One of the Jewish religious authorities presents a conversation between Adam and his heirs :

---

[113] Brantl, *op. cit.*, p. 58.

The righteous descendants of Adam upon whom death has been decreed ... approach Adam and say, "You are the cause of our death". Adam replies : "I was guilty of one sin, but there is not a single one among you who is not guilty of many sins".[114]

Man's sinfulness, or the Adam in every man, calls for a redeemer. Since man as man (as cultural man) is necessarily guilty or sinful, he cannot remedy himself. This can be done only by someone without sin. Judaism maintains the Messiah as the redeemer, that is, as the remover of man's sins and therewith the restorer of man in his Paradise milieu, that is, of man no longer man, but superman. According to Christianity, the Messiah is Christ, who returns to man his supernatural rights of birth. The re-acquisition of his supernatural rights constitutes, according to Christianity, the destiny of man. "The historical need of man for God is the need for the friendship of God for fulfillment of his supernatural destiny".[115]

The restoration of the full or complete, that is, supernatural, man — broken by the natural — even though it is not in his own hands, nevertheless demands man's understanding of his sinful (natural) state and his co-operation by his response to the supernatural Grace. In other words, the natural or the cultural is a necessary basis constituting his thrust propelling him toward his supernatural fullness.

Because of Adam's sin, "death has been decreed" [116] upon humanity. This means that man, when he became man, he *ipso facto* became a mortal. According to the Bible, God principly did not mean man to be mortal. Only because of his sin did he become so. Man, having become mortal, in God's eyes is a deviation (sinning) from his intended status for man. Consequently God wishes man's immortality. " 'For I desire not the death of anyone', says the Lord God; 'therefore return and live' ". (Ezek. 18:30-32).

Reincarnationists understand this invitation of God to man to return and live as his going through a series of incarnations, that is, as his repeated returning to live until he reaches completedness which cannot be achieved without the Messiah or Christ, but which (repeated incarnations) requires strong efforts of man to restore, straighten out, or compensate for previous guilts or sins.

Adam's sin can be compared to a pendulum which swings in a certain way, throwing the primordial fullness of man (his supernatural status) out of balance or out of harmony, of the peace of Paradise. Only man, thrown

---

[114] Hertzberg, *op. cit.*, p. 196.
[115] Brantl, *op. cit.*, p. 58.
[116] Hertzberg, *op. cit.*, p. 196.

off balance, is a "thrown" (*geworfen*) man, which means that he is natural and thus cultural and mortal.

Man, who sinned, lived out his life : instead of in the pre-natural or Paradise's totality — the *no-way*, he had a certain *natural way*. To make good his sin, he had to be born again to proceed in a way opposite to the way of his former life. In this restoring way, he again sins by embarking another way, which always is other than the pathlessness of the holy whole. Man, throughout the series of incarnations, always lands (is thrown) on a way, and thus he always lacks the true pathlessness, the whole, the Ever-hidden; he lacks Nothingness or Nature. Nevertheless, he always has an awareness of the whole in his innermost hidden self — the inner self (how else could he lack it?).

Man always lands on this or another way because, with his own power, (including his participation in the play of Nature or the dance of gods) he cannot attain full reconciliation — attain totality, the no-way or pathlessness. Man — because of his sins — enters a series of lives and thus a series of births and deaths. The aim of these births-deaths is the Peace of Nature, which, as the Ever-hidden, *could be* supernaturality.

We have touched upon the aspect of reincarnation, and previously Adam's myth, only to demonstrate a possible original source where the natural and the supernatural are the same. In no way are we trying here to affirm man's pre-human, that is, pre-natural, origin. It is beyond a *natural* venture (which we maintain) to decide the above point in one or another way. We also do not subscribe ourselves to the reincarnationists' theory; we feel, however, that it helps to make the issue (eventual relatedness of culture to the supercultural) more graspable.

Both of the above treated problems — Adam's myth and man's reincarnation — can be somewhat solidified by the problematic of man and animal.[117]

An animal is always placed on a certain way, where it fully belongs and, in this sense, is complete. Man belongs in the pathless totality. However, he is never at home in it. He is "thrown" off from pathlessness onto a certain path, which, however, does not fully befall him, but onto which he gets by his own participation. Man, the dweller in pathlessness, is never at home here, but always on the way leading to home. Thus man has two selves : one of pathless totatlity, his inner self, and the other — the self of the path or way on which he actually is. This latter peripheral self changes or constantly becomes different with each successive life. His inner self, on the con-

---

[117] Cf. V. Vycinas, *Search for Gods*, (The Hague : M. Nijhoff, 1972) Chapter" Man and Animals".

trary, prevails : it belongs in Nature's play — in Nature's ever-flickering rhythmics of disclosure-concealment. Man's inner self outlasts all his incarnations.

The constant change of man's peripheral selves — even though his innermost self-prevails — presents man as an erring being. The history of all cultures around the globe at all times is a continuous series of man's attempts to attain his completedness. In all these attempts man does not have a control over his self-completion. On the other hand, he necessarily participates in guiding himself toward it.

As long as man will be man, he will be on the way toward his primordial home. Having attained this home, that is, his completion, he will no longer be on-the-way; he will no longer "ex-sist". He then, perhaps, will overcome his being-locked into a series of peripheral selves and enter his inner self, the self of man in Paradise.

Man's dwelling amid a multitude of gods, some of whom are benevolent, but many others of whom are hostile, makes his life (cultural life) risky, insecure, and often merciless and hopeless. Cultural man always is chaotic; always confronted by obscurities, by impenetrable problems, by the unknown, by the Ever-hidden, the ultimate grounds of reality — by the holy Abyss.

Perhaps the real meaning of Christianity is hope in hopelessness, security in insecurities, grounds in groundlessness?

The culturalization of Christianity serves as a warning or cautioning gesture as regards finding a secure and easy way "home", to the eternal abode with God. The above mentioned insecurities, hopelessness and obscurities of the natural or cultural life prevail also in this life's Christianization (even though Christianity in itself may mean the hope and security!). Christianity does not take away or solve our cultural problems; however, it grants more strength and endurance to us in carrying the burden of being-man, because it gives us the promise of completedness and fullness, that is, of being above being-man. To attain this, man, in every epoch of his cultural life, must constantly re-interpret Christianity anew into his cultural milieu — let the supernatural radiate in the natural.

With these efforts of culturalization of Christianity or Christianization of cultures, no definite or absolute security is attained, except perhaps by a man of faith, that is, by a man gifted with the supernatural gifts, the graces. As looked at from the viewpoint of man *as man* nothing is absolutely or definitely disclosed or established in Nature; nothing is absolutely or definitely disclosed or established in culture, and finally, nothing is absolutely or definitely established in Christianity. All is flicker! All is play! Yet this flicker or play is holy, is sacred.

CHAPTER IV

NATURE'S PLAY

All beings and their functions are more or less obvious, they have their persistent natures, and they are well set on the ways on which they proceed in a predetermined manner. Man is the only being which is mysterious, problem-burdened, puzzling, and never exhaustibly comprehensible in his essence as well as in his way of being. Such a being is a cultural being.

1. *Historicity*

The events of cultures, unlike those of things, are never static. Cultures essentially are historical. Historicity means man's erring under the sway of Nature's determining powers, the gods, in his attempt to find his place (his home) wherein he belongs, along with his attempt to get hold of or to acquire his own essence. Man, a historical being, is *quasi* split : he is and yet he is not. He is on the way to and never at home. The split is the split between him as on the way which he possesses, and him as at home, which stands out from him or where he is possessed.

Things and animals are not cultural in themselves. They, however, always are cultural in the sense that they can be meaningful in man's cultural world, his *Dasein*. The non-cultural aspect of things and animals means that neither their essences nor their being are split and, because of this, they can be considered as completed, while man, as a historical being, principly is uncompleted.

Man's uncompletedness does not mean his inferiority to things or animals. It rather means his "primitivity", and this not in the common sense of this word, but in the sense of pristinity, meaning man's being withheld or retained in Nature's unentitative milieu. A historical or cultural being essentially is unentitative. Because of this, man lacks an entitative way of being. In spite of this, man, yet, is a being and thus he has an entitative essence and entitative ways of being. However, neither this essence nor these ways are

man's distinguishing marks. The "heavyweight" of man's essence and
of his ways of being is existential : it stands out from him and he is on the
way towards it.

To know man in his historicity is to know culture. To know culture is
to know Nature in her eternal play. Man, a historical or cultural being, is
a participant in Nature's play. He is such firstly, because he is uncompleted
(by the work or play of Nature) and secondly, because he himself contributes to the process of his completion by being responsive to Nature's
play — by cultural means.

From here we can see that any inquiry into the background of all-entitative
reality, necessarily is an inquiry into man and his cultural sway — into
man's historicity. Consequently, man is placed right in the center of the
ultimate dynamic reality, the center of the Event of Being, the center of
Nature's play. In spite of this, we do not maintain an anthropocentric or
man-centered standpoint. This is so because in the Event of Being or in
Nature's play, man plays second fiddle, while Nature plays the first. Our
standpoint here is Nature-centered. Since Nature's play breaks into disclosure
or openness through man's world or *Dasein*, that is, through culture, the
Nature-centered standpoint is the cultural standpoint.

The contemporary prevailing standpoint considers itself also cultural,
and even the most advanced. However, contemporary culture is anthropocentric in the sense of it being rooted in man as its founding ground. Our
standpoint is the primacy of culture over man. In an anthropocentric culture,
historicity is the story of man, while in a Nature-centered culture, historicity is Nature's play as responded to by and thus as disclosed by man. According to this latter standpoint, an inquiry into man, into his historicity or
his way "home", necessarily is first of all an inquiry into Nature.

2. *Nature's Play*

Explorers of ancient cultures almost always find gynecocratic or matriar-
chic traces in the dawns of mythical cultures. Thus, for instance, the Chthonian, gynecocratic mythical culture precedes the Olympian one in Greece.

In the midst of the earliest cultures stands Mother Earth or the Mother
Goddess, representing Nature as such. Mother Earth is the source of everything. Everything has its start in Earth and here it has its end. To be a thing
is to have a start, as to be lit and have a sparkling duration by which this
thing draws a shiny line of duration which ends with its losing its light and
sparkling. Thus every thing has its beginning (the lit-up point), its duration
(while drawing a shiny line) and its end (point of its losing its light and shini-

ness). Mother Earth alone has no beginning or end and therefore she does not draw a shiny line of duration — is never disclosed herself — remains always in the dark, mysteriously veiled or concealed.

Even though concealed, Mother Earth, Nature, announces herself : she discloses herself. Her disclosure occurs not merely by the being lit-up of things and their having a length or duration which ends by merging into darkness of Nature again, but most significantly by the upcoming of the gods of light, her children. The words "god" and "light", especially "daylight" in many ancient languages are practically identical.

The transcendental powers of light have their light by penetrating or permeating man's world. This is why these powers, the gods, are always the powers within man's world, within his cultural *Dasein*. Gods, understood apart from the cultural world, are not "lightful" and therefore they are not disclosed. In the womb of Nature gods are just as much concealed or hidden as is Nature herself.

Nature's play means her coming to light through her transcendental powers, through gods. These can be born and also die in *Dasein*. The birth of the gods is their arrival in and their stepping into man's world — the dawn of gods — and their death is their withdrawal from it — the twilight of gods. Gods, because they are transcendental, cannot start and end, be born or die, the way things or animals and also men (in their peripheral selves) come into being and fall apart.

Ancient symbolism indicates Nature's play by the symbol of the swastika. The center of the swastika symbolizes the source of the Ever-hidden, creative womb of Nature; it has no *disclosed* essence. From this center radiate *disclosed* structural orienting or ordering lines — fundamental criteria or principles. They constitute the network of light, the world of *logos*. On the ground of these structuring principles of *logos* all things — everything entitative — become disclosed, get their start in the light of *logos*, prevail there for a limited time, and step out from it, thus falling apart or plunging into the source of the Ever-hidden again.

While the source of transcendental and of entitative realities, the Ever-hiddenness (the center of the swastika) seems to be static, the principles of *logos*, the gods (the lines of the swastika) speak of dynamics. Their dynamics is geared and guided by the Ever-hidden, whose dynamics is concealed. In the mythical world this means that the Mother Earth (Nature) is not really a goddess. She ,however, is the mother of the gods — of the ever-lit transcendental powers of her. The swastika expresses the dynamics of Nature by the works, by the dance of gods, Nature's principles. The lines crossing each other in the center (Nature-centeredness) "move" clockwise; the angular

tips of these lines indicate the direction of motion. This presents symbolically the play (disclosure) of ever-hidden Nature. The swastika thus symbolically indicates the dynamic background of all that is real : it indicates Nature's
play, thought of by the early Greek philosophers as *physis*-is-*logos*.

The mythical meaning of this dynamics or transcendental motion is
creativeness or fertility. All things necessarily have a beginning : they spring
up from Nature's creative, birth-giving source. They last in Nature's shine
in the light of the cultural world, and they fall back into the source again.

In the Mycenaean (Chthonian) culture, preceding the Dorian (Olympian)
in Greece; in the peninsula of Asia Minor and in the area of Mesopotamia
(the Sumerian, Assyrian, Babylonian cultures) jewelry, ceramics and statues
of Mother Earth, goddess of fertility, have swastikas engraved on them. In
Egypt the symbol of the lotus flower is related to the swastika and also means
Nature's creativity, her fertility or play.

The swastika, symbol of Nature's play, stands for Nature's movement
in its transcendental or unentitative milieu. This movement sets all things on
their ways and man on his pathlessness. Thus the swastika indirectly or
mediately stands as the symbol of the source of all things. Nature's movement is the founding ground of things. This ground itself — having no
entitative foundations — can be considered as groundlessness or an abyss.
Briefly, Nature's play means a disclosure of the movement of her transcendental powers and simultaneously it means a disclosure of things or
immanent realities. Both of these disclosures go hand in hand and are
inseparable. The milieu of their belonging-together is man's cultural world,
his *Dasein*. Accordingly, Nature's play, her movement (*Be-wëgung*) is the
ground of cultural movement; it is historical.

3. *Man in Nature's Play*

The historicity of Nature's play inevitably means man's belonging or
being implied in it. This means that man is involved not just in the break-
through of things into their disclosing light — into their truths — but,
first of all or most essentially or principly, in the break-through of the disclosing light itself from its ultimate, ever concealed background of the Ever-
hidden itself or Nature herself.

An individual man is not the truly cultural being — the being which is
involved in the break-through of the ever concealed grounds of reality,
into the disclosed grounds of reality which sway and dominate all things.
An individual man does not really have a culture all by himself. Culture
belongs to a society, a clan, a tribe, a nation. Or, perhaps we should say,

trying to be more strict, that a society, clan, tribe or nation belongs in the event of culture.

Nature's play takes place in *Da*, in man's cultural milieu, his stead. Only in this stead can Nature's play break through into openness — it *is* or it "essentiates". Only in man's cultural stead can Being (not just a being or beings) *be*. This stead is the stead of Being, it is *Dasein* (in the German language *Da* means "stead" and *Sein* — "Being").

The most true and most intense *Da* is the one which involves the whole nation with its festivities. In the Egyptian cultural life, the main festivities which electrified with transcendental enthusiasm every cell of the nation's structure, were the pharaoh's coronation and burial. Since the pharaoh was considered a god, participation in his coronation and burial ceremonies meant participation in the movement of Nature's play — in the variously diversified interplay of various deities.

Besides these events, which were irregularly spread in time, there were festivities occurring regularly — annually, seasonally. These festivities were of the agricultural kind and all were connected with the seasonal flooding and drying up of the Nile, the holy Egyptian river.

Behind both kinds of festivities the same holy backgrounds were at work : the god Osiris' birth to Isis, the holy Throne of ruling Mother Earth in which the royal throne of the ruling pharaoh was founded, and his death as his return to the holy womb of Isis, of Mother Earth. The concealed background of Isis is the birthbed of Osiris. His mighty sway is as Isis' bridegroom, and his deathbed is Isis, as his return to the life-granting source or milieu.

Isis' close companionship with Osiris indicates that the divinity of Osiris consists of his close relationship to Mother Earth, who herself steps forward into disclosure as his birth-giver, his bride, and his death-bed.

In his reign a pharaoh too, is a representative of the Ever-hidden as having sprung up from it. The pharaoh is the Horus-child, son of Ra, the god of the sun. With the king's coronation the in-itself ever-hidden sun (sun as Ever-hidden, as "nameless", as the god Atum) rises to openness, just as the actual sun emerges above the horizon. This procedure is just another variant of Mother Earth's coming to light through the gods of light. The king's burial parallels itself to the sunset or to the return of the god of light back to Mother Earth.

From what was said above, it follows that the annual festivities of the agrarian kind belong to or serve the same transcendental background as does the historical sequence of the ruling pharaohs. Just as Nature's play continuously goes on, so does cultural or historical life.

Each year, the god Osiris is born and dies with the rhythmics of the annual seasons, most manifest in the Nile's, the holy river's, fusion. Also, Osiris is born when each new pharaoh takes up his throne, and he dies with the king's death.

Nature's play thus is self-contained : it does not start with a lack in order to reach fullness. This is the case on the level of agrarian life as well as on the historical-cultural. Pharaoh Tutankhamen's reign did not remove all obstacles before the accomplishment of the Egyptians' cultural aims. The subsequent kings, Ay, Horemheb and others had to carry on Tutankhamen's unfinished deeds and leave them to their progeny after their deaths.

The lasting rhythmical play of Nature holds its sway over all natural events, no less than over cultural lives. In this transcendental rhythmics of Nature the ground is provided for things to rise, to flourish, and to sink back into it; simultaneously such ground is provided for man and his cultural enterprises, by which he essentially contributes to the works of Nature's rhythmics in co-disclosing natural things and his own cultural makings or deeds.

Nature's play goes on and on, but it depends on man, on man's cultural world, his *Dasein*, to break itself through into openness. Man is the bulwark, exposed to the mighty transcendental flooding forces of mightily oncoming Nature. Thanks to this opposing-responding bulwark, overwhelming powers of Nature are strikingly exposed or brought to light — they are disclosed and become true in man's opposing-responding milieu, in the stead which principly is owned by Nature, by Being.

The most fundamental truths are the truths of transcendental reality, mythically thought of as gods. The subsequent or subordinate truths are those of things. These latter truths are rendered possible by the former ones. All truths — be they transcendental or immanent — occur in the cultural world, occur with man.

While the philosophical understanding of reality foremostly has been (and to a great extent still is) concerned with the truths of things, rather than with the transcendental or unentitative truths, the mythical world and, in addition, the early phase of philosophical thought (Early Greek philosophy) principly was concerned with the disclosure of transcendental, unentitative truths, which found and carry — moreover which are presupposed by — the immanent or entitative truths. The very heart of transcendental truth, truth *par excellence*, is Nature's break-through from concealedness or hiddenness to transcendental ways of disclosure. These ways of disclosure are gods.

Nature, the Ever-concealed, breaks into disclosure in the sway of gods; in their dance. Gods, consequently, are, to a certain extent, a misrepresentation of Nature's very-own character of concealedness. Here, therefore, the sort of antagonism between Earth and gods, between *physis* and *logos*, is abiding. The very fundamental or central truth of culture as culture simultaneously is just as intensely untrue as it is true. Man, the cultural being, does his utmost in serving Nature's disclosure-concealment, Nature's play.

The previously mentioned rhythmics of gods' births and deaths, for instance, expressed by the myth of Isis and Osiris, well characterises Nature's play. The same truth can be found in the Greek myths with a somewhat lesser impact. The change of sovereignty from Uranus to Kronos and from Kronos to Zeus, however, undoubtedly maintains the point. With Promeetheus' upheaval against Zeus' rule, man's contribution to the births and deaths of the gods comes to sight. The most dramatic, mythically expressed, rise and fall of gods — the tragedy of gods — takes place with the Teutonic Twilight of Gods.

The depth of man's wisdom consists of his grasp of the gigantic event of Nature's play — the rhythmics between concealedness and disclosure of the ultimate transcendental reality. This monumental event of Being never is presented or expressed for once and for all. For man to be culturally alive means to continuously surrender to this flickering everlasting and ever-elusive transcendental event with his highest activity and total surrender.

During the ceremonies of the ancient Egyptian king's funeral banquet slices of mandrake, "the famous love-fruit" were served. During these ceremonies the goddess Hathor was honored — the goddess "who watched over the dead and presided over love".[118] Here we can see that burial or death was closely related to life, love or procreation. These elements emphasize or stress the interbelonging of death and life, *qua* love, of concealment and disclosure, of Nothingness and Being.

An animal has everything he needs placed right on his way by Nature. If by some circumstance, some of these vitally important things are missing on the animal's way, he perishes, being unable to provide himself with what he misses or lacks. Man, on the contrary, clears a site for his homestead. He uses rocks and logs for his dwelling. The earth's clay is suitable for man's pottery; metals — for tools or weapons; some roots, berries, mushrooms, wild animals on land or water constitute his food supplies, and so on. All these things are not really standing there ready on man's ways. He must use his own initiative, his own creative activity to receive these gifts of Nature responsively — co-operatively. Nature provides man with what he needs, but not without his own contribution in this provision. Man cultivates wild plants, domesticates wild animals. He modifies rocks and trees in making

[118] Desroches-Noblecourt, *op. cit.*, p. 244.

them suitable for his needs. In this way, through his work man contributes to Nature's act of disclosing things as what they are. Only man is a working being. Animal activity really is not work.

If the world was inhabited by angels rather than by men, would there be any comfortable dwellings with nicely panelled living rooms, with fireplaces, with mirrors, bath tubs, sewerage systems, porches, and so on? Would there be shoes of good leather, beautiful ladies' hats, combs, lipsticks; refrigerators, televisions, cars, milking cows, cultivated fields, roads and bridges? All these things step out as meaningful, that is, as true and real, in the world of man. Without man all these things would lack clarity, meaning and realness : they would be shrouded in impenetrable veils of reality, Being or Nature.

Things or beings come forward with their clarity on the grounds of their being backed by their founding cultural principles, the gods. The forthcoming of gods in man's cultural world owes itself to Nature's fluctuation or flickering. This occurs with Nature's self-disclosure, which being concealment rather than disclosure, calls for renewed disclosure again and again. Man, by providing himself with the things he needs discloses not only these, but also the principles of all entitative disclosure — the gods; and that is not all : he simultaneously discloses Nature in her play, that is, the breakthrough of Nothingness (*physis*) into Being (*logos*).

Early man was much more intensely exposed to Nature's elements than the man of today, who — surrounding himself with successful technological devices — constructs a defensive barrier isolating him from Nature's playful sway. The early man was plagued by diseases, by sudden storms, by dangerous beasts, crop failures, and so on. He, much more than the man of today, was aware of the powers which control the course of things and events, including his life and the lives of his beloved.

The powers of Nature, for the most part, were hostile. Comparatively few of them were benevolent. All of a man's life, all his major activities, consisted of his rites or ceremonies for appeasing his hostile gods, thus aiming to soothe their adversity, and of praying to the benevolent gods for help, by seeking their support. Temples, prayers, songs, hymns, statues, and various other religious creations or performances during various seasons of the year or at irregularly occurring historical events — all these were the outcome of man's encounter and thus his responsive "under-standing" of his gods. These things of cult are things of culture. They closely belong together with the things of man's living world. Therefore to draw a line between "material" things and "spiritual" (cultural) things is to overlook the transcendental grounds of reality, mainly — to overlook Nature's play, the Event of Being.

4. *Animism*

Things are immanent reality permeated by gods and Nature's play — by the transcendental reality. Since man is involved or implied in the transcendental realities, he too, is a transcendental force which permeates the things of his world. Would an apple tree all by itself be — even in a million years — what it is in man's cultural world, if the world was manless? The apple tree is as though permeated by man's being-man thanks to its (the tree's) prevalence in man's *Dasein*. Neither the beauty of this tree while it blooms, nor the beauty or the flavor of its fruits would have the clarity, truth, and unquestionable realness if not for man, for his world. This permeation of things by man in some ancient cultures is presented in a peculiar way by animism — by man's taking an abode in a thing, mostly a tree, after his death. Many mythical Lithuanian stories or legends tell about trees bleeding when cut or chopped.[119]

The meaning of animism, as the permeation of things in the human world by man, has its roots in man's close standing to creative, that is, playing Nature. Every thing or every animal can be considered as let loose from Nature's very own transcendental event — from her play. Man, on the contrary, is withheld in Nature's play, and because of this, he can be seen as himself active in it. And this is not the main point! Man's being withheld in Nature's play means his not being placed on a certain way of an entitative being. Without actually belonging on any of many ways of Nature's playgrounds, he potentially has the capacity or potency to be on any of them — on all of them. Things or animals have their very own natures, due to their being firmly settled on certain ways in Nature's territories. Man has no definite, assigned way — no path on Nature's map. His very own assignment is the finding of his way, his path. He must find it by his own efforts, corresponsively or responsively (or even irresponsively) to Nature's play. Man is as though able to take any way or any path in Nature's territory. He can be all things. Without having given to him firmly forged distinctive qualities for his specific being in Nature's milieu, he *quasi* possesse all these qualities or traits in a way of his own posibilities. In other words, man — an unentiatative reality, not a thing — potentially can be anything or everything in Nature's world; he can take any path in her territory. He is unprepared to live in a raw environment by not being equipped for it. However, he can provide himself with an environment controlled by him :

---

[119] Cf. Balys, *op. cit.*, p. 68.

he builds a dwelling for himself, wherein he determines the conditions which are suitable for him in his primitivity or uncompletedness to survive by his actual qualities or capacities in his raw environmental conditions. Man has no protective natural coat; he provides himself with various garments responding to various climatic conditions. He naturally is incapable of living on water, but he can live for months or years on it by building a water craft. He has no wings, but he can fly. The time is near when man will be able to live on the moon or even on some distant planets. The qualities which man lacks biologically and with which he can provide himself due to his insight into and his responses to Nature's creative working patterns, her play, can hardly be exhaustively enumerated. Man seems to stand right at Nature's inexhaustible wishing well, where everything is accessible to him. There is hardly any quality possessed by anything which man cannot have as well. Often it is said that Nature to man, unlike to animals, is a stepmother rather than a mother; nevertheless, man, her neglected child, has an access to Mother's (Mother Earth's) treasures, to her inexhaustible source of all goodies or all qualities.

Man's having access to all the qualities of things or animals, even though not having them as naturally given to him, makes him, at one and the same time, more primitive and the least gifted, and on the other hand the most capable and extraordinarily gifted. On the one hand, man is almost a nothing — totally lacking in quality — and on the other, he is all things, having all their qualities. He is the most finite of all beings, and yet he has infinite potencies. Because of these he stands close to gods; moreover — he stands close to Nature. No being except man is creative in the way that Nature is creative. Man is in need of Nature in order to have his stead in it. Since man — in the way indicated above — is (although potentially) the criss-cross network of all qualities of all things, his stead is the *locus* wherein all things are rooted. This latter point becomes most obvious by recalling the frequently pointed out aspect that man's cultural world, his stead, is the *locus* where all things come to light or are disclosed. Nature needs man in order to bring her creative play into man's world by man's creative response to her. Man's stead thus principly belongs to Nature. We call this stead man's because of his responsive, attuning participation in it — in the birthbed of all things.

Animism must be seen as meaning the permeation of all things by Nature, by her play. Such a permeation necessarily and simultaneously means the permeation of all things by man as well — by his culture or by his responsive attitude toward Nature's play. Man's response is the integral part of Nature's play.

A consideration of the cultural world as principly belonging to Nature and only secondarily (by a response or according surrender to Nature's swaying powers) to man, maintained by the mythical man, distinguishes him from the attitude of the modern man. Modern philosophies — it is true — are quite aware that the meanings of all things or beings are rooted in man, in his subject. Here they acquire their forming or structuring onto-logical grounds. Modern man, however, ignores that the foundation of man's being-man, the foundation of his subjectivity, is not in his hands, or is beyond man. Modern thought stops at man, the subject as the grounds of all reality. It does not go any further. This is why the modern world is anthropocentric, while the mythical world maintained a Nature-centered understanding according to which, the being-man is founded in that which lies beyond man — is founded in Nature.

The ancient world knew well that when Nature plays, man is alive (as far as his true being-alive is concerned — the being-alive of his inner self). This profound thought is expressed in the Egyptians' prayer-hymn to their supreme deity, Atum, the Ever-hidden, in the "Song of Atum". Atum is the sun beyond the horizons. The sun ever rises and, because of this, it disrupts his very own character of ever-hiddenness. This disruption compels the sun to set again, to conceal itself. In this way, the sun heals its disruption of self-disclosure. Sunrise and sunset are Nature's play, the function of Atum. They are eternal.

Because man is rooted in Nature, his mission is to respond to her eternal play in an eternal manner. The meaning of culture consists of granting the hue of eternity to man's cultural works or creations, which respond to Nature's play. The "Song of Atum" says :

There is no death! On the earth everything proceeds according to thy will, because you did create man. You rise, and we live; you go under, we die. You yourself are life's aim. One lives only through you; all men are looking up to you, o god of the sun until you go under. All work is laid down when you sink down into the West. As soon as you light yourself again, you permit all men to grow on Earth.[120]

Due to the finitude of his world, man is incapable of getting hold of Nature's eternal play in an eternal manner. Nevertheless, every culture, and even every cultural phase, must try to come forward with eternal cultural creations by which it *quasi* arrests the majestic flicker of Nature's play which sways mightily in it or in its phase. Of course, Nature's play in itself eludes all arresting; a caught, fixed or arrested span or fragment of

---

[120] Zierer, *op. cit.*, Band II, p. 74.

Nature's play results in a grand monument and remains a living testimony of the grandeur of this play. An arresting of Nature's play in some culture or in its phase by "eternal", "immortal" creations of culture's great men is possible and efficient only within this particular living culture. In no way are they absolute : they can never be extended over to or placed above all other cultures as the ultimate, indisputable and unshakable values, criteria, or principles.

The Egyptian culture is especially noteworthy for its monumental eternalizing of Nature's play within the Egyptian *Dasein* by the pyramids, sphinxes, obelisks, mummified bodies, prayers deep in ancient wisdom, hymns or mythical stories of gods. In spite of this, all these majestic monuments are such within the Egyptian cultural world itself. Even though they can be of great contributive importance in other cultures, they, nevertheless, remain alien to other cultures, and can make only subordinative, complementary contributions to the latter. In other words, the principles of the grand Egyptian culture are not superculturally valid. The cultural monuments of Egypt are eternal creations *in the perspectives of the Egyptian culture itself, having grandiose significance principly within it.*

Nature's play is the theme of every culture, and the mission of every culture, or its phase, is to bring as though to a stand the mode of Nature's play, holding its sway within this culture, by mirroring it within its *Dasein* in its own way.

5. Individuality and Selfhood

All things are gifted by Nature with clarity : they have ways and aims; they are meaningful and valuable. All this means that they are well founded in Nature, who herself breaks through into the openness of a cultural world and thus *is* this world.

Nature or the world differs from things by not being founded and thus by lacking the clarity of things in the way of their aimfulness, meaningfulness, valuability, and so on. Nature or "the world in itself is aimless and has no value and always remains outside of any moral valuation, is 'beyond good and evil'. Without foundation and without purpose, without meaning and without aim, without value and without plan — it, however, contains in itself all the grounds for the thoroughly founded mundane beings; it even — though purposeless itself — implies in itself all the ways in which purposes and aims are pursued; it — itself valueless — comprises all the scales according to which all the manifold grades of the intensity of being are determined; it holds spaces and times open for spatially and temporally fixing the established, purposeful, meaningful and value-loaded being of things".[121]

Man — even though a being or an entity — has his distinguishing mark from everything entitative in that he is open to and is implied in Nature's play, within his cultural world or *Dasein*. Accordingly, man's distinguishing marks must be such as those of Nature. In other words, we must assign to man as his traits the purposelessness, valuelessness, meaninglessness — briefly the lack of entitative clarity, or, perhaps, the lack of that which is essential to everything entitative. This can be to a certain extent exemplified by the Nietzschean indication of man (or rather of superman) as of the being which stands beyond good and evil.

Needless to say, the above mentioned "negative" features applied to Nature or the cultural world and to man do not in any way mean a degrading of Nature or man below things or beings; nor does it indicate any nihilistic or sceptical standpoint. These features principly pose Nature and man as essentially unentitative — as transcendental. It is obvious — as what we have stressed over and over again — that Nature (the world) and man are "stronger" realities (transcendental realities) in which the "weaker" realities of things (entitative or immanent realities) are founded or by which the former are presupposed.

Man's purposelessness, valuelessness, meaninglessness, his obscurity as regards his ways and aims, his "immorality" — all mean here that he does not stand on a road well provided with directing signs, which leads him securely "home" : towards the completion of the mission of his being. Man stands in the whirlpool of Nature's creative sway which also dominates his cultural world. He himself must, by his own co-operation with Nature and her gods, provide himself with a purpose, values, meaning, moral codes, and so on. To do this, he must have his pristine stance prior or anterior to any purposes, values, meanings or moral codes; in other words, he must be purposeless, valueless, meaningless or "immoral". To co-operate in Nature's sway or play, in the swaying powers of his cultural world, man necessarily must be a pathless wanderer in pristine chaos. Such a wanderer, the cultural being, is bound to be creative : he is bound to open up the new ways, to establish purposes, values, meanings, laws, and so on; he must establish systems or doctrines which explain things and the world around; he must create works of aesthetic beauty in which the chaotic backgrounds of reality come to shine with their eternal splendor; he must disclose the gods of his

---

[121] Fink, *Spiel*, p. 238.

world who announce to men the holiness of Nature and who hand over to them their criteria or standards of life.

Nature, culture, man — these are the grounds on which the clarity of things is resting or is founded. Everything-clarifying grounds themselves elusively withdraw from clarity. We cannot determine either Nature or culture or man's innermost self with the exhaustive clarity by which we often determine the entitative realities of our world. Nevertheless, we can and we must constantly try to disclose the ultimate realities within the framework of our culture. Such an attempt constitutes man's cultural mission. What is Nature? What is the world? What are the major powers which sway our world? What is man's very core and what is his way in his world? These questions — essentially obscure — determine the answer to the following — mainly clear — question : What are the meanings of the things in man's world?

All the above questions constantly confront man, and they cannot be answered with absolute exhaustiveness once and for all. They are answered again and again through man's very own inner self; through his very own cultural works which are such by their correspondence with the swaying transcendental powers in his world. There can be no absolute system explaining Nature, the world, or man with rationally proven clarity, which would be totally complete and valid for all times. Nevertheless, since Nature, the world or man are known, even as reality which founds immanent realities or things, *they yet are known*! Moreover, on the grounds of this knowledge, the knowledge of things — of everything entiative — is founded. The knowledge of transcendental as well as immanent realities always is culture-bound. The clarity of entitative knowledge here rests on the essential obscurity of transentitative or inentitative foundations.

A thing or — let us say — an animal functions orderly on his clearly given way of road. Because of this, he is a member of his species — one like all the others, and an individual among other individuals like he. Man, unlike the animal, being an inompleted being, "a sick animal" (Nietzsche), is transspecial as he does not have a definite road or way on which he stands with others like him. We could say that each man is bound to embark his own way or find his own response to the superior powers which rule or govern all things; he thus to a great extent is a species of his own.

A member of a species rides the rail of his life. A cultural or chaotic being is "railless". He works co-operatively with Nature's working powers in establishing the rail of his life. If in his cultural milieu man has his firm rail (even though this never is a rail for all the members of all cultures, for all humanity), it is of his own making. Even within the same culture, every member of it must ride his own rail; this never can become totally objective, without the hues of the riding personality. A true member of a culture never can be faceless, which is the case within an animal species.

Because of man's chaotic essence — because of his pathlessness — he is not a member of a species. A human individual (a person, an inner self) has his own link with Nature, which link is not as yet crystallized into a road, a way, not as it always is with the road or the way of any animal species. Man thus constitutes *quasi* a species of his own. This species of his, however, is in a fluid state: it is not definite, stabilized or petrified.

All this means that man, an "unspecial" being, has, as an assignment of his being or life, to form or, perhaps we should say, create his own species responsively to Nature's swaying criteria. This does not mean that each man heads in totally his own way by co-creating his own species co-operatively with Nature. He does so by drawing his own line in "under-standing" the gods, with his cultural co-travellers. A bird builds a nest totally identical to that built by any other member of his species. An architect of the Egyptian culture builds a unique temple. Nevertheless, his temple maintains definite hues of the Egyptian culture as do the temples built by other Egyptian architects.

Human society has the tendency to drift away from its primordial implication in Nature's play — from its very own manner of standing in this play. Because of this, there always is a danger of erring and going astray from a nation's true cultural pathlessness. It takes intense efforts of creative men — great men of society — to uphold the basic cultural standards like guidings stars and not just to follow them, but through the creative works of these men to keep these ideals in an accessible manner in front of their people — their nation. Comparatively only a few individuals in a society have the strength to stand under the pristine cultural chaos of their *Dasein* — to stand in the milieu of primordial obscurities, insecurities of dancing gods. Only the high priests, the singers and the wise men of the community can keep their people culturally alive. This difficult situation of a great man is well formulated by Heidegger, according to whom the utmost being-man (his being rooted in his *Dasein*, his cultural world) consists of his "being-held in Nothignness",[122] in chaos, in pathlessness. Cultural creations of society's great men — men with he sight of Nature's pristine chaos — provide their society with paths, with rails, which assign to men their ways of being and functioning in their world — provide their society with the book of codes. Cultural works of great men in society —

---

[122] Heidegger, *Was ist Metaphysik?* p. 32.

epics, stories of gods, decrees of wisdom, formulations of the laws of the
gods, creation of hymns and prayers, building of temples, statues and other
monuments, and so on — all this provides the man of society, a pathless
being, with a dependable path.

According to this, the cultural works of a nation or society render man
— a "speciesless" being — to a being of species. Now, as we already know,
the cultural backgrounds are a fluctuation of the ultimate reality — are
Nature's play. This play occurs by Nature's coming to light or disclosure and
immediately becoming veiled or shrouded by the impenetrable veils of
primordial Night. Man, whose mission is the bringing to light of this primordial Event of Being, the sunrise and sunset of the Ever-hidden, accomplishes
this mission by opening up the ways or rails with his creations wherein the
clarity — the emergence from the pristine chaos — of Nature's play is
assembled or reflected *along with its becoming extinguished or falling back
into the chaotic shrouds of this clarity* — its becoming veiled again. Nature's
play is responded to well by the great men not merely by their openness
to its dawns, but also to its twilights. Accordingly, the works of great men
of a cultural society, by establishing a path for their people's dwelling, must
make this path unsteady — they must make it a path of pathlessness. Great
men must transcend their creations by showing them as merely a flicker, as
a flashing light, which — born in cultural night — fall back into the abysmal
chaos of this night. Thus they disclose the ultimate grounds of reality as
abysmal.

Festivities, the days of celebration, in the mythical world were not the
days for entertainment and amusements for a man interrupting the serious
days of constructive work (as is typical of the contemporary modern man).
These days were the days for deepening and revitalizing of a man's personhood, his selfhood, by re-relating his daily activities to his gods and thus
placing them under godly standards. Festivities were the days of the intensification of man's personhood, of his self-hood.

Festivities — as we already know — occurred seasonally with the more or
less regularly occurring holy days in the agrarian society. Besides these
there were holy days occurring historically with no interdependence with
the seasonal agrarian festivities. These days, for instance, were the coronation or burial ceremonies of kings or other great men of society. Or they
can be the days heavily permeated with cult ceremonies or rites invoked by
unexpected, mostly disastrous events, such as floods, epidemics, enemy
invasions, and so on.

These holy days — be they regularly or historically occurring — were the
days when men sat down at the tables or the altars of the gods of their

culture and — after certain religious acts, almost always of a sacrificial kind, performed by the society's holy men, its priesthood, which (these acts) made the men entitled to sit down at the tables of gods as their part-ners — responsive, surrendering themselves to or "under-standing" their gods.

Man's ritual common meals with his gods principly mean his drifting back to the pathless state, where he is in full touch with or genuinely ex-periences Nature's play and her gods. Such a getting-in-touch, obstructed by man's daily involvement with entitative realities, encumbering every move or pace throughout his living situations, awakens man to his pristine "under-standing" of his gods. Simultaneously, cultural holy days, the days of man's direct encounter with his gods, mean the shattering of the apparently solid and firm cultural path established by him — the shattering of his "rail", and thus his drifring back into pristine pathlessness again. Festivities mean that man cannot for once and for all establish his "true beyond doubt" cultural ways. His efforts toward this establishment are his incessant mission.

Culture must stay alive; that is, it must constantly seek out the ultimate backgrounds of reality — of Nature, of the world — and its diversified principles, the ordering criteria of *logos*, the dance of gods. Culture means man's incessant "under-standing" response, in which he actively and co-operatively works with Nature, partakes in her holy (whole) sway. With his "under-standing" response man is actively and constructively establish-ing his own species, paving his own way, pristinely unprovided for him by Mother Nature.

As soon as man has a definite "table of values", a "book of codes", valid to all humanity for all times, he ceases to be cultural. Such a man, for instance, is the Communistic man with his "unshakable" and "unquestion-able" doctrine. Such also was Thomistic philosophy-theology which "proves" everything logically-rationalistically from dust to God. Such is, perhaps, American democracy, which, however, does not claim complete elaboration in fine details of everything in the world; it still leaves areas which can be worked out or elborated according to the basic "democratic" principles which themselves are beyond any question. The basic principle here is the posing of the anthropocentric world — a world where everything is determined by its being related in one or another way to man, the axle of the universe.

We call a member within a species an individual. In the sense we maintain here, an individual is much like any other individual of the same species. Man, being "species-less", is then principly not an individual. He is a person, a cultural being with an inner self, a soul. An individual here is "faceless" due to his entitativeness. A person for us is marked by transcendental qualities.

In a cultural world, man quite often, to a great extent, becomes individual-like comparable to a thing or animal, thereby becoming well directed on a firmly drawn out way of life and being guided by clearly set norms for his being and functioning.

Even though man can and often does became an individual, he — in order to be culturally alive — must break the formation of a species-like shell around himself, or rather around the society of which he is a member, and must drift back to his pristine standing of "being-held in Nothingness". This means that he must maintain the state of personhood and selfhood instead of becoming merely an individual.

The mythical distinction between man's peripheral or individualistic self — a cultureless self — and his inner or personal self — the cultural self — in our modern times is just as good as completely ignored. In some psychologies, however, mainly in various types of psychologies of the subconscious mind, the two "mythical" selves in man are remotely revived. These two are the conscious self as distinct from the subconscious self. An attitude typical of the modern understanding or grasp of these selves has the tendency to treat the subsconscious self as degraded or even banned from man's "true" self (his conscious self), and it places it on the same level as the animal "self", that is a special individuality.

A man as an individual or peripheral self, may know, may be well informed of or have a good understanding of the various laws, rules, and regulations governing complex areas of inorganic, animated, or human realities; he may know extensive areas of things with their manifold meanings; nevertheless, he may he ignorant of the transcendental event of reality : of Nature's play, the ever-concealed background of the cultural world; he may not "under-stand" Nature, gods, or his living world in the cultural, that is, personal sense.

An invasion of a living culture by another does not necessarily mean cultural destruction. It may be an enriching process which stimulates the invaved culture by opening up new vistas within its own horizons. It may even promote an intensification in its growth, by helping it to gain deeper insights into the meanings of its own native gods, along with the acquisition of new gods, who (as it has been the case in history) often merge with similar native deities thus endowing them with richer and deepened traits or qualities. This has happened in a number of great ancient cultures.

On the other hand, however, an alien culture may prove to be destructive.

This, almost always, is the case, when the conquering nation imposes by force its own "true" gods, customs, moral codes, and truths upon those conquered. This is done with the motives of conquerors being culturally superior. Cultural destructiveness or suppression usually takes place by casting down the gods of the conquered culture with the light of the conquerors' own negative deities, spirits, or powers. In this way, the gods of the European nations were proclaimed devils by the young Christianity in Europe.

With the theocide and outlawing of cultural standards and customs of conquered people, these people cease to be their true selves — cease to be persons. A conquered nation whose gods are outlawed becomes depersonalized; becomes existentially dead. Unable to adjust to "new" alien gods, it becomes the new society's lower class citizens. Conquered people lose the inner core of their selves. With a theocide, the souls of the conquered as well are killed, even though these people continue to live on physically.

No culture has a right to re-interpret the basic structures of any other culture strictly according to its own viewpoints or principles. This applies to Christianity (or any other superculture) as well. Just as any culture may constructively contribute to the living procedure of any other culture, as long as it does not violate or drastically distort its very-own principles, so Christianity may have its *constructive* supercultural influence upon a society's or nation's cultural principles. Christianity must heed, have a gentle or tender care regarding the gods or basic principles of any *natural* culture, that it Christianizes. Any violation of these basic principles (or gods) is a depersonalization of the Christianized people, along with the thereby committed theocide.

A person, soul, or the inner self, even though he belongs to the same cultural world as others, never is an individual like the others within the same world : in standing together with the others, he, nevertheless, always has his very own) (*jemeinig* — Heidegger) standing. A person, unlike an individual, has his finger against the finger of some god, of gods, or of God. He cannot just be in mutual accordance or conformity with the others. A soul is a being which is rooted in the abyss of reality — in the grounds which found all things and provide them with meanings. The founding of things and their being set into meanings in no way is a matter of conventional-mutual agreement in which all the members of a society are concerned.

A person, loyal to his cultural codes, most of all or first or all, is loyal to his gods. This constitutes his transcendence into pathlessness. In the mythical world, this transcendence was manifested by every person's having his own goddess of destiny. In the Lithuanian *Dasein* this goddess was Dalia. She was the universal goddess of destiny, swaying all of Lithuanian mythical society. This goddess simultaneously was the goddess of the destiny of every particular individual in this society; she definitely had a personal character in the sense of her being related to or her being concerned with every person in the society dominated by her. Dalia's sway was well stressed in the living situations of every member of Lithmanian mythical society especially when this member, instead of "in-sisting" in the immanent or entitative matters around him, maintained an openness to or "under-standing" of the transcendental godly powers of Nature. In attitudes of this kind, the person, referring to the goddess Dalia, addressed her as "my Dalia". Much the same should be said regarding the Roman goddess Fortuna. Just as mythical society's way simultaneously was everyone's personal path through his "ex-sistential" (standing-out into the openness of Nature's play) living situations, so the goddess Dalia always was *his* Dalia. Even the Christian God is called "my God" in a believer's heartfelt prayers.

In the cultural world, every person is the paver of the way of his life. The cultural road or way, established by society, never is a common high-way — the very same to everyone —; it always is a man's very own personal way, it always is *his* path trodden by himself along with his fellow men. A genuine person does not face the gods of his nation collectively (this would mean impersonally!) with others. He faces them by his innermost self, totally exposing all his dynamic essence and applying all his innermost creative powers — even though, by doing this, he works along with the others acting in their own way in facing the same gods. *Dasein* is always co-*Dasein*.

Consequently, we must say that true freedom always is co-freedom. The facing of gods means freedom to gods. In a cultural society persons are free : they "under-stand" their gods. A close association of persons, properly understood, does not mean a cutting down on their freedom. When a person admires another person or even considers him a hero, he admires his way of standing under their gods on their pathlessness. This admirer may enrich his own standing by imitating his hero. True imitation is such, where the hero is imitated not as an individual, but as a person, that is as one who "under-stands" his Dalia. Strictly speaking then, this imitation of a peron's hero is the imitation of the goddess Dalia. Hence, such an imitation, instead of curbing personal freedom, expands it to the vast areas dominated by the goddess. When two persons assume the bond of marriage, they both, hand-in-hand, follow their Dalias. By such a following they mutually enrich their "under-standing" of this goddess (which simultaneously means the "under-standing" of the gods in general!), thereby expanding, deepening, and strengthening their inner selves, their personhood, along with intensifying their freedom. True marriage in no way restricts persons, freedom; on the contrary, it expands it.

The inner self or personhood always maintains a responsive being-in-touch with gods. This is the very source of man's wisdom, his knowledge of truths; it is the root of his awareness and appreciation of true beauty and, before all else, it is the being-anchored in the true holiness. Undoubtedly, man may increase his wisdom and appreciation of beauty, and cultivate holiness through his communication with others *qua* persons. Such a communication in the ultimate sense is not a communication with others. It is a communication with them *in their openness to gods*. Ultimately, thus, it is an intensification of communication with the gods.

Contemporary or modern man, by his interests in and concern for things in their variously interrelated, complex intricacies; — by his apprehension of their essences, appreciation of their harmonious beauty, even by discovering in them the elements of holiness, may learn a lot about them. He, however, does not increase the intensity of his inner self — does not cultivate his personhood, as long as he is unconcerned with the transcendental backgrounds of the essences, beauty, and holiness of the things — the transcendental backgrounds of all immanent realities. All of man's entitative learning contributes nothing to his inner growth, to the cultivation or development of his personhood. The contemporary anthropocentric culture, scientifically and rationalistically well founded, explored, and explained with precision — be it very informative to the peripeheral self — says nothing to man's innermost self, to his personal selfhood. "In pains and longings", says Jurgis Balstrusaitis in his poem "The Strings of a Wanderer", "I understood how blind art thou, earthly reason. In the night I observe the swarms of stars, but I am deaf, because I do not hear their psalms". Only when our sight and hearing penetrate things by looking right through them as if they were transparent, only then can we see or hear the ever-elusive gods, the psalms of earth and sky. Only then can we constructively see and hear. Without these backgrounds we see or hear nothing but a vacuum. Without these holy backgrounds — by losing them — we lose our very own selves.

In "democratic" society, usually every man is considered as fully a self. We now see that man, even though a self in the sense of a "democratic" individual in society, most of the time lacks his truer self : his inner self, his personhood.

According to almost all mythical stories concerning theogonies and the birth of the world, the most ancient or pristine times have been called 'the golden ages". In the Jewish myth these golden ages constitute the phase of man in Paradise.

During the golden ages, every man was a person and every thing in the
world was divine — manifestly permeated by the glaring transcendental
backgrounds of holy Nature with her harmoniously dancing gods.

With his own guilt man lost the holy pristine world with the fullness of
his inner self. This loss — strange as it may sound — precisely was the instance of man's birth, since man is a being which lacks completeness : he
lacks the fullness of himself along with the fullness or holiness of his world.
Man's existence is his "ex-sistence" — his standing out from his innermost
self and from his holy world, Paradise. His self-completion or self-realization, along with his co-operative or responsive partaking in Nature's play,
which is the principal power in the bringing about of dynamic *Dasein*, the
flickering event or basis of Nature's self-disclosure along with her self-concealment is his existential assignment or mission.

Paradise lost during the twilight of the golden ages left man marked
by immense lack : left him pathless and without any guiding star which would
lead him on his way or ways. Such a man was thrown on the ways (though
pathless!) of a search for gods and of all that which is founded in gods. This
search is inseparable from man's search for his own innermost self. The
guide — or guiding principle — in man's search for his gods, for his world
and for his inner self is *yet* his inner self which, lying concealed in his subconscious depths, is possessed by man and now and then announces its
hints, suggestions or cautioning safeguards as his living inner voice known
under the name of conscience. Moreover, man did maintain knowledge (or
rather "under-standing") of gods after the times of Paradise lost, even
though this knowledge did undergo phases of black-outs. The true meaning
of festivities with impressive rites and celebrations precisely meant the "recalling" of gods, meant man's "under-standing" of them and his renewed
communication with them. It is true that during the post-golden ages of
mythical culture, gods no longer were obvious everyday companions of the
human race.

In spite of this, however, they brilliantly and with overwhelming might
invaded man's living situations during the ecstatic intoxication occurring
with man's being filled with godliness in the heights of the festivities and
celebrations. Unlike in the golden ages, when gods were constantly present
in man's every living situation, the mighty approach of gods in man's living
situations and their withdrawal from them during the "prosaic" days between
one festivity and the other, meant the *elusive* presence of gods in man's
Dasein. During the prosaic days which always interrupt the "poetic" ex-
hilaration of the holy days and which excessively outnumber the latter,
the world loses the aspect of holiness. Moreover, things during these periods
lose the halos of their holiness.

We must make sure that we here do not identify the golden ages with the mythical world as such. The golden age is a phase (perhaps, the most important) of a mythical world; it is the earliest or pristine phase. While during the golden ages all things were holy, during the "prosaic " (yet still mythical!) times only certain things were holy. Not all the earth was then holy, but only some segments of it : a lake, a river, a grove, a rock, a tree, and such like. Not all man-made things were holy, but only some few ones, such as certain bread, certain wine, a certain table (an altar), a certain staff, crown, a flag and so on. Not all men were holy, but only a few, mainly the priest, "medicine man", magician, or some hero performing extraordinary deeds. Not all days were holy, not all days were festivities, but only those, when man was meeting his gods and re-establishing the standards to estimate or valuate things or events of his world. These latter days were firmly fixed seasonally or by historical occurrences.[123]

Holy places, holy things, and holy persons are the points of orientation in the accomplishment of man's mission in his world. This mission is man's attempt to re-discover his gods, his world, and his selfhood, lost through his guilt. Festivities with their rites of cult recall the golden ages, thereby setting man back into his pristine pathless world and into his truer self, his personhood, while unholy everydayness makes man drift away from his gods, his genuine *Dasein* and his true self; it depersonalizes him by making him only peripherally a self.

The structure of man's life, of his dwelling, is a rhythmics of his self-estrangement and his self-rediscovery. Festivities, presided over by a society's holy men with holy things at holy places repeatedly set man back into his pristine childhood, making him thus the child of his gods. In a certain sense, man as a person outlives himself and comes back *quasi* being-born anew into a new childhood. "Man's departure in death is his assembling of himself /into his inner self/. By this assembling, man's 'essentiation' is re-implicated in his serene childhood, and this furthermore into the dawn of another beginning".[124] The reincarnationists take this latter point in a direct sense. According to them, the dying person is reborn in order to straighten out his deviations from godliness which occurred during his former life. Often in his new life he proceeds in an opposite direction, which, however, instead of removing his karmic guilts completely, may burden him with new deviations, with new guilts. Only when he succeeds in atoning

---

[123] Cf. Fink, *Spiel*, pp. 130-131.
[124] Heidegger, *Unterwegs zur Sprache*, p. 67.

for all his guilts without incurring any new ones does he attain his holy
fullness and is no longer reborn.

The life of fullness, lost since the twilight of the golden ages or since the
days of Paradise, reoccurs in mere sparkles or flash-ups during the rites
of cults, the ceremonies of festivities, where "man encounters the divine
and the divine encounters man".[125]

The rhythmical death-birth of man's inner self or his personhood is
man's existential play. In this play man's gaining of his true self easily may
be its loss. Culture is much like Nature swaying over the world of things and
animals : she builds and develops them, in order — often it seems so — to
shatter and destroy them. Culture, like Nature, plays.

The man of Paradise, of the golden ages, must be thought of as standing
wholly in harmony with Nature and with the works of gods. Post-Paradise
man principly is disharmonious. Cults — and thus culture — precisely
are man's attempt to restore his harmony with Nature. The major activities
of mythical man were accompanied by ceremonial rites. This took place
in the world of hunters before the chase and after its success or full accomplishment; in the world of the agrarian culture, such ceremonies were held
at various phases of seasonal climatic fluctuation, mainly at the time of
breaking the soil with the plowman's share and at that of the harvest; in
the warriors' world the principal religious ceremonies were held before
battles with the enemy or when celebrating a glorious victory, In all these
activities the mythical man was aware of the disruption of Nature's order,
her *logos*, and he felt a need to reconcile his gods by his diverse cult ceremonies, by his libations and sacrificial donations, by his dances, songs, and
various magic acts.

Early man's disruptive acts were an outcome of man's disharmony in
himself : his lack of his true inner self and of his true or holy world.
Culture thus is a process of healing. First of all, it is the healing of man's
"sick inside"; secondly — of his disturbed or ill world and finally, of Nature's
play, which disrupts man's world and his inner self, since both are rooted in
this play. It is this play which disrupts and heals — which plays.

All animal activities are executed by Nature's play, without an open
participation or co-operation on the part of the animal. Therefore the
re-establishment of harmony between the animal and his environment is also
done by Nature. This means that an animal has neither cult nor culture.
An animal, a being without cult or culture, cannot be a person. Each animal
individual is more or less rigidly set to function in more or less the same

---

[125] Fink, *Spiel*, p. 143.

way as every other individual. Man, a cultural being, even when participating in his cultural world as a member of a cultural group, society, or nation, himself undergoes a cultural event and himself creatively partakes in paving his own way and in building up his own self. To do this is to be a person.

Because of this, the cultural achievements in a society or nation have the character of "innermostly my own" (*Jemeinigkeit* — Heidegger). In Nature's play, in the dance of gods, a man — every man — plays. On the ground of this playing occurs the founding and disclosing of things : these become true. The truth *par excellence* (the transcendental truth) is the Play (along with all playing transcendental powers). The immanent truths of things are a result of their derivation from the truth of the Play. Both of these two kinds of truths abide or are rooted in the "innermostly my own" world, in my living situations, in my days, in my *Dasein*.

Man in his *Dasein* is a pathless being, and because of this, his *Dasein*, his playground, is his "stray ground" (Adamczewski), where man's venture of culture — venture into truths — along with all his successes and godliness implies all his failures and his godlessness. Without gods man cannot even be properly godless.

The mirror of man's play with his ways under the gods, and his strayings on the anthropocentric straying ways void of gods, is his language. Language or *logos* is the milieu of truth — transcendental as well as immanent. When man speaks, ultimately it is Nature herself, via the rainbows of gods, who speaks. "Language *alone* is that which truly speaks".[126] Man is a person insofar as he makes himself available to the speaking of Language, which prevails in his world (rather than being encapsuled in his subjective consciousness). Man himself is silent; he merely allows Language (Nature's play) to speak through him. *Personal* speaking, then, is true, "poetical" and holy.

Nature's play — Being's self-disclosure — is chaotic. It is an ever-waving ocean into which man is plunged. In this grand whirlpool of Nature, with no ultimate clarity, no ultimate assurances or securities, man is exposed to manifold blessings and ever impenetrable blows or crushes. Nature's play is full of sunshine and rainbows; it also acts as biting frost which makes living leaves shrivel and die. Nature never is a straight road with rows of roses on both sides; it rather is a complex cluster of trails — it is pathlessness well suited to man's getting ever lost, to his perpetual straying.

We must plunge into Nature's play. We must be thrown onto its pathless terrain. If we would ease out from this play and live securely in an ivory tower

---

[126] Heidegger, *Unterwegs zur Sprache*, p. 265.

which we would build for ourselves, we inevitably would end up hanging on an invisible string in the vacuum of endless nothing. Only by setting our feet on Nature's pathless earth and heading in a certain direction, can we discover earth and sky forming the openness of our world, pervaded by manifold directions of the deeds of gods which guide our steps on our earth. By responding to these transcendental powers, which constantly come at us with every thing in our living world, we discover and explore our world, discover our own innermost selves and we *are*.

6. *Philosophical and Mythical Thinking*

Philosophy cannot tell in its philosophical way, what Nature and what her play is. And therefore it principly is impotent to give an account of gods or also of man's innermost self, his personhood.

A careful inquiry into philosophy's methods and its procedures — moreover, an inquiry into its starting points — would show us that in its proper (classical) phase it already had presupposed noteworthy thoughts — pre-philosophical thoughts — along with pre-philosophical man's acquaintance with his world and the principal powers within it; — the powers which sway everything, including man. "Philosophy, as man's thoughtful relatedness to world, has been decisively determined in such a way that man's initial openness to the swaying wholeness of the world closed itself off from it, and thus his theoretical insight, directed toward the intra-mundane being, the thing, the substance, took over the predominance".[127]

Philosophy in its properly accepted sense, throughout its whole development, its whole history, principly is thing-bound. It degrades or mostly totally overlooks the transcendental principles of reality. These principles are of such a nature that they cannot be revealed theoretically — by the means proper to the so-called classical philosophies — instead they can only be disclosed or brought to light by man's deep dwelling, by his culture.

Culture is pre-philosophical, and is of a much wider range than is theoretical inquiry into reality. Culture, as cult, is a confrontation in the way of man's being-exposed to the holiness of Nature and of gods; it is a way of man's being captivated by the beauty and harmony of these transcendental realities; and, finally, it is a way of man's "under-standing" of (in the sense of his standing under) the fundamental principles of reality, which (these principles) govern the structures of entitative realities and which provide man's life, his dwelling with the norms or codes rationing his ways of life.

---

[127] Fink, *Spiel*, p. 140.

Mythical man's exposure to Nature's holiness, his being overwhelmed by her beauty and his "under-standing" of her principles, which sway everything in his world, precedes any philosophical insights and is more ancient than these. "Older than philosophy is cult", says Fink, "Before men were able to think in a strict manner, before they could manipulate with the concepts, they beheld the images which present that-which-is, and which show what *is* properly and essentially, what are the assignments of whatever is on earth, what is the destiny of whatever-is and what is its mission".[128]

Images, of course, here must not be confused with the images of imagination, which principly are mere copies of existing things, while the images in pre-philosophical thought were transcendental, expressing the structures of reality anterior to any thing, entity or being, and which, therefore, were anterior to any abstract concepts. Images of this kind are the overwhelming sight and experience of Nature's playing principles. From the basis of these principles all entitative realities spring up and have their origins; furthermore all concepts have their beginnings here.

It is true, that philosophies in the dawn of rational thought, as well as those prevailing in contemporary existentialistic thought, maintain an attitude of the "under-standing", rather than conceptual domination regarding the ultimate structures of reality. These philosophies thus still maintain or re-acquire the characteristics of mythical thought. Because of this, they have a pre-philosophical character and, as a consequence, they are qualified to inquire into the transcendental realities : the world, gods, and man's innermost self.

Philosophies in the ordinary sense (mainly the classical philosophies) are incompetent to make an inquiry into gods — either in the way of affirming them or in denying them. This aspect marks these philosophies, along with the scientific or theoretical grasp of reality by modern man in general, as godless. Accordingly, the theistic philosophies which prove God's existence, and the atheistic, which prove God's non-existence, both venture into the milieu which principly is trans-philosophical.

Philosophies with pre-philosophical tendencies differ from the philosophies in the ordinary sense, and simultaneously they resemble pre-philosophical mythical thought by not really having concepts in the proper sense of the word. Heidegger's main "concepts", such as Being, *Dasein*, historicity, the four "members" of the foursome (earth, sky, gods and men as mortals), language, Nothingness, and so on are not concepts in the traditional sense. The same must be said of the "concepts" of the Early Greek philosophers,

---

[128] *Ibid.*, pp. 140-141.

such as *physis*, *logos*, water (Thales), *apeiron* (Anaximander), Being (Parmenides) or Fire (Heraclitus). Here "Fire does not mean that of which everything is constituted, but it means the ordering-founding power which casts all detached beings into certain quiddities within a beautiful, brilliant order of wholeness".[129]

Heraclitus' Fire means Nature's play. This play is transcendental chaos (immanent chaos is mere confusion!), and it stands at the beginning of Being's Event. It *is* this Event. Not gods, but Nature constitutes the ultimate source of everything that is real in any way.

Gods and men are what they are not on the basis of their being related to some intra-mundane being, but on the basis of the ever-living world's Fire, which molds everything singular into the definite outlines of its appearance; Fire allots everything its shape, place and duration; Fire brings everything into prevalence and takes it away from it. Even gods and men are, as participating witnesses of enlightening, temporizing forward-bringing play of the world's Fire. Men gain from such witnessing by acquiring themselves the traits of the world's Fire : they are poetical, are disclosing and have the understanding of time.[130]

With the gain of creativeness of Nature's play (the world's Fire), men gain their very own selves — their personhood.

Heraclitus' Fire is the same reality which is thought of in the Greek Chthonian mythical phase as Mother Earth or the Mother Goddess. Mother Earth — we must state here — began to be known as Mother Earth in times when her soveregnty was shaken up and disputed by the lightful powers of the Olympian gods, especially by those ruled by Zeus, the god of thunder and lightning. In the pre-Olympian period, Mother Earth was the holy chaos, the everabundant source of plenty — the everconcealed source.

The prototype of Heraclitus' Fire in Egyptian mythical thought is the Ever-concealed, which well corresponds with the Chthonian chaos. The earliest transcendental image of the Ever-hidden in the ancient Egyptian world was not the sun beyond the horizons, but mother Earth, thought as the Throne — the thorne of Mother Earth, the ground of the ultimate strength, the all-ruling, ordering and founding stead, where the mighty transcendental powers have their support and the source of their divinity. This stead is also the stead of man's cultural world, his *Dasein*.

The Fire sheds light upon all things. In this light things are founded. Moreover, the Fire initiates and carries even transcendental realities (such as earth, sky, gods and men) while holding itself in constant concealment.

[129] *Ibid.*, p. 27.
[130] *Ibid.*, p. 36.

"Nature likes to hide", says Heraclitus (Fragment 123). We are barred off from knowledge of the Fire, the ever-elusive play of Nature. What can we say of Nature, of her play, of the Fire? What is Nature? What is her play? What is Being? According to Fink, Nature or Being cannot help but plunge into time, that is, into a world. "Temprizing" or "worlding" is Being's truest mark. Being plays the world and it never gets tired of this play.[131]

7. A Search for Gods

Everything in man's world is perishable. The things we like, admire, seek, and enjoy, as well as those we avoid, reject, or hate — everything which we run into on our ways of life, in our particular situations, sooner or later is no longer there.

Even men — those whom we love or respect and those to whom we are indifferent, whom we disregard or hate — cease to be; they leave our world, even though we may be reluctant to say they turn to dust in the way almost anything else does.

What about our culture? our cultural world? Don't we have to say the same regarding them? A culture is a stage which opens itself up, flourishes and bursts into often brilliant creations. After a certain length of time, it, inevitably, gradually crumbles, faints, sounds away and disappears just as everything else in the world.

Nevertheless, in the limited span of its duration and through its limited perspectives and often mighty and efficient principles, a culture allows that which is eternal, which never begins or ends — the sway of which holds all cultural principles, along with everything that comes to light with them, to be often breathtakingly present in the midst of human living days : it allows the eternal sway of reality, the majestic play of Nature, the drama of the gods — to be disclosed, even though often in a broken way in its cultural milieu. Majestically playing Nature, who depends or leans on nothing else and who always rests in herself, even though always playful and dynamic, holds herself in a lasting concealment; she is ever shrouded in impenetrable veils. In spite of this, Nature incessantly steps forward and mightily breaks forward in a diversified, harmonious array of transcendental principles. She steps forward with the drama of gods.

Nature's abysmal stepping out as firm grounds for everything and, most of all, for the transcendental principles, which found everything entitative,

---

[131] Eugen Fink, Lectures during the Winter Semester 1947-1948 at the University of Freiburg (Germany).

may be illustrated by a glass prism. A ray of light invisible in itself, when breaking through or penetrating the prism, bursts into a multitude of rays with rainbow colors.

Culture's function is to guide the event of the ultimate reality, or rather to allow it to be disclosed in an observable manner — the reality which is unobservable in itself — thus presenting within the cultural world, within the living *Dasein*, that which principly is outside of the cultural milieu and thus outside of the human *Dasein*. Such a presentation necessarily and inevitably is a misrepresentation. This misrepresentation is not exclusively a failure on the part of man : it is rooted in Nature's flickering play. The crumble of cultures, as well as that of everything entitative, belongs in the way Nature plays. A sad hue rests on man's greatest and most enthusiastic deeds, his brilliant creations, as the mighty cultures with all their gigantic, "immortal" achievements sink into oblivion like the dying melody of the Volga boatsmen drifting away on the immense stream which flows slowly over vast steppes towards the sea.

All around the globe there are ruins of once great civilizations, and who can assure that our civilization will be of a lasting kind or that it will attain the eternal fullness of disclosed Nature's play?

The ancient Egyptian culture to a great extent seemed to have captivated Nature's eternal play, the everlasting forthcoming and withdrawal of the Ever-hidden in the transcendental light of the living gods. This culture was capable of majestically holding the eternal event on a cultural stage of Egyptian *Dasein* which was gliding away. Even today, anyone beholding the grand monuments of the Egyptian past cannot but be overwhelmed by the everlasting power of the magnificent transcendental backgrounds beyond the passing by of the little events of the day, of daily life. We can be sure that the ancient Egyptians, in the numbered days of their lives among the perishable things, lived within the rhythmics of the grandiose self-disclosure-concealment of Atum, the most holy, nameless and ever-hidden. Amid things they simultaneously were amid gods.

Even though everything in man's world is perishable, he stands in the event of that which is imperishable : in the rhythmics of Nature's play. The mission of man is to guard this imperishable event of Being open in the openness of his cultural world. Even though desert sands have covered the great cultural monuments of the ancient Egyptian *Dasein*, nevertheless, the pople of this *Dasein* lived a great life : they were able to light up the ultimate, everhidden, pristine Chaos within their own cultural milieu, in their own living days. Such a majestic accomplishment cannot be carried over into other cultures in their own, the Egyptian, way; it, however, may serve as a pattern for attempting a break-through from the shallow ways of life into the ever-concealed abysmal grounds which found or serve as the most firm foundation for everything else.

Things come and go. So do cultures and their gods. Nature alone plays on. This shows that neither things nor objects (objectivism) nor man, the subject (subjectivism), nor also gods (theism), but only Nature, along with man who is involved in her play, expresses or manifests the lasting event of reality; and constitutes the basic orientation point elucidating all the ways of all things that are real; she constitutes the basic point for understanding man's ways and mission in his world; and finally she constitutes the basic orientation point for understanding what the world is, what culture is, and what gods are.

In our godless contemporary world, a creative and forward-looking man must, first of all, discover his own self, lost on the pathless terrain whereon he is set or whereon he is thrown by the powers of destiny. Trying to size up his own situation without any well explained, prejudiced system or without scientific or philosophical "blueprints", he can discover or experience genuinely man's true, pristine pathlessness. Man on his pathlessness has no clearly marked out direction with easily readable signs — directions making his dwelling without problems and without self. With obscurities and the unknown all around himself, he is bound to embark the ways of a search for some fundamental points of orientation, for absent cultural principles — he is bound to embark the ways of a search for his gods, the gods of the future. Doing this, he is bound to free his inner self toward the gods — to free it from the captivity of anthropocentric principles and from the objects ruled or dominated by these principles.

A search for gods in no way means a removal or rejection of the former moral codes or systems of thought. Instead of demonstrating our "new" culture by destroying the "old" prevailing culture, we rather must reconsider or reinvestigate their principles without blindly succumbing to them; we must reinvestigate them with the forward looking view which seeks new dawns.

In a situation where we are freed from the whole array of proven or self-evident facts, where we no longer succumb to former ideals or values, we can enter with our whole essence and with our full and complete self-exposure to meet the oncoming gods of the future. Once gods begin to radiate in the world freed from well elaborated anthropocentric truths, the ideals or values hitherto accepted are bound to become absolete without a need to oppose and combat them. Any destructive cultural revolution is cultureless. A sight open to gods is cultural. With such a sight, godlessness is bound to evaporate like morning dew after the sunrise.

The search for gods is a search for cultural principles. In today's anthro-pocentric, godless, and thus cultless, times, such a search means a switch from an anthropocentric standing to a properly cultural one, that is, to Nature's play. Accordingly, the main issue which is bound to concern future humanity is not man, but culture. Attention to culture is attention to gods — not necessarily to the gods of the past but certainly to the gods of the future.

Responsive approaches to gods, such as were maintained in the stories of the gods of mythical times, according to Edgar Dacque, "are not mere tes-timonies of the events of former times, but of that which is perpetual".[132]

Even for Christianity, which brings the supernatural or supercultural message, the principal problem is culture and not man. The increased au-thority of the bishops principly does not mean a turning from monarchy to democracy within the Church, it rather indicates a shift towards the cul-tural. The Bishop of Rome (the Pope) cannot be a genuinely "Good Shep-herd", let us say of the Eskimos, the whale hunters; he cannot be such to some African tribes who can face Christianity only in their own ways — mostly by raging, spiritually intoxicated dances.

The participation of lay people in the work of the Church also is not a copying of anthropocentric democracy. It rather is a letting or absorbing of local cultural aspects into the circles of the Church. It means a maintaining of the Natural or the cultural as the living medium for the supernatural or supercultural. Christianity cannot reach man without reaching his culture first. By penetrating his culture, Christianity acquires living colors; it becomes a living part of his world.

There is no cultureless man in the true sense of this word, and if the im-portance of culture is overlooked — as it often was the case in the history of the Church — the work of the Church is vain. This does not mean that Christianity in the historical times of the past was totally unconstructive. It was not so! But this was only because she often took into herself many cultural (pagan) elements without being fully aware of it, and construct-ively developed them and contributed thus to cultural growth.

The way of man is a way through the fields of culture, which even though pathless, are full of wayfaring gods. The cultural way of man begins with disruption. This disruption principly is the disruption of Nothingness by Being, along with the falling back of the latter into the former — along with the healing, remedying or restoration of pristine tranquility. Man participates

---

[132] Edgar Daque, *Das Verlorene Paradies* (*Zur Seelen geschichtedes Menschen*) (Mün-chen & Berlin : Verlag von R. Oldenbourg, 1938), p. 154.

in this disruption, and his ultimate ideal is Nature's peace. However, as long as man is man, he is meant to heroically maintain his course in the waving ocean of Nature's play with no absolutely definite guidance. Man is meant to play in Nature's play — on the ultimate and abysmal grounds, his stray-grounds.

BIBLIOGRAPHY

Balys, Jonas. Lietuviu Liaudies Pasaulejauta. Chicago : Lietuviu Tautinis Akademinis Samburis, 1966.

Boelen, Bernard J. Existential Thinking. Pittsburgh : Duquesne University Press, 1968.

Brantl, ed. George. Catholicism. New York : George Brasiller, 1962.

Carrington, Richard. The Mammals. New York : Life Books, 1963.

Daque, Edgar. Das Verlorene Paradies. München & Berlin : Verlag von R. Oldenbourg, 1938.

Desroches-Noblecourt, Christiane. Tutankhamen. New York : Graphic Society, 1964.

Fink, Eugen. Spiel als Weltsymbol. Stuttgart : W. Kohlhammer Verlag, 1960.

Heidegger, Martin. Hölderlins Erde und Himmel. Pfullingen : Verlag Günther Neske, Long play record, NV 7, 8, 9, 10-33-0196 A, B.

Heidegger, Martin. Unterwegs zur Sprache. Pfullingen : Verlag Günther Neske, 1959.

Heidegger, Martin. Vorträge und Aufsätze. Pfullingen : Verlag Günther Neske, 1954.

Heidegger, Martin. Was Heisst Denken? Tübingen : Max Niemeyer Verlag, 1954.

Heidegger, Martin. Was ist Metaphysik? Frankfurt a.M. : Vittorio Klostermann, 1949.

Hertzberg, ed. Arthur. Judaism. New York : George Braziller, 1962.

Larousse Encyclopedia of Mythology. New York : Prometheus Press, 1959.

Nietzsche, Friedrich. The Philosophy of. New York : the Modern Library, 1927.

Riga, Peter J. The Church and Revolution. Milwaukee : The Bruce Publishing Co., 1967.

Ritter, Christiane. A Woman in the Polar Night. New York : E. P. Dutton & Company, Inc., 1954.

Schlosser, Friedrich Christoph. Weltgeschichte. Band IV. Stuttgart und Leipzig : Deutsche Verlags-Anstalt, 1900.

Sinn, Dieter. "Heideggers Spätphilosophie" Eine Vieteljahresschrieft Für Philosophische Kritik. Tübingen : Hans-Georg Gadamer und Helmut Kuhn, Mai 1967.

Vycinas, Vincent. Greatness und Philosophy. The Hague : Martinus Nijhoff, 1966.

Vycinas, Vincent. Search for Gods. The Hague : Martinus Nijhoff, 1972.

Zierer, Otto. Bild der Jahrhunderte, Band I. Gütersloh : Murnau Gesamtherstellung & Co. G. m. b. H., n.d.

INDEX

Adam 120, 122, 127, 131, 158, 159, 161.
Adamczewski, Zigmunt 187.
Anaximander 190.
animal 34, 35, 36, 37, 39, 60, 61, 74, 75, 81, 85, 92, 93, 94, 99, 100, 101, 102, 103, 104, 105, 106, 107, 113, 114, 136, 139, 143, 144, 145, 147, 149, 163, 169, 170, 171, 172, 176, 177, 180, 186.
anthropocentic 3, 4, 5, 7, 10, 11, 14, 15, 18, 20, 21, 24, 25, 26, 28, 30, 33, 38, 41, 44, 49, 54, 55, 60, 63, 64, 72, 73, 78, 81, 82, 84, 85, 89, 90, 95, 98, 108, 109, 111, 116, 129, 130, 136, 137, 153, 164, 173, 179, 183, 187, 193, 194.
animism 171, 172.
Anysas, Martynas 151.
Aphrodite (goddess) 101.
Apollo (god) 157.
a posteriori 38.
a priori 4, 6, 17, 28, 38, 89, 96.
archetype 98, 141.
Aristotle, Aristotelian 5, 27, 67, 88, 89.
Artemis (goddess) 43, 65, 157.
'assemble', 'assembler' 30, 43, 50, 54, 56, 57, 69, 74, 85, 94, 96, 98, 139, 178, 185.
Assurbanipal (king) 61.
Athena (goddess) 43, 101.
Atum (god) 40, 41, 44, 59, 158, 167, 173, 192.
Avyzius, Jonas 52.
Baltrusaitis, Jurgis 157, 183.
Balys, Jonas 152.
Being 26, 28, 38, 50, 90, 94, 98, 100, 115, 158, 159, 167, 168, 169, 170, 178, 187, 189, 191, 192, 194.

'*Be-wëgung*', *be-wëgen* 37, 43, 45, 49, 74, 94, 105, 116, 166.
'blue', 'blueness' 49, 72, 73, 81, 86, 117.
Boelen, Bernard 29.
Britons 152, 153.
Budreckis, Algirdas 79.
Bultmann 148.
Catholicism 128
chaos, chaotic (also abyss, abysmal) 40, 44, 49, 60, 76, 87, 88, 89, 90, 91, 104, 136, 159, 162, 166, 175, 176, 177, 178, 181, 187, 190, 192, 193, 195.
Christ 120, 122, 123, 127, 129, 135, 140, 144, 145, 147, 148, 149, 150, 151, 157, 160.
Christianity, Christian 13, 15, 23, 46, 47, 113, 119, 120, 121, 122, 123, 124, 125, 127, 128, 129, 130, 131, 134, 135, 136, 137, 138, 139, 140, 141, 142, 144, 145, 146, 147, 148, 149, 150, 151, 152, 154, 155, 156, 157, 158, 159, 160, 162, 181, 182, 194.
Chthonian 42, 164, 166, 190.
Church 127, 128, 129, 130, 135, 136, 137, 140, 141, 145, 146, 148, 154, 194.
civilization 47, 48, 54, 55, 63, 65, 66, 118.
Communism, Communistic 4, 5, 6, 7, 19, 22, 23, 25, 46, 48, 61, 66, 79, 80, 83, 84, 128, 153, 155, 179.
community 30, 31, 79, 108, 109, 110, 111, 112, 134, 138, 144, 145, 150, 177.
complete, complition, completedness 9, 10, 11, 77, 78, 87, 95, 105, 118, 120, 136, 160, 162, 163, 164, 172, 175, 176, 184.
conceal, concealment, concealedness 4, 26,